Living *in* Sonshine

Compiled by
Marjorie Ebersole

ISBN: 978-1-933753-84-3

Compiled by: Marjorie Ebersole
Text Design: Larisa Yoder

2673 Township Road 421
Sugarcreek, OH 44681
1-800-852-4482
Fax: 330-852-3285

Carlisle Press
WALNUT CREEK

Acknowledgments

Thank You, God, for blessing our home with boys. This book would not be in existence without Your moving in our lives. May You receive all the glory.

Thank you, Rendell, for supporting my brainstorm, for reading the contributions and giving your advice and opinions, and ultimately, for helping me understand the life of our sons.

Thank you, sons, men-in-the-making, for adding spice to my life and for giving me something to write.

Thank you, contributors, for feeding the book. (Mail time isn't as exciting anymore.) The added notes of encouragement and anticipation were inspiring.

Thank you, editing team, for blessing my life:

Meredith, for your interest in the book and your encouragement when I realized I didn't know what all was involved when I got started.

Juliann, for your point of view as a mother of girls and for the observation that our worlds do have some similarities. (When will we see a book about girls?)

Diane, Annetta, Edna, and Esther, mothers of boys, for your helpful insight. You are friends I've never met in person, though I feel a kinship from working with you.

Effort has been made to give proper credit to writers. If there is any error, your corrections will be appreciated and changes will be made in future printings.

Preface

Toothpaste dribbled the spigot. Chocolate smeared the washbowl. Sand gritted across the counter. Drips dried on the toilet. Puddles decorated the floor. The rug lay dirty and askew. "Filthy!" I muttered under my breath. Cleaning the bathroom was not on my schedule for today, but...I set to work.

It was one of those days when I was eager for Daddy to walk in the door. It is always a highlight when 6:00 PM rolls around and Daddy comes in. Sometimes I feel at the end of my string. The "sonshiny" world in which I live turns cloudy.

Task accomplished, I turn to throw my rag into the laundry basket. *What...?* I bend to investigate further and discover water in the laundry basket. The basket is not beside the sink nor is the roof leaking. *Someone* purposefully put water in there. Apparently, Son had decided that would be a bright idea. Lightning sizzled within me, proof of how stormy things were. My husband appeared at the bathroom door. Thunder rumbled ominously. "I *can't* keep up anymore!"

He calmly replied, "It's just boys!"

It was not a new thought. I already knew I mothered three sons. However, one fact remained: *I* was not a boy!

If you had asked my mother twenty years ago, she would have admitted that of her three daughters, I was the most boyish. Even my uncle said I should have been a boy. (I've forgiven him.) It's ironic that I struggle to view life through the eyes of my sons. Maybe my mother, who was never in her life a tomboy, breathed a lady's demeanor into me.

Thus the seed for this book was planted and begged to be watered. When I told my husband I would like to hear how other mothers cope with the responsibility of raising sons, he thought it was a good idea. Therefore, I thank each contributor for your help in fertilizing, and I thank God for giving the increase. This book is for mothers of boys. God bless you as you labor from son up to son down...and beyond.

Marjorie Ebersole

Table of Contents

In Training

SARA BOWMAN

During the three years before our first child was born, I thought it would surely be a girl. As the youngest in a family of three daughters, there were disadvantages to growing up without brothers. I knew little about the masculine gender, but I did know they were different from girls. Being married had reinforced that. What would I do with a boy?

When our baby arrived, "it" became "he," namely Matthias. After a flash of disillusionment, I quickly adored my hearty nine-pound, six-ounce son. I watched Timothy care for our little boy; I loved them both. A boy baby is still a baby. I learned they need cuddled, fed, loved, fed, bathed, fed… This was as brand new to me as Matthias was.

As every mother knows, babies grow quickly. Soon Matthias was showing boyish instincts. When he was twenty-two months old, I bought a little bag of cars at Goodwill. Immediately fascinated, he drove them back and forth, making car noises. I recalled that an aunt had told me, "A boy spends more time looking at wheels than into people's eyes."

Around the time Matthias was three, he became even less a toddler and more boyish. The next summer his older cousins, Tyler (8) and

Jase (6), came to visit. Three boys instead of one were very different. They helped us clean our new home's construction site. When Timothy picked up a large scrap board, granddaddy long-legs ran everywhere. "Spiders! Spiders! Smash 'em! Smash 'em!" the cousins shouted, scrambling for sticks to poke them. Matthias watched wide-eyed before jumping in the fray. A repeat happened when we uncovered common black spiders. When a frog hopped away from the trash pile, all the boys chased him, shouting and calling. Timothy called them back so the frog could escape unscathed. My mind revisited the thought, *Boys are different!* And, in Tyler's words, "Boys are rowdy!" Jase built a boat. For weeks afterward, Matthias claimed scrap wood and built his own boats. They didn't float; that was superfluous. Tyler built houses. The cousins' visit taught Matthias many boyish things.

As Matthias continued to grow, our living room furniture became a dump truck, skid loader, and pickup, with sound effects. "Vrroooom, vrrroooommm!" I have a picture of my youthful sisters with me wrapped in a blanket, with a baby bottle, taking trips on the couch, but we never dreamed of using the recliner footrest for a skid loader bucket.

Matthias was five when our third child, second son, arrived. Matthias had wished for a brother; apparently, his cousins joined him in that. After I gave my sister our baby news, she told Jase, "Uncle Timothy's have a boy!"

To Jase, the name was inconsequential, but the gender was newsworthy. "Can I go tell Tyler?" he exclaimed. Without asking the name, he sped away.

The Lord must have things to teach me as a mother of two boys. I appreciate my sons' easygoing personalities against the backdrop of my daughter wailing, "I can't get my dress ooofffff!" and other similar distresses multiple times a day.

Boys are much like men. They need respect, encouragement, and admiration. They need someone to laugh at their funny jokes and watch them ride their bikes. They need a mother to visit their Indian houses and to watch them sled. They need the responsibility of chores, indoors and out.

And they need chocolate chip cookies.

These little men-in-training need me to teach them that a joke isn't funny when it hurts someone. They need me to teach them to respect ladies by respecting their mother and sister. Don't wrestle with your sister (which causes the aforementioned wailing). Don't step on my foot. Keep your elbows (and knees) to yourself.

I am blessed when Matthias tries to joke his sister out of grumpiness. Those times when the children are washing up and giggles abound are rewarding. Even when they play creatively and messily all morning, it's worthwhile.

Matthias is our handyman-in-training. When he was almost five, Grandpa gave him a pliers and screwdriver set. He replaced many batteries with them. His tools are handy for taking apart old appliances or engines. Have extras? Give me a call.

We have one disadvantage in raising boys—our daddy works away. Matthias says, "I wish every day was Saturday." He loves to follow his daddy around, pounding nails in his projects, mixing cement, and picking up rocks. I know the frustrations of a boy who just needs *something* to do! It is a challenge to make that something profitable. Matthias spends a lot of time looking at books. Since the children were small, my sanity saver was to have them sit with a stack of books when they got rowdy.

Matthias does many jobs: unload the dishwasher, set the table, and sweep the kitchen and dining room or his bedroom. If the noise and squabbles are intolerable, I call him to help make supper. As we gather around the table, he announces, "I helped make this soup!" He sweeps the porch, picks up trash outside, gathers eggs, and forages for pinecones for me. Working is a great time-filler; he is not making a mess. He is learning, I hope, to be a cheerful, diligent worker. The key word: learning.

One day, I told my son, "Stand up! You are not a crab or a caterpillar! Right now you are a *boy* who is picking up toys."

The day passes; we welcome Daddy home. Then the males outnumber the females three to two. Although I didn't know much about males before I was married, by the grace of God I am learning.

A Boys' Mom

MARLENE BEILER

Before I was a mom, I dreamed of someday having a blonde-haired, brown-eyed little son. Our first child fulfilled that desire, and a little lass of similar coloring followed him. Three more lads have joined our family since.

I dearly love being a mama; but some days I despair, thinking, *I don't know how to be a boy's mom!* I want our boys to be boys, but I also want them to be respectful, to grow up to be pleasant young men. How do I teach them manners without smothering them?

Sometimes I fret that they won't know how to treat girls, for they have only one sister. However, maybe they will be great husbands someday, for they know how to do laundry, sweep the floor, and wash dishes. I hope that someday they will automatically hang up their clothes, clear the table, or put away their books since they don't have a houseful of girls to clean up after them.

Although I don't understand all about it, I enjoy their tales of hunting and fishing. Today most of us no longer rely on wild game for survival, but this passion for hunting and fishing is a gift from God, a man's inborn desire to provide for a family.

Boys chatter about narrow escapes, how many home runs they hit, and the great jump they needed to perform to catch the ball. I want to listen, truly listen, so that someday they will share their bigger triumphs and struggles with Mom because they know she cares about their life.

It is an overwhelming responsibility to raise these young boys to become Christian men, who we need to lead homes and churches. Let's never forget to ask our heavenly Father for guidance and wisdom. After all, boys were His idea!

Of Buds and Boys
DONNA J PETRE

Our four-year-old and I got home
From school-drive one gray day,
And found our first two daffodils
Were opening—Hooray!

"May I pick them for you?" he begs.
"Be sure you get a stem."
I show him how. "Now let's go in
And fill a vase for them."

Warm days pass, buds burst to bloom,
Son meets me at the door.
"Look, Mother, what I brought for you!
I found a couple more!"

I'm stirring supper. Doorbell rings.
I go to take the call—

"Guess what's behind my back," Son grins,
Then wails, "They're getting all!"

That night I think how God has placed
Four sons within our care.
They're metamorphosing to men;
My thoughts become a prayer:

"Lord, fan my flickering interest in
Each treasured stone or stick,
Sulfuric acid stories and
How dying pigs can kick…

"Oh, keep me kind and caring in
Each interrupting call,
Because, behind my back it seems,
Our boys are… getting… all!"

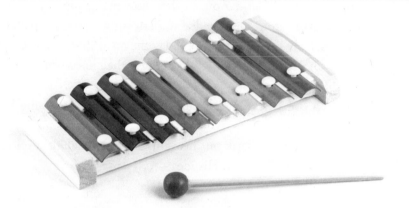

ENERGY, NOISE, AND FUN = BOYS

MABEL REIF

"Five boys….busy, busy mama." Several years ago, my family doctor shook her head as though a mom of boys was much busier than any other mother was.

I was busy. I'm still busy, but not busier than any other woman with a family. I definitely did not deserve the admiration of one friend who marveled at all the work our sons do around the house. Of course, they help. There is no one standing around waiting to clean up after them, so the boys pitch in. Like it or not.

While some are more patient with household chores, no one may complain. "Dishes are a part of life," I've said more than once. "I wouldn't feel bad to see you occasionally do them three times a day. After all, you ate that many meals." And to myself I think, *That doesn't include all the snacks and cold leftovers you devoured out of the fridge.*

Cooking might be fun, but baking is a coveted job (until it's time to wash up the dishes) because one gets to lick the spoon, the beaters, the bowl, and the fingers. Then if the cake isn't ready for the oven yet, lick some more. I've been amazed at the small size of some of their cakes. The same recipe fills a normal cake pan when I do it.

A pet peeve of mine is messy rooms. I detest clutter, dresser tops included. I bought wash baskets for dirty laundry because boys who love basketball could shoot their clothes into the basket. Wouldn't that be the perfect way to practice? Guess again. Open drawers have pant legs and shirt sleeves draped over the edges, rejected clean clothes are scattered on the floor along with the dirty ones, and why is the curtain hanging by one arm? According to my friends with girls, I can't blame the gender. It must be more of a personality thing.

Whatever the reason, it bugged me, so we set up a coin system. Each week I put over a dollar's worth of coins into a small container. Anything misplaced allowed me to remove a coin. (I picked out the quarters first.) If there was anything left over at the end of the week, the occupants of that room were allowed to buy a pack of gum or save it for something bigger. Believe it or not, after doing this for a while, I hardly ever collected coins. We eventually discontinued this, and for months afterward they kept on being tidy out of habit. But…all good things come to an end…unless Mama stays on their case.

One good thing about the dirty clothes—they also get practice with laundry. The wringer washer is more fun than the automatic washer is. Hanging out wash? Not so much. Each one knows how to sort clothes—and fold and put away—and no, they never check pockets. At this house, if you still value it, get it out when you take off your pants.

A mom of mostly girls commented, "I don't see how you do it. I have my hands full with one boy. He's loud, dirty, and rude." That hurt. Not as much for myself as for that little boy whose mom couldn't accept the diamond in the rough God gave her to work with.

Boys *are* loud. Listen to five of them jumping bikes over a ramp on the lane or playing trucks and tractors in the kitchen on a rainy day. At least they're not traveling around the room without touching the floor or piled on the desk chair spinning at top speed yelling with delight or, worse yet, wrestling.

Rainy days, icy days, late-in-winter-slushy days—if I get gray hair, that might be when. My house shrinks several sizes during the winter while my husband works away from home for a few months.

Don't try to suppress this vigor; it only erupts—kind of like a bottled volcano. Quiet times seem to defeat the purpose for us. Instead, help them channel that voltage into something creative like work or a project. Exercise and fresh air (even in cold or drizzle, but likely not in a downpour) works wonders on restless, picking-on-each-other boys and saves the sanity of moms.

During the summer when we spend most days picking and grading produce, we don't require them to do as much housework, except for helping with freezing and canning. What I can't clean doesn't get done. (Call before you stop in!)

I'm glad trapping season, along with skinning and tanning hides, falls during the slower months of winter. The younger boys also enjoy trapping, but instead of muskrats and coons, they downsize the mouse population. Ever see a mouse skin without the mouse? It stretches perfectly around two boyish fingers.

The rudeness my friend dislikes can be a problem. A shoulder bump in passing, a friendly (or not) whack on the back, a kick under the table—boys interact with their bodies and muscles. Back and forth. Give and take. How do you know when to let boys be boys and when to make them stop? One day I read a note that I try to apply to these situations: *We're not raising boys; we're raising men, the future leaders of our churches and families.*

A bit of rowdiness (they're like overgrown puppies), a burping contest—there is a time for fun. But my husband and I decided devotions and story time are when we'll practice sitting still, and at mealtime, we'll try to be mannerly. So we started to use our little pink pig, an idea I got from a maid. We chose three of the worst behaviors: belching out loud, passing gas (isn't anything private?), and reaching across the table for food. The guilty one got a toy pig beside his plate. If anyone else broke a rule, he got the pig while the first one sighed with relief to get away from the reward of washing dishes, vowing to be extra careful for the rest of the meal.

The dirt part of having boys? Mostly it's contained in the wash-house, but a produce farm offers plenty of opportunity for getting dirty. Produce needs picking, muddy or not. And mud leaves trails *everywhere*. Thankfully, summer evening soaks in the pool take care of the dirt and fade the shadows on the neck and behind the ears.

Besides mess and clutter, dirt is my greatest challenge. It's hard to remain sweet with dirt on the floor and mud streaks on the ceiling (don't ask how) and caked boots strewn on the rug inside the wash-house door. Most times I can handle it if they keep it where it belongs. It's the times they find a mud puddle complete with a mud slide and pretend they are otters or roll in the dust and fill their shirts with it—even the ten-month-old in the stroller—that I feel overwhelmed.

But I loved the way one lady put it: "Think of all the fun they'll have!" They do have fun—lots of it. I enjoy that even though it means bikes in the yard and street hockey gear scattered on the produce shed concrete. They can pick up the balls, bats, and gloves after a game just as they pick up the leaves and twigs that clutter up the grass after an afternoon of tree climbing. I remind myself that playing together builds friendship and communication skills for life, and teaches them to clean up after themselves in the bargain.

Yes, there's always laughter heard, and some creative project found on the shop floor or cluttered on the washhouse counter. I am talked into helping make bows and arrows or letting them try to sew moc-casins on my sewing machine. Daddy loves to show them how to do the heavy projects like build a tree house, craft little sheds with scrap wood, or weld steel equipment parts.

Come to think of it, aren't most inventors men? Somewhere along the years, there must have been more than one mama willing to ignore a mess in order to encourage her son's creativity and help him channel his energy. Maybe, like me, that mama needed to set guidelines. Rules are a part of life: "The overhang of the barn roof is no place to play catch," or "No snow forts on the shop roof," shouldn't damage their creativity a whole lot. If other moms could do it, so can I. (Just clean up after yourself, please, without being reminded.)

It's the way God made them. Girls have brains, too. Judging from the difference in the size of certain areas of the brain, the type of hormones He gave them, and the amount of spinal fluid in the brain stem, God created boys to be more aggressive, more competitive, and less nurturing than girls. He created them to be conquerors and leaders.

Boys carry on a different type of conversation. Working side by side in total silence gives them a sense of comradeship. A mama needs to be ready to catch the start of an in-depth talk. My boys love if I listen to their accounts of sports or hunting or whatever captures their interest. No matter how much they talk, they don't waste any time in chitchat or rehashing an issue as I might.

I never wished for girls and was delighted with each boy as he came, but sometimes I fleetingly wonder what it would be like to have teenage girls instead of boys. Would they like cooking, cleaning, and pretty arrangements? Would we have girl-type conversations about this and that and nothing in particular? Then I look at women with no children or with special needs children. Even mamas with lots of girls aren't guaranteed an easy life. The family God blessed us with is not to only be endured; it's to be enjoyed to the fullest because one day we'll no longer have our boys. They will have become the men we were raising all along.

And [Jesus] took a child, and set him in the midst of them:
AND WHEN HE HAD TAKEN HIM IN HIS ARMS,
he said unto them,
WHOSOEVER SHALL RECEIVE ONE OF SUCH CHILDREN IN MY NAME,
receiveth me:
AND WHOSOEVER SHALL RECEIVE ME, RECEIVETH NOT ME,
but him that sent me.
Mark 9:36,37

My Choice

AMANDA HORST

There was so little to be glad about. The constant commotion was getting on my nerves. The boys and their daddy were always talking about men things: trail cameras, hunting rules, sawmills, welding, firewood, snowplows, and trailer lights. All I ever got done was feed and clothe and clean and then start all over. There was no time to scrapbook or sew new kitchen curtains. The reality was I barely had time to sew the coverings on order, or the dress (note the singularity) for my sister's wedding in four weeks, especially since I was trying hard not to let my housework fall too far behind in the process.

You see, I am the only lady in this house. Dwelling on this fact had spiraled my being into a funnel where I felt like, in order to survive, I was left with two choices. #1: Fling all my femininity to the wind, forget the pretties, get dirty, and be boisterous with them. Or #2: Build a dainty shell around myself so everyone knows that I will break if touched. Then a friend shared this poem with me:

> Lest We Lack True Men
> God, give us women, women of such mold,
> Preferring ever honor unto gold,
> Women unspoiled by luxury or ease,

Of nobler type than ancient Rome or Greece.
Women who wear Thy beauty as a flower,
Whose homely virtues are their richest.
Say you, "The age needs men?"
I say again, "God, give us women,
　　　　　Lest we lack true men."
　　　　　　　　　-H. Shuyler

So—two choices? This new perspective is the third and best choice. I can actually be the Queen of this house. I really may set out a tea party with fancy china for my husband and sons and burn candles and prefer to stay in the house on a cold winter day. I don't need to go hunting or clean out the chicken pen or tumble on the floor. I will probably scream about the dead mouse dangled in front of my nose. I will teach my boys to do dishes and fold wash *neatly*. Sometimes I will order my rowdy sons to just sit on the sofa and look at books for the next half hour to keep myself from becoming frazzled. Occasionally, I might spread the table full of scrapbooking things at the expense of my other housework. In addition, I think I may even dream of someday using those pink sleepers still tucked away in the attic.

On the other hand, I can also growl like a bear for my baby to imitate. I can look at the pictures on the trail camera and take a ride on the new sled with my four- and six-year-old. I will decorate the birthday cake with a backhoe instead of a kitten with a pink ribbon around its neck. I will give full attention to my husband's detailed account of his day of sawing. I can even sometimes let my boys play deer hunting with rubber bands in the living room. I may decide to go out in the cold to help stack firewood. I will cheerfully feed, clothe, clean, and then start all over.

For now, I am *joyfully* playing a very important part in the lives of these four men who love me unconditionally. My sons will someday be measuring their ladies by what I have been to them. I want to teach them to appreciate the finer qualities of life, while helping them develop their manly potential. Therefore, desiring more than anything else that my men would be true, I will again commit myself to being the woman God has intended me to be for them.

A Heart Full
of Joy

M EBERSOLE

It was Christmastime. The second Christmas since we moved into the snug Bedford stone house in a non-Mennonite neighborhood. Last year, my sister and I were together and made cookies to share with our neighbors. I wanted to keep up the tradition of giving something to our neighbors at Christmas. It seemed appropriate to reach out to the neighbors in a way that spoke of the true meaning of the joy of the season. But this year I didn't feel inspired about a big cookie-making project with my sister. Between the two of us, we had six boys to mother. I would do something in my own kitchen, myself. Like making sticky buns.

The closer Christmas came, the bigger the project looked. Just the thought of my baking day overwhelmed me. I'm not the type of person who makes a BIG mess when I'm working in the kitchen. Every big baking project does involve a sink and countertop full of dirty dishes, a splattered mixer, and a sticky counter. Some ladies wait to clean up until they get finished baking. And they get the food made more quickly, too. Me? I tend to befriend the dishrag and wipe up any splatter, any spill. I like to keep dishwater in my sink and sort of keep things clean while I'm baking.

My sticky bun project would have looked a whole lot more doable if I were alone in the kitchen. But I'm not just a baker. I'm also a mother. I considered the combination: Sticky bun project *and* sons. I saw boys on the table. Flour on the floor. Dough on the pants. A frustrated mom. It wouldn't be worth it. After all, what's good about doing good deeds for the neighbors when you feel cross with those nearest and dearest to you?

I greatly admire mothers who make things like donuts and sticky buns along with their children and no other help. I rarely make cookies. Just making a cake or casserole involves more than my own two hands and usually results in an internal temperature gauge that gets dangerously high.

That's when the cupcakes entered my mind. I could use a cake mix and make cupcakes. Keep it simple. Well, maybe I'd use a decorator tip for the icing. That would make them special. I had red and green decorating sugar to sprinkle on top. Just the thing!

I started mixing the cupcakes, when two more hands appeared... and shortly after, another two. Such licking and fighting and begging to clean off the utensils! I was taught you could get sick from eating raw batter. If that were the case, my boys would be sick a whole lot more often than they are. Before long, one boy had batter on his sleeve...then on his shirt front. I'm not sure how often I cleaned them, got them to go play, and quickly put their chair away only to have it pushed back up to the counter.

Eventually I gave each boy a cupcake. (A baked one!) That kept them occupied for a while, but then I needed to mop the floor because they didn't stay in their seats, and chocolate crumbs got scattered around. I got the icing mixed and was frosting the cupcakes when it was time for lunch. When my husband came home, I felt rather accomplished, in spite of everything. Yet also exhausted. The rest of the cupcakes still needed icing. I decided to do it while the little boys were napping.

Of course, my six-year-old wanted to help. He wanted to sprinkle the sugar on the icing. I feared they would get an abundance of sugar, but I let him try. After he had done a few, and they had turned out nicely, he said, "I like to put the sprinkles on. It fills my heart with joy!"

I chuckled. Sonny looked a little sheepish. But I thought about what he said and realized how true it was. Helping Mother gave him joy. How can I deprive him of joy and feeling needed for fear of it not getting done just the way I want it to…or he'll make too much of a mess …or I can do it faster? On the other hand, there are times I need to help find joy in doing a job he despises.

I looked into the joyful eyes of my sugar-sprinkling six-year-old and said, "Thanks for your help! They look lovely!"

You've Been Jingled!
MARILYN WEAVER

A Christmas snowman brought you a treat;
You're a favorite neighbor on our street.
We're wishing a blessed Christmas for you
And for all whose lives you touch then too.
Please make a copy and a treat to share;
Within two days, show someone you care.
Drop a treat at your neighbor's door;
Homemade or purchased from a store.
Ring the bell and run away fast;
A smiling neighbor is my forecast.

Boys love a fun little prank! Help them fill a gift bag of goodies and add a copy of this note. Deliver it to a friend's or neighbor's house after dark. Set it at the door, knock, and run away fast! Your boys will have fun and so will the family receiving the gift.

Boys in EVERY ROOM

EVELYN FISHER

Everywhere I look in our house, there are signs of boys. What would it be like to have girls instead of boys? I'm sure the activities, noises, and decorations would be quite different! There is a crow wing and a cage with a mouse family on the laundry counter. There are wooden rubber band guns uniquely fashioned with a trigger and scope. On the back porch sits a bucket of hickory nuts for sling shot ammunition.

In the sewing room

My sewing room is decorated with skulls: a deer skull and a mouse skull. By the outside door stands the gun cabinet. On the chest of drawers by the steps is a squirrel skin complete with its tail and head shape, eyeholes and all. In the corner are a deer hide and a groundhog skin. The whole room has a boyish look, with boyish projects that even include sewing projects from time to time. Our weekly cleaning and putting away of material often involves lumber and woodcarving/woodworking projects. In one corner of the room is a garbage bag with material scraps left over from cutting out comfort patches from scraps. The little boys want to sew up a big ball someday. That is what you call recycling to the smallest material scrap!

In the living room

Living room decor. In the corner of the room is the showroom for a variety of woodworking projects that give a glimpse of the small business one son started. The crane he made as a nine-year-old, the wooden puzzles, marble rollers, and pens all start conversations in Sunday afternoon visits. A number of wood-burning plaques tell of interest in wildlife or illustrations of life's lessons. During the summer, his toolbox sat in the living room. He calls it a toolbox, but I call it a cedar chest. I guess mine's the more feminine term, and I have dreams of how I would be using it. He made the chest for carrying his small tools for woodworking when he travels the twelve hours to and from his teaching job. The chest is beautifully made of cedar, wood burned and engraved on the lid and sides with boyish designs of wild animals.

In the kitchen

Boys give expression in the kitchen. Birthday cakes consist of forklifts and trucks, tractors and barns. Our last birthday cake was chocolate, and from the green grass surface rose a rock pile with gummi worms crawling around it. To make the scene more complete, there was a man standing in the corner with a gun carved from a popsicle stick aiming at the snakes. This handiwork was all done by the nine-year-old birthday boy and his next older brother. The rock pile and the man were cut out of a cake that came about by accident. The birthday boy wanted to make his own cake. As he carefully followed the recipe, he suddenly realized that some of the ingredients were for the icing. He had already put in the brown sugar that was meant for the icing. That was easy to take care of. All he needed to do was double the ingredients for the cake since there was enough sugar for a double recipe. Then he had exactly what he needed for the making of a rock pile and a man.

In the kitchen there are other boyish influences. Why put the food on the table in pretty serving dishes when the kettle works so well and saves on dishes? Why bother with dessert dishes or knives or forks when we don't need them? The dishwasher likes to be given the option of extra utensils. Dishwasher? Indeed, I have had a dozen dishwashers. Sometimes they get a lazy streak, but really, my dishwashers are all very special. My dishwashers have all been specifically designed and given as gifts to me. Sometimes it bothers me that my big boys need to take turns washing dishes. However, someone told me, "If your husband puts their names on the dishwashing schedule, let them wash dishes. Someday your daughters-in-law will thank you for it." So I learned to enjoy watching my big boys in the kitchen. Little stories come back of things that other boys do not know how to do, like cracking and frying eggs or going ahead in the making of a meal.

When our oldest daughter got married and the second daughter was asked to teach school, I was left at home with nine boys and a daughter still in school. Without the aid of my boys, I could not have done it, but they met the challenge. They helped pack lunches and make breakfast and even made bread.

One Sunday, my youngest daughter came home from church and said, "The girls at church were wondering what we were having for dinner, and I didn't know." A couple Sunday mornings later, she got up a little earlier and came down to help get dinner in the oven. But her brother had been up earlier this time, and dinner was already prepared. When we had little ones who needed help getting changed after we got home from church, I did not need to worry about dinner. By the time I got to the kitchen, our boys had the table set and dinner ready. One time we had gone away for the weekend and left some of the big boys at home. They had some boys over for Sunday dinner, and it was a feast. (Wish I could have been a little mouse in the corner!)

In the basement

Well, maybe I would not want to be a little mouse in the corner with a table full of big boys. Our old house has many places for mice to make their entrance; even rats have gotten into the cellar. When someone shouts, "Mouse!", there is a wild scramble to end the life of the rodent as furniture is moved or appliances are pulled out. I smile and wonder what life would be like without my boys. If we had a family of girls, would they make a wild scramble to perch high and scream because of the appearance of a rodent? Our son came home from work one day with a gaping cut on his head. They were chasing a groundhog, and in the scramble, he was hit on the head with a rake. While others wondered how the accident happened, I could just picture those wild scrambles in rodent chases!

One evening the big boys snuck to the basement with one of their friends and enjoyed a bowl of ice cream. To add adventure, a rat ran across the room. We heard the commotion and wondered what was going on down there, but by the time we got to the scene, one of the boys was holding the rat by its tail. He had pounced on it in his stocking feet! Another time, our boys with some company boys were in the basement getting ready for bed when a rat came in the open basement window. Might the story have had a different ending if it would have been a group of girls getting ready for bed?

In the great outdoors

I grew up on a one-hundred-twenty-three-acre farm, and I loved outdoor work. To me the less than two acres that my husband and I owned seemed very small on which to raise nine boys. One day a gentleman who lived on the eleventh story of an apartment building came for a meal. He was a broker for the recycling business of which my husband was a partner. This man exclaimed repeatedly about what all we can do where we are. Our boys could have pets. Our boys had a nice driveway for riding bikes and skateboards and rip-sticks and unicycles. (And they didn't need to bring their bike into the house every night.) There are trees for building swing sets and tree houses as well as for dangling ropes and tree climbing. Our boys have room for a woodworking shop and room for doing mechanical work. Suddenly I realized what a big world we had!

In butchering

Recently the eight-year-old found a snake skeleton in the hay that

Daddy just bought. He brought it in and wondered if he could cook it and clean it. After finding the perfect kettle, he boiled the skeleton. It turned out better than an older brother's experiment years ago, when a kettle of starling skulls on the basement stove ran out of water! The lad had been sidetracked from his project. We smelled it for days! That time a son was beginning to set up a little taxidermy in the basement kitchen. It was a time of adventures as he tried out my butchering skills when he did not know where to begin. (He was not the first of the boys that wanted help to butcher a groundhog.) Teaching our sons to skin a groundhog was not impossible, because once you know how to skin one creature, it is a foundation for skinning the next. But being a mother of boys brought a new dimension to skinning. Never before did I skin a groundhog! And then the question comes up on how to dig the brains out of the skull. Of course, that was information Mother had no experience in, but we tried measuring spoons and all sorts of tricks to scoop out brains. (And I think how different life would be without my boys! What if I had girls instead?) After a few disappointments, the trial and error of a few years, and the reading of books, today a beautiful mallard and a lovely squirrel sit mounted on their logs perched in the living room.

There's not a dull moment in the house for a mother of boys. I would not trade any of my boys for another girl. After twenty some years, I am discovering that God first blessed us with sons. With time, our sons have continued to grow and develop so that eventually they have brought more daughters into the family circle.

Boys will be boys. As earthly mothers we can enjoy the boyish things of life with them. As Christian mothers we can help our boys develop their interests in a God-honoring way. So soon our little boys are grown men with boys of their own, and our house becomes quieter and quieter with many fond memories of boyish projects and tricks.

Of Boys and Housecleaning

MRS ALLAN MARTIN

"Guess what!" Hannah said brightly as she poured granola into her bowl. Pausing, she smiled at her sons. "We're going to houseclean today!"

"Houseclean?" Caleb groaned.

"Oh, please," Daniel echoed dismally. "What a way to spend our school vacation!"

"I planned to houseclean your bedrooms when you boys can help," Hannah explained, unfazed by their lack of enthusiasm.

The boys headed out to do their animal chores after they had finished breakfast. Soon Caleb was back. "Ready to start, Mom?"

"That sounds better," Hannah said approvingly. "Your enthusiasm at the breakfast table left something to be desired."

"Oh, we were just teasing," Caleb reassured her. "Housecleaning is better than having nothing to do. Lifting the furniture builds muscle anyway."

"Of course," Hannah said, smiling. "All right. I need to put Abigail down for her morning nap before I'm ready to start."

"What shall we do while we wait for you?" Caleb wondered.

"Why don't you start by stripping the beds?" Hannah suggested. "I'll put the bedding in the washer when I get down."

"Lord, help me to be patient and pleasant with the boys while we house-clean today," Hannah prayed as she rocked Abigail. From experience, she knew that housecleaning with a group of energetic boys was not for the faint of heart. Hannah remembered housecleaning with her sisters when she was a young girl. They had meticulously cleaned and sorted everything in their bedroom. Now she was the mother of five sons, and she had done some learning along the way. There was more than one way to houseclean.

Nearly half an hour had passed by the time Hannah headed downstairs. She heard muffled sounds from Caleb and Daniel's room. Upon entering, she saw that an elaborate fort had been created using two single bed mattresses, box springs, the dresser, and an assortment of bedding. Giggles and shouts indicated that five boys were having a good time!

Daniel stuck out his head. "Hey, Mom! Check out our fort!"

"It's nice!" Hannah said after a brief inspection. "Now we'll have to dismantle it so we can houseclean. Then I'll clean the ceiling and the light fixture while you get everything out from under your beds."

The boys set to work.

"Oh, Mom!" Daniel shrieked gleefully a moment later. "I found my fishing pole! The last time we went fishing I couldn't find it anywhere!"

"Take it up to the garage," Hannah instructed. "That's a more likely spot to find a fishing pole."

"Mom, someone is at the door!" Kenton's voice floated down the stairs. Hannah hurried up to see who it was.

"Hello, Ma'am," an older gentleman in a suit greeted her. "I'm Bob Mason, and I'm running for mayor..." his voice trailed off. "You probably don't vote."

"No we don't," Hannah assented. "But the Bible commands us to pray for our authorities; we try to do that."

"Why, thank you, Ma'am," the gentleman said, surprised. "Have a nice day."

Hannah was unable to tell whether it was the ringing of the doorbell or Kenton's yelling, but Abigail was awake again. After a diaper change, Hannah took her downstairs. A hullabaloo sounded from the bedroom.

Slap! Caleb's rag hit Daniel in the face. Daniel howled and sent his rag whizzing across the room at Caleb.

"Boys! Boys!" Hannah scolded. "What is going on here?"

"We're having a rag fight. It's fun!" Daniel explained.

"Fun?" Hannah shook her head in disbelief. "Well, throwing wet rags around makes a mess. No more!"

"We're ready for the next part," Caleb said. "We were waiting for you to come tell us what to do."

"Let's clean your dresser," Hannah decided. "You can each do the drawers that belong to you. Carefully sort through your paper drawers and put anything you don't want in this garbage bag. The more things you throw away, the less you need to organize and put back."

Daniel opened his top dresser drawer and stared at the accumulation inside. Caleb pulled his drawer out and dumped it upside down on the floor.

"Good idea," Hannah approved. "I can wipe the drawer for you."

Whoosh! Hannah lifted her head in surprise as a paper jet whizzed by.

"Sorry, Mom!" Daniel apologized. "I was aiming for Caleb."

Already a paper from Caleb's drawer was fast forming into a jet. Hannah rolled her eyes in mock exasperation. "There ought to be some kind of prize for mothers who attempt to houseclean with their sons," she said.

Caleb stopped folding his jet. "A prize for mothers?" he asked in astonishment. "I thought you'd say there ought to be a prize for the boys who houseclean!"

Hannah laughed. "There is. Your prize will be a nice, clean room."

She set down the drawer.

"I'll wipe the outside of your dresser too," Hannah continued. Eyeing the shotgun shell collection on the dresser top, she asked casually, "Do you want to keep your shell collection?"

Daniel's head jerked up. "Our shotgun shell collection?" he asked, incredulous.

"It's up to you," Hannah reassured him. "It's just that it takes a lot of room on your dresser, and it's hard to dust."

"We've had it quite awhile and haven't added any new shells recently," Caleb observed. "Maybe we could throw it away."

"Well, maybe if I kept a few of my favorites," Daniel conceded.

"Throwing stuff away is a part of housecleaning," Hannah encouraged. "It makes room for new collections and interests."

"Should I throw out my letters from Miss Yoder?" Caleb asked.

"The letters from your teacher?" Now it was Hannah's turn to be incredulous. "Of course not! Daddy wrote his teacher a letter every summer and got one in return, and we still have them!"

"It was fun to get them in the mail," Caleb said. "But I never reread them."

"Your wife might find it interesting," Hannah maintained.

"Hmpf!" Caleb said. But he put the envelope of letters back in his drawer.

Kenton was at the bedroom door. "Mom, Josiah stinks!"

"I'll come in a minute," Hannah said as she gave the dresser a final swipe. Turning to Caleb and Daniel she said, "After you finish your drawers, you can each wash two walls. Rinse your rag carefully and wipe the wall like this," Hannah demonstrated. "If there are dirty marks on the wall, use your muscles and scrub until they are gone. After I change Josiah, I need to start dinner, but I'll be back."

Hannah heard shrieks and giggles, thumps and bumps from the direction of the basement bedroom as she made dinner. *I wonder what it would be like to houseclean with a couple of girls,* she thought to herself. *It has to be different than refereeing a boys' housecleaning bee. I wouldn't trade my boys for a minute though.*

"How's it going?" Hannah wanted to know when she returned awhile later. She set Abigail in her infant seat again. Both boys were sprawled out on the floor reading.

"We're done," Daniel said. "Is there anything else?"

"The floor…" Hannah's voice trailed off as she looked closely at the wall by the door. "Whoever did this wall missed some spots."

"Wasn't my wall," Daniel said quickly.

"I didn't do it either," Caleb admitted. "I must have missed one wall."

Missed a wall? Hannah thought to herself wryly. *That was half his assignment!*

As Caleb scrubbed, Hannah noticed the empty spot on the dresser. "Did you get rid of the shotgun shell collection?"

"Yeah," Daniel answered, "we decided we don't want it anymore."

"Is it in the garbage bag?" Hannah tried not to sound too excited.

"Nah, the little boys wanted it. We helped them set it up on their dresser. We let them have our rock collection too."

Hannah stifled her groan.

Abigail was fussing. Hannah jiggled the beads hanging from the toy bar. "What's with the pile of clothes on the bed?" she asked.

"It's all stuff we don't want. Either it's too small or it's scratchy or something," Caleb answered.

"All right. I'm glad you kept those clothes out," Hannah said. "Whose socks are on the pile?"

"Not mine," Daniel said, tossing them at Caleb.

"Not mine either!" Caleb exclaimed, throwing them back.

Hannah intercepted and caught the socks. Pulling them apart, she looked at the innocent brown socks. "Why don't you want them?" she asked. "They look like good socks—no holes!"

Daniel wrinkled up his nose. "Blech! Those socks are yucky!"

"They have a falling-down habit," Caleb supplied.

"And they just don't feel nice," Daniel added.

"Then I'll wear them," Hannah declared. "They can't be that bad. Now I think we're finished except for the floor, and I'll do that."

Abigail's whimpers were changing to wails.

"What about the closet?" Caleb wondered.

"Oh. The closet." Hannah picked up her crying daughter. "We really should clean the closet too. You boys go ahead and empty it while I put Abigail down for another nap."

Finally, just before supper, Hannah finished the floor. The closet had been duly emptied and reorganized. Though exhausted, Hannah was pleased with the day's accomplishments. Caleb came to the door. "Looks good, Mom!"

"Why, thank you," Hannah said, feeling her spirits lift a little. "I appreciated your help."

"It was actually fun," Caleb said sincerely.

Hannah's spirits rose further. "Oh, I'm glad to hear you say that," she exclaimed, rumpling his hair. "What better prize could a mother wish for?"

Hannah was feeding Abigail the next morning when her twelve-year-old niece, Julia, arrived to spend the day. "Welcome," Hannah said with a smile as Julia let herself in. "The boys are all downstairs in the storeroom. We're housecleaning the freezers today."

"All right," Julia answered, laughing. "I'll have no trouble finding them—I'll follow the racket."

Hannah listened to the rumpus coming from the basement as she rocked. *Poor Julia! Was she feeling up to working with her noisy cousins?* Being the youngest in her family, and only having two brothers, Hannah was sure Julia had never housecleaned amid such a commotion. *I suppose she is learning that boys' housecleaning and girls' housecleaning are two entirely different things,* Hannah mused as she put her sleeping baby into the crib. *I'd better go down and see how it's going.*

Hannah entered the storeroom just in time to see Daniel flick ice from the freezer at Julia. "Daniel," she gasped in dismay. "It's one thing to treat your brother like that. But don't do it to Julia. She's your cousin, and a girl at that!"

"But Mom," Daniel protested, turning to face Hannah. "She put a hunk of ice down the back of *my* shirt first!"

On Mothering Boys

ANOTHER MOTHER

I am a mother of four boys, ages six and under. How dull my life would be without them! I've learned that boys will be boys, and although they must not be turned loose to do as they please, they will do some things that most little girls wouldn't do.

Our boys love to climb. Trees, stepladders, or their daddy's trailer ramps in the up position are all fun to climb. Even the baby, not yet a year old, likes to climb.

They don't mind a mess either. When I ask them to take the watermelon rind out to the pigs, they'll get forks and sit in the grass and devour the red that remains on the rinds. There's a thrill in watching them sit together, not talking, concentrating on getting another bite.

Mud puddles are a great attraction to little boys. It's such fun to sail little "boats" on the water or simply walk through the puddles. Is that something I allow? It makes a big difference whether it's in the summer or if it's chilly outside.

A more serious mess is paint. Now *that* is not allowed! Once they got into some brown paint and ruined the oldest son's school pants.

Another mess that our boys often create is spilled water. I sometimes forget to yelp when it happens; it's getting so common. (When I get frustrated at their clumsy little hands, my husband or I spill the next one.) One day I even ran out of tea towels, which is what we grab for spills.

Cookies or snacks surely don't last long. Sometimes I wonder how much they'll eat in another five years if they already eat this much. But imagine how much help I'll have by then! I think they do well at helping with dishes even though they don't like doing them.

One day I went to the garden and picked many tomatoes. Our four-year-old surprised me by bringing in two loads for me. Another time our two oldest cleaned out our garden shed. It's such a good feeling when you see that they are realizing how good it feels to do something for someone else.

Fathers and mothers have such a high calling. Too often through the hustle and bustle of the day, I get my priorities mixed up. I am thankful for new days, new chances to do better, and more practice in patience. By nature, I am not a patient person. I think God is trying to teach me patience—through our sweet little boys!

Stay Small, My Son!

LORAINE J BATES

Stay small, my son!
No need to run
into the arms of manhood;
you'll get there soon enough.
You're made of better stuff
than that.
You're stronger than the strongest man
to get this mama-heart to stand
for you.
I'll do
'bout anything you ask
with one small cry of yours.
You have no wars
that I'll not fight.
Your whimpers smite
the depths of me
more than a muscled man, you see.
Your eyes speak out in dire demand,
and I'm a puppet in your hand.
There is no willpower left in me
whenever you relentlessly
hold on with hugs and kisses.
I have no other wishes
but this one—
stay small, my son!

The Bustle of Boys
&
Creation of Clutter

MARY ANN MARTIN (ALTERED)

Why hot pads on the bathroom floor?
Who smeared the glass on our front door?
The milk that's on the front porch mat—
Who spilled it dashing to the cat?

Why is there soap on someone's desk?
And what's this here? A robin's nest?
The washer makes an awful sound
As it goes 'round and 'round and 'round!

While standing at the closet door,
Because of things, I see no floor!
Just paper, strings, some screws, and scrap—
Son hauls it here just like a rat!

I scan the living room's full floor;
Two bathroom plungers here? What for?
The boys were bored, too bored I say
If they had nothing else to play!

Now what's this rolled-up ball of stuff?
Perhaps some…socks. Why, sure enough!
Rolled neatly to the tippy-toe;
The ones we searched for high and low.

The measuring cups just disappear,
Although they recently were here.
They must have thought, *Cute, handled cup—*
Mom won't mind if I fill it up.

"A sale," I hear, "junk sale today,"
He shouts, "Come see my great display
Of doodads, gadgets, trinkets, more."
Some shoppers gather at his store.

Crazy contraptions of Legos and blocks,
Inventions that function with balloons that go
pop,
Crafty creations, and great gizmos too,
Homemade flying objects that will "amaze"
you.

They are boys, they are boys, they are here and
then there,
They swing open the door, and they stomp up
the stair.
Not minding the dirt and the laundry undone,
It is home life to us, and we are all having fun!

Recipe for a Sunday Dress for mother

BEEN THERE

Ingredients:
  1 well-rested mother (for the sweetest results, do not
  substitute*)
  4 lively preschool sons—
          1 five-year-old
          2 two-and-one-half-year-old twins
          1 six-month-old baby
  1 telephone
  1 book—*The Big Red Barn*
  1 dress, cut out, but not sewn
  1 sewing machine
  1 spool light blue thread
  1 spool white thread
  1 ripper
  1 Sunday dress (Well-Worn brand)
  1 can genuine smiles
  (*Sometimes it has become compulsory to substitute, but I have found it sours
very quickly.)

While the baby plays in his walker and the rest of the boys play farm, thread sewing machine with light blue thread. Sew one skirt seam. Use a twist-tie to hook five-year-old's toy manure spreader to his tractor. Rebuild the fence that the twins knocked down on their farm. Replace all the toys that fell off the baby's walker tray. Sew half of the second skirt seam. Answer telephone. Fifteen minutes later, remove twins from sewing machine chair. Rethread machine. Reset tension and stitch length. Finish second skirt seam. Retrieve crying baby from walker. Rock him to sleep and tuck him into bed. Once more, remove twins from sewing chair and punish them. Search for light blue thread. Rethread the machine with white thread instead. Reset tension and stitch length. Thread an embroidery needle for five-year-old so he can sew on his embroidery patch while Mom sews. Sew third skirt seam while reading *The Big Red Barn* (mostly by memory) to the twins. Rip out third skirt seam that you sewed inside out. While ripping, read *The Big Red Barn* twice more; sing "This Little Light of Mine" three times, and "Cling to the Bible" once. Dig a knot out of five-year-old's embroidery thread. Re-sew third skirt seam while one twin stands behind you with his arms around your neck and the other stands on a stool beside you and tries to catch the hand-wheel on the end of your sewing machine. Set twins on couch with a stack of books. Get crying baby out of his crib and settle him into his swing. Answer telephone. Sew fourth skirt seam while baby grumbles and twins quarrel over *The Big Red Barn*. Turn off sewing machine. Pick up baby and settle onto couch between twins to read stories for twenty minutes until dinnertime. Thank God for four healthy sons. On Sunday, pull the well-worn dress out of your closet and wear it one more time. Garnish your face with the can of genuine smiles. The effect will be beautiful!

And let us not be weary in well doing: for in due season we shall reap if we faint not.
Galations 6:9

WORMS, WORMS, WORMS!

M EBERSOLE

It all began with frequent complaints from my two-year-old son of his sitter hurting (to put it in modest language). It was puzzling. He couldn't sit still. (Most normal two-year-olds can't, but this was a significant bouncing.) He seemed to think that maybe frequent trips to the bathroom would help. I didn't spend an undue amount of time thinking about it. Perhaps it was just one of those passing things.

One day my five-year-old casually informed me that, "We like to bite the cats and then spit out the hair."

My response wasn't "I-see-but-you-shouldn't-do-that." At that moment, we had Health Class—both of cats and of humans. This was a lightbulb moment. Two plus two equals four. Using the same equation, I was adding Boy plus Eating Dirty Cat Hair and getting the sum of Worms. WORMS! My husband agreed that my mathematical figuring was correct.

What were we to do? This was worse than horrible. Those worms dogged my thoughts. Weren't worms something that only third-world inhabitants had? Surely not something common in America, was it? Or if it was, maybe back in the sticks where low-class folks lived in unsanitary conditions. Certainly not worms in *my* children!

I consulted my medical books. Most of them suggested seeing a doctor. Only one gave the hope of getting rid of them without medical help. But these words ballooned the situation: *By contaminating food, drinking glasses, sheets and towels, the child may pass pinworms on to other family members.* End of Quote, but definitely not End of Stress.

We're not the kind of family who always has designated cups. We rarely give leftovers to the cats. My husband and I don't gag about cleaning up our children's plates. All the boys still bathe together. I visualized these fierce worms swarming through our house...and bodies, with their mocking grins! HORRIBLE!

I told my mother. Of course, her response was the same as mine. She had heard that pumpkin seeds were a cure for parasites. Boys who eat cat hair should easily be able to tolerate pumpkin seeds, but I didn't have pumpkin seeds.

When I talked to my friend, her response matched mine. After she heard what my sons had done, she laughingly said, "That sounds like something that would happen here." Interestingly, she only has experience mothering girls! Maybe I wasn't such a negligent, careless mom after all.

My friend offered help. She had a daughter, who as a toddler had tasted anything within reach. Once this little girl had tasted something unmentionable, so my friend bought some herbal medicine known to cure parasites in children. A just-in-case type of thing. I was welcome to try it.

Well, why not? Something had to be done. It couldn't make this horrible situation worse. An herbal cure seemed a little easier than pumpkin seeds, and a lot easier than a trip to the doctor. Sheepishly I received a pink-striped plastic bag containing the glass bottle of Olive Leaf Extract in the church parking lot one Sunday evening.

That week we began the cleansing process. I diligently mixed the medicine into my son's water. I have boys who like to take medicine. If one is sick and takes medicine, the non-sick one needs some too.

So my son felt very pleased and quite privileged to take medicine! At first, that is. After several doses, it wasn't going so well. (It should taste better than cat hair, not?) Mixing it with juice helped it flow down easier. Eventually, all signs of the Might-Be, Probably-Are worms vanished, and the herbal treatment was discontinued.

Later I told the story to my sister-in-law who has served in Haiti. She had experienced parasites in her children. Her description of the illness was not at all similar to our situation. My son's problem was likely misdiagnosed. Oh, well. It made memories that we can laugh about! I guess it proved how tough boys' systems are to accommodate their uncouth ways!

After the Worm Episode had gone down in history, I found my son drinking from the cat's water bowl. Just in case you wished to know.

A Boy's View on the Structure of the Body

AUTHOR UNKNOWN

A young boy was requested to write an essay on anatomy. The results are as follows:

Your head is kinda round and hard and your brains are in it and your hair on it. Your face is the front of your head where you eat and make faces. Your neck is what keeps your head out of your collar. It's hard to keep clean! Your shoulders are sort of shelves where you hook your suspenders on, and your stomach is something that if you don't eat often, it hurts and spinach don't help it none! Your spine is a long bone in your back which keeps you from folding up. Your back is always behind you no matter how quick you turn around. Your arms you gotta have to pitch with and to reach the butter. Your fingers stick out of your hands so you can pitch a curve and count up arithmetic. Your legs are what, if you don't have two of, you can't get to first base. Your feet are what you run on and your toes are what *always* get stubbed. That's all there is of you except what's inside and I never saw it!

On Raising Men for God

MRS SHARLA BORNTRAGER

"*A little boy is the only thing God can use to make a man.*" Boys come with a great need for guidance and many prayers. Be prepared to learn things you never cared about or even knew existed. Many idle moments can turn into learning for them, and the most important thing we can do for them is to guide them to the Fountain of Wisdom.

What if Daddy is gone? We must do our best and leave the rest. A worldly lady once gave me a tip on raising sons. "Daddy must be involved," she said. If your sons have a godly father at all, even if he has passed away, they are richer than many boys. Many godly men have grown up even without a daddy coming home.

We must focus on the eternal good of our sons and hold loosely to the gifts of time, money, and things. Boys need to be allowed to dig, build, explore, and take things apart. When we shift our priorities, we will allow them to do this.

On the doing of jobs, the hard question is not, "What can they do?" Instead it is, "How can they be taught to *want to* do it, *keep at it*, and *work with others*?" Diligence and willingness are of greater worth than quantity and quality of work. For the sanity of the mother, it works best to give only one or two boys an assignment while the rest play or do their own projects. If they all must stay indoors, the basement, garage, an extra room, or enclosed porch can be turned into a shop, science corner, or pet area.

Boys can cook, bake, clean, wash, launder, and even sew. Just expect extra noise, extra messes, and extra action to get it done! Lists help a lot so they know where the finish line is.

True, strong men never purposefully hurt the weak and the small. They are protectors. We must teach our sons when fun is not right. Never, ever allow mocking or tormenting of animals or humans. Not even bugs. Our boys must learn to be gentlemen.

Our boys might not remember what we said, but they likely will remember what we did. We must listen more. Our boys need our example to show them the importance of truly listening from the heart. Someday they may have a wife who needs a listening ear and heart. We also need more trust. It takes faith to let them be boys, to let them climb, use power tools, ride a horse, drive, swim, and shoot. If they have a daddy who teaches them, trains them, and allows them to experiment, they do not need a hovering mother. Rather they need a praying mother. Pray more! Every man needs a woman who believes in God's plan for him and to pray for him.

Each of our sons has a purpose. We need to go forth with courage, and God will grant wisdom for those who ask. If there is anything that will bring parents to their knees, it is the raising of sons.

Is Pink a Girls' Color?

M EBERSOLE

One day as Son cleared the table, he innocently asked, "Mother, why do you always give the pink cup to yourself? Isn't that being selfish?"

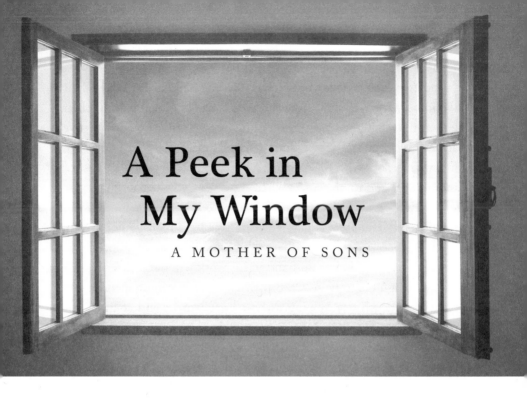

A Peek in My Window

A MOTHER OF SONS

After our ninth son was born, our only daughter, who was four at the time, asked why I don't put dresses and girls' clothing on him. After explaining to her why, she said that she thought if we would give the baby a girl's name when it is born and put girls' clothing on it, then it would be a girl. Afterward, I couldn't help but think, *What if it would be that way? What if we could decide? Oh my, wouldn't that be fun! Why, I just might have every other! A boy, then a girl, another boy... Or maybe I would pick two boys, two girls... Or even three or four or five boys followed by just as many girls would sound appealing.* I'm sure I definitely wouldn't have waited until after seven boys to tell my husband that I think this baby will be a girl now, then afterward choose to add even more boys to our family! Instead, we are not in control and need to be content with what God chooses for our family. But at times, I do wonder what God is trying to teach us by giving us so many sons.

Some women wonder how to remain sane and sweet when their feminine nature clashes with the rough and tumble spirit in their boys. I find that amusing. My husband doesn't think I qualify to give advice since many times I don't remain sane and sweet. Yes, I fail many times, but with God's help, I try very hard to make the best of these rough and tumble years when the boys are still all at home.

I believe one of the contributing factors to how much a mother will miss having daughters is how well she is able to manage her household. Chances are that a mother who has no other occupation and is not required to help her husband in his work will not as keenly miss having daughters to help her. But when a mother must spend hours of her time each day helping to be a breadwinner and at times get maids to help her stay on top of the workload while the teenage boys' help is needed by their dad, most likely she struggles more with not having daughters.

When the children were younger and our family was smaller, I knew our boys were helping me in the house just as well as anyone else's families. But over the years as our families grew, I started noticing more and more big differences in homes where older daughters were versus homes with just boys to help. It is as another mother of boys said, "All these years I was longing for the cute little girls, and all of a sudden, I look around and realize that I'm now longing more for that teenage daughter instead." I couldn't have agreed more.

As a family grows, a mother's workload grows too. The amount of food it takes, the amount of laundry there is, and the amount of cleaning to do is much greater with a family of ten than with a family of five. Yet often a mother of sons doesn't have much help in those later years, because as soon as the boys are old enough, they are likely needed by their dad on the farm, in the shop, or in the business. Even if they were taught when they were younger how to make that jug of iced tea and that handful of cookies they grab before they leave on the tractor, they now won't have time to make them. Neither will they have the time to wash the grease-covered pants they were wearing when fixing machinery!

As our family got larger and the workload heavier, I had to decide what was priority and do the rest only as time and energy allowed. The things I used to love doing—hobbies, sewing, charity work (taking meals to others), or sending birthday cards, scrapbook pages, and letters—rarely happens. I knew God's blessing wouldn't be there if I neglected my family while doing these things. I realized I needed to be content with the things I could manage and let the rest go. There were many times I longed to take a meal to someone, but instead just stopped in with a plate of cookies the boys made or some cut flowers. It was humbling, but it was all I could do at that point of life. My husband told me not to feel guilty since he and the boys often help people when needed.

Can boys help in the house as well as girls? Preschool and lower grade boys can be as much help in the house as any girl the same age. But most times, older boys' interests aren't in housework or helping Mom. The work gets finished as fast as possible so they can be out with their dad. We mothers need to be careful in how we treat our sons when doing housework. Just because one son might be better in the kitchen than the other, do not take advantage of it. I found it best to work side by side with my boys. It went more smoothly, and in the end, I didn't have a bigger mess to clean up than the work they helped with, as can happen while baking or making food.

There are limits to what boys should do around the house. Mom should still be in charge of the laundry even if the boys know how to do it. It isn't proper for boys to be handling women's undergarments while sorting laundry or hanging out loads of wash. Babysitting is another challenge. We should not make our boys responsible to babysit if there are little girls in the house. Even if they are all boys, we shouldn't require them to frequently change diapers or rock the baby to sleep. We'll never regret the inconveniences we may have dealt with in trying to protect our sons' purity. Over the years, our boys did a lot to help with the little ones by giving toddlers rides in pull-behind bike carts till the child fell asleep, playing with them, or taking them along while they worked to keep them happy.

Our boys helped in the garden and with canning and freezing. They enjoyed outside work, such as mowing and mulching flowerbeds. With so many boys, I was very thankful when the day came that I wasn't needed in the dairy barn anymore. I enjoyed staying in the house with my little children, doing housework, and raising a family. So many times when my workload is too heavy I long for that teenage daughter. Instead, I have to be content in still getting someone else's daughter to give me a lift.

One of the biggest things I noticed after the boys were seventeen and joined the youth gatherings was how Sundays were when our boys brought their friends home for meals. For example, one Saturday was a beautiful fall day, so I spent most of the day outside. The evening found me trying to prepare enough food for Sunday and cleaning the house besides giving haircuts and bathing the little children. After the little ones were settled for the night, I was again back in the kitchen finishing my work of peeling potatoes, washing dishes, sweeping floors, and picking up toys. I did not finish until 11:30 PM. The next day after church while I was preparing lunch, I kept watching out the window trying to count how many extra boys there would be. Boards had to be added to the table, more chairs set up, the table set, water poured, food dished out, and the little ones changed out of their white Sunday shirts before we ate. I was more than thankful when my husband pitched in to help where he could. But after the meal when I was again left alone in the kitchen washing dishes, I couldn't help but think how different it would have been if my seventeen- and nineteen-year-olds would have been girls, and this would have been a bunch of girls coming to our house for lunch… I had to think back to when I was a girl, and my sisters and I had friends over. We did most of the work, and our friends pitched in and helped. What did my mom even have to do?!

There are many joys and blessings in raising boys! Probably the biggest one is that they are not as moody! If something doesn't suit them, they will be quicker to speak what is on their mind instead of spending the day moping. They tend to be friends with all the boys, not snubbing or excluding one because of things that are said or done. Recently, my niece told her grandma that the only other girl in her grade told her she didn't like her. I almost had to smile because in all the years we had boys in school, a problem like that never occurred. Also, when you're running late in going somewhere, there is no need to comb and braid hair. As long as the shirttails are tucked in and the faces washed, they will be the ones out waiting on you and your husband!

My favorite poem and song is: "Hold him while he's little; he won't be little long; For all too soon will come the day he won't need Mama's song…" We are never promised tomorrow or how long we are able to keep our children before they are called Home to Heaven. One of our boys has already answered the Master's call.

Umpiring
Brothers

MARLENE BEILER

B aby Michael enjoys lying under the baby gym and batting his toys. Being our fourth boy, he has lots of encouragement:

"Good hit, Michael!"

"Strike! Good try!"

"Home run!"

"That was way out of here!"

I hope Michael's brothers will keep up their encouragement to him as he grows out of babyhood.

Hold Him While He's Little

SUSAN NOLT

Hold him while he's little;
He won't be little long.
For all too soon will come the day
He won't need Mama's song
Nor cuddling on the rocking chair.
He's joined the busy throng.

Guide him while he's little
And show him how to be
A good, obedient little boy,
One not obsessed with "me."
Then you will find in years to come,
A blessing he will be.

Love him while he's little;
He needs your touch of grace.
He needs the comfort you can give
In just a sweet embrace.
Thoughts of Mom will bring him back
With smile upon his face.

Teach him while he's little
To love the Bible true,
For it has all the answers
To what he needs to do
To make his life fulfilling
And keep heaven in view.

Hold him, guide him, love him;
He'll soon be grown, you'll see.
Teach him while he still is small
And sitting on your knee.
For if you do these while he's small,
'Tis for eternity.

THE HUMOR *of* BOYS

DIANE STUTZMAN

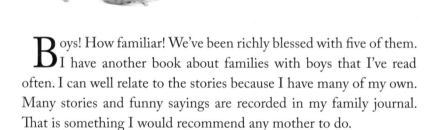

Boys! How familiar! We've been richly blessed with five of them. I have another book about families with boys that I've read often. I can well relate to the stories because I have many of my own. Many stories and funny sayings are recorded in my family journal. That is something I would recommend any mother to do.

We discovered that toads don't like music. We were butchering, so the little ones were running free all day. I stopped to feed the baby when I heard the three- and four-year-old in the kitchen giggling like crazy. *Oh, no, what now?*

I went to investigate. The two boys were on the floor. Between them was a large toy pickup truck that had a loud horn, loud music, and flashing lights. The speaker was on the bed of the pickup. They had caught a large toad and put it on the bed of the pickup, right on the speaker. When they pushed a button to make music, that toad got so scared he would take a flying leap right out of the truck! The two would bend over double with giggles! When they finally caught their breath, they would catch the toad and do it all over. The poor toad probably lost his hearing during that episode!

My husband loves to hunt and fish, so naturally the boys follow in his steps. They fish in any old water hole they find, sometimes even on the lawn or in a snowdrift. One afternoon I looked out the window toward the backyard. One boy was sitting in a baby stroller; the other had a small lawn chair perched on top of a snowdrift. Both were bundled up in snow pants, coats, and mittens. Both were casually casting fishing rods out into the snow as if that was perfectly normal. We believe they had a bad case of spring fever!

Now that our boys are getting older, there's almost not enough Daddy to go around. He can only take them hunting one at a time, although the oldest goes alone now. We have some private hunting land where they go to hunt sometimes. One morning my husband took Luke, our eight-year-old, there to hunt. They saw four deer coming their way and ended up shooting all of them! Luke remarked, "The neighbors probably thought the British were coming with all those gunshots!"

My husband thought he had it made this past year. He shot a deer one day. The next morning he took one of the boys hunting and came home to find yesterday's deer in the freezer, thanks to the boys!

Here are some short sayings and stories that I've recorded in my journal:

• The boys just couldn't wait for the strawberries to ripen. They were only half-red, but finally Grandma said they could each pick one. One boy said, "Grandma, that strawberry was green, but it tasted red!"

• Our boys went through many butterfly nets. One frustrated boy said, "Mom, we need a butterfly call; I can't catch any!"

• Once when we were at the lake fishing, one boy caught a baby perch. I told him to throw it on the trash pile because it was dead and too small to butcher. Guess what I found the next day as I was checking pockets and getting ready to do laundry? Yup, this cute little perch with a not-so-cute fish smell!

We've had our share of ponies, rabbits, ducklings, dogs, and wild bunnies. No cat, sparrow, or starling dares come near us. If they do, they won't be there long!

And food. Lots and lots of food! We used to be able to make it on the fish and deer meat we caught with an occasional pig thrown in. But last year we got ten deer, and the meat was still gone before the hunting season started. We had to butcher our first cow. Our boys aren't picky eaters. They soon learned if they won't eat it, someone else will, and there won't be any left for them. The boys like to butcher, eat, fish, eat, tear around, eat, hunt, and ... oh, did I mention eat? But we love it!

I had my share of struggles over not having any girls, but we know of a few couples who haven't been able to have any children. I think that's what helped me the most. I had five healthy children, no disabilities, only one broken bone (so far), and only one hospital stay. Also, many, many people (many strangers) have told me girls are harder to raise than boys. Therefore, I am very satisfied with what I have. I will enjoy my boys all I can, while I can.

BOYS AND NOISE

MARTHA SCHMUCKER

Boys screech and scream
To let off steam.
They laugh and sing
Till echoes ring.
They growl and roar
Behind the door.
They holler and whoop,
Whistle and toot.
They cheer and chatter,
Clash and clatter.
They moan and mumble,
Groan and grumble.
They yell and shout,
Indoors and out.
But...who wants boys
Without their noise?

A Boy and His Pig

JUDITH MARTIN

Our son Landis was six years old when he wanted a pig to raise. Oh, he wanted a pig in the worst sort of way! We decided he could get one from a neighboring hog farm. Finally, I went with him to see if they had any runts. They said they'd bring us one the next day. When they came, there were two pigs on the back of the truck! We dropped them into the pen we had prepared in the barn. It was only a matter of minutes until they discovered a hole. They were out the back of the barn and running through the young stand of corn with Landis and me puffing and panting after them in hot pursuit. After a long, winded chase, we got them into the barn again. The long story short is that by the time those hogs were fattened and ready for market, Landis was so tired of feeding them he wished he'd never ever begged for pigs! But, oh, was that bacon good!

LED BY MY SON

M EBERSOLE

Oh, they grumble on Monday, Tuesday, Wednesday... How many of us sing this song to our children, partly in rebuke, but mainly in hopes of producing a change of attitude? Yet how many times would our children be justified in singing this song to us, their mothers, if they knew how? I'm ashamed to say that I was dramatizing the song very well, but it took a six-year-old to tell me so.

I wanted to host company for a meal, and my husband and I agreed to invite them for Friday evening supper. I cheerfully made the calls on Wednesday morning and gave the invitations. As soon as the phone was back on the hook, I was flying around—or at least trying. But the baby was following me, whimpering and begging to be held, and the other two boys were not playing well. My flying turned to buzzing, and the boys were getting stung.

That evening one boy came down with the flu. My noble goals were threatened, but I held out as long as possible. When Friday dawned with a still sick boy, I called our invited friends and un-invited them.

Something needed to be done with the food I had managed to prepare. Some of it went into the freezer...except the potato salad. I had overshot in the making of it, and now had nearly two gallons. My husband didn't mind; he relishes potato salad. I enjoy it too. And our one son eats a little bit. But two gallons would last a lo-o-ong time. I would send some to our neighbor family who had a five-week-old baby, but I wouldn't send only potato salad. I decided to send some of the company cake and make a casserole to go with it.

I was reaching into the cupboard when it happened. I bumped the glass lid, and it hurtled downward. I shrieked. It landed on the counter in one piece. I turned, and there stood my three sons. This time it was Mom's fault.

A few minutes later my six-year-old said, "Mother, God must have had His Hand on that lid and kept it from breaking." I heartily agreed. And I pondered it in my heart. *God has His Hand in all things. When I feel out of control, He is in control. If only I could remember that instead of flying off the handle.* Such lofty thoughts and ideals.

That evening the baby came down with the flu.

"Boys!" I snapped. "Would you please be quiet and calm down!"

It was Sunday evening, and our family was at home. Sadly, I had reverted to buzzing. I had good reason. I had missed church in the morning due to a sick child. The baby was not sleeping well, and I longed for an undisturbed night of sleep. I was tired. Tired of the whining. Tired of the coughing. Tired of the sniffling. I was tired of the croaking cries: "I need a hankie!" "I want a drink! Of juice!" "I want some medicine!" "I want ice in my cup!" "I need a hankie! A hankie!"

At the moment, there obviously was not a need of medicine. The boys had manufactured a sliding board using sofa cushions. Their shrieks and giggles and thumping was too much for my somnolent brain.

The hymn singing we had been listening to on the phone was over, and the ordained brother was closing the service. He mentioned that when we get to heaven our voices won't wear out. "And we won't need to hang onto frayed knots," I wryly told my husband.

We were preparing for bed when my son complained, "I'm getting tired of you grouching around and sighing." My husband rebuked him for not being respectful, but I felt condemned. If I want my sons to respect me, I need to act in a way that deserves respect. God doesn't give us more than we can bear. I had no good reason for my irritability. God placed me in these circumstances—three sons, sick children, missing church… He will give the grace to keep sweet. All I need to do is ask Him. How often in my haste to regain control do I push past God's Hand? God also blessed me with a godly husband, and that evening after the boys were in bed, he helped me to get refocused. God, in mercy, led me by my son, and He gives me courage for… one… minute… at… a… time.

A Word of Wisdom

BY ONE WHO WAS THERE

A group of young mothers were visiting at a family gathering. The discussion was lively as each related the ups and downs of mothering a row of small children. When their aunt walked up and sat down among them, one young mother leaned forward, asking, "After raising a family of seven boys and two girls, can you tell us what is the most important thing to remember while training children?"

The aunt thought for a few minutes, and then replied, "Keep their heart. When you've lost your child's heart, you've lost it all."

A Song of Surrender

LUCINDA EBY

Spring was here, and the promise of new life was sprouting forth. The tulips and daffodils were blooming again after the barrenness of winter. We, too, had spring in our hearts after years of barrenness. We were anticipating the bloom of a new little life. But God had another plan for us. After several weeks, our hope began to flicker and fade. Soon our fears were confirmed. The new little life had slipped into eternity.

Stephen, our six-year-old, was excited about his plans for the day. It was Saturday, and Daddy did not need to go to school. Today it was his turn to go with Daddy all by himself. He was anticipating the simple joy of eating a packed breakfast with Daddy after Daddy's blood work at the lab. The remainder of their day was going to be spent helping a church brother on a building project.

As I was praying that morning, I was continually interrupted with the sound of Stephen coughing. I pondered, *Should Stephen stay home today? He really should get a nap. But how could I disappoint him?* The pain of our own disappointment, the loss of our wee little one, still lingered in my own heart.

When I mentioned Stephen's cough to my husband, he replied, "I know Stephen is going to be really disappointed, but it won't hurt him. I think he should stay home."

Stephen was heartbroken. My heart ached for him, and I squeezed him tightly as he cried. Soon it was time to sing in family worship, but Stephen did not want to choose a song. He wanted to cry and pout.

Daddy gently commanded, "Sit up and be cheerful."

It was hard for Stephen, but he was obedient. After singing two songs, he said, "I know what song I want, 'There's a Cleft in the Rock.'"

When it was time for Daddy to leave, Stephen cheerfully waved good-by then went gleefully to help his big brothers wash the van and rake the grass. Stephen had surrendered, and he was happy.

Later as the quietness settled over the house, I meditated on Psalm 40, *Many, O Lord my God, are... thy thoughts which are to us-ward: they cannot be reckoned up in order unto thee: if I would declare and speak of them, they are more than can be numbered.* As parents, we have tender thoughts toward our children in their disappointments. We try to help them bear their thwarted plans. God cares about our disappointments, too. He lifts us up and sets our feet on a rock.

We do grieve our loss. And our Father grieves with us. Then He says it is time to move on, to bear our disappointment with joy. As we sacrifice ourselves to His will, God will "put a new song in [our] mouths" —a song of surrender.

"There's a cleft in the Rock of Ages, Where my soul may safely hide. While the storms of life are raging, And the billows roll o'er the tide."

THE GIFTS OF BOYS

JUDITH MARTIN

A year ago at Christmas we exchanged names for the first time. That meant the boys had to think of gifts. At twenty-three, our son Bruce has grown up (some!). One day I brought a package in from the mailbox. It was in a gray plastic bag, and I felt there were straps of some sort in it. It was common for Bruce to get packages for his shop things, so I never gave it a second thought. When he came in, he swiped it off the counter and took it upstairs to his room. Christmas rolled around, and we were exchanging our gifts. A package, in a Cabela's bag, was thrust on my lap from Bruce. I said, "Oh, is that why you went to Cabela's?" I proceeded to open it, and to my total astonishment, I pulled out a black Vera Bradley purse! I couldn't believe it! As one who likes purses, I had often jokingly talked of owning a Vera Bradley purse. Bruce had searched and ordered one with my daughter-in-law's tip on which one to get. Inside the purse was a wad of cash, and scribbled on the envelope, I read, "To the best mother a boy could have." Even though I knew that wasn't true, I soaked it up like a sponge. (And no, it did not come from Cabela's!)

One evening we went to a viewing and left the five children at home in a messy house. "Perhaps you could surprise us and have the house cleaned up whenever we get home," I said as I hurried out the door.

When we arrived home and stepped through the door, we stood transfixed. The kitchen and living room were tidy. There was some dirty laundry on a pile with a torn paper on top that read, "Wash thees." On the counter, Philip had put a note— "Mom, I love you and ponies." Bruce had even changed the pillowcases on his bed. (Who would have thought of that?)

I love getting notes! In later years, I made a Sunday evening meal for Philip and his friends. He left a scribbled note on the table—"Mom, thanks for the sup. It was good. Phil."

When our son Anthony was five, he surprised me one day with a heartwarming gesture. Our neighbor lady had come to visit, bringing her out-of-state sister-in-law. We sat in the living room, and the next thing I knew, Anthony had brought us each a little bowl of popcorn. He had made a bag of microwave popcorn, and it was sweet, coming from a round-faced, five-year-old boy!

Our son Clinton is a loving boy with a soft heart. Another Christmas memory comes to mind of several years ago when he was eleven. He placed a gift in my lap, crudely wrapped in newspaper as only a boy could wrap. I opened it to find a tiny paint can, about a cup size, of "Bumblebee Yellow" paint. I heard Landis, his younger brother, say to his dad, "It cost $52.00."

I said, "This paint didn't cost that much!"

He answered, "No, altogether with that," and pointed to a screwdriver bit set which was on my husband's lap. Gradually, we pieced together the story. He had biked out the back lane and then two miles farther to Hoover Lumber, the closest place he could go alone to shop for Christmas gifts for us. I thanked him sincerely and told him I would use that paint on some old wooden blocks in the toy box. Now whenever I see those sunny yellow blocks on the floor, I am reminded of the little boy who used his "copper money and walnut money" on gifts for us.

Our boys give us many things in life, but the best gift is themselves! How we accept their gifts means much to them, but how we accept their person means so much more!

A Son! What Fun!

ERLENE STOLTZFUS

*E*xcept the Lord build the house, they labor in vain that build it (Ps. 127:1). The Lord is the One who plans our families and the One from whom we receive wisdom, guidance, and grace to raise our children for Him. After all, these dear souls are His and only lent to us so that we might teach them the ways of God.

We are a richly blessed family. Yes, a family of boys. But before God gave us any sons, He gave us a daughter, the only sister to all her brothers. She is the only one of our children who remembers our oldest son. She was only four years old when God chose to take her only playmate and our only son of two years out of the world to join the children in heaven. (His life on earth ended in a skid steer accident.) God is good, and this was part of His plan for our family. In the next ten years, the Lord has added four more boys to our family. They are all precious to us, and we thank God for the privilege of loving and caring for these sons.

A wise son heareth his father's instruction... (Prov. 13:1). There is so much involved in teaching our sons to be wise. First, they need us as parents, especially fathers, to be wise examples for them to follow. Then we need to teach them parental respect. I appreciate how my husband requires our sons to respect their mother. After all, how they treat their mother is most likely how they will relate to their wife in later years. My observation in our own home is that when we fail to command respect, then there is also a lack of prompt and cheerful obedience. When both are present, there is a joyful, peaceful atmosphere. *A wise son maketh a glad father...* (Prov. 10:1).

Every normal family of boys will have its challenges with noise! I mind it the most in the winter when everyone spends evenings in the house. What do you do when your boys are bouncing balls off the walls or racing their little coupe cars through the rooms or being plain silly and chasing each other around and around? Once you think enough is enough, then come up with something profitable for them to do. Maybe it's reading a story to them, playing a game of Sorry, or singing together. If they happen to get rowdy at other times of the day, it may be time to give them jobs to do. They can do dishes, sweep the floors, wash windows, and fold laundry. Oh yes, boys can bake, too. Our boys enjoy making Best Brownies. One of the first times our son Lewis baked these, he dumped in one cup of baking powder instead of one teaspoon! I caught up with his mistake before he stirred up the batter, so we scooped out what we could. As it was, the batter baked to the very top of the pan, but the finished product was still scrumptious! We had a good laugh!

Boys can also create all kinds of messes that require mothers to clean up. Our son Nevin has been the most famous for getting into trouble that resulted in major cleanups. He was between one and two-and-a-half years old when most of the incidents happened. I clearly remember the time he threw a china sugar bowl onto the floor for the sheer delight of watching it break. Another time he awoke from his nap as hungry as a bear, spied a pan of freshly baked bars on the table, and reaching up, pulled the glass pan until—CRASH! It landed on the floor! He didn't get to eat any of those yummy bars! I also remember the time he smeared Desitin all over the front of his shirt, on the wall, and on his crib when he was supposed to be napping. Once we caught him squirting toothpaste into the toilet, but at least that was an easy cleanup! Too often I would become impatient because my precious time was wasted cleaning up a mess. Thankfully, my patient husband helped me to see the uselessness of that. Now I try to see the humorous side of the incident and remember to be grateful for a healthy boy. To add to that, it makes memories to jot down in his baby book!

We are a singing family. Our boys helped sing at a young age. Once they got older, we needed to coax them to sing. We wondered how to get them enthused about participating wholeheartedly. We started with music lessons since music isn't taught much in our school. We sing the scale and do the scale drills in the back of the *Growing in Music 1* book. It wasn't long until they could take it on by themselves. We sing and pray with them at bedtime. Then we had our eight- and ten-year-old sons stand up by the wall and sing a familiar song by themselves. Now on occasion my husband will ask them to lead a song in family worship. We still need to give reminders when we see them slouching and looking bored. "Remember, we are worshiping God when we sing."

It is very important to have chores and daily jobs to occupy our boys profitably. We have enjoyed raising boys on a dairy farm. By the age of five, they wake up around six AM to help feed calves. This helps give them a hearty appetite for breakfast! I do the evening milking, so the whole family is out doing chores. In the last year, two of our sons have also been feeding heifers on our rented farm a mile from here. We bought a mini Japanese truck (which we call Jap) that our oldest son drives around to headlocks and barns to do the feeding. On Sunday afternoons, I accompany him to feed heifers. I enjoy working with my boys in this way. Working one to one gives opportunity for personal sharing. We also have rabbits. These friendly pets supply our young boys with just the right kind of chores and responsibility. If the boys become lazy or distracted when it's time to do chores, their father will remind them that they don't get to eat their supper until the animals are fed.

We find it rewarding to take time to make special memories with our boys. Every spring and fall, we set up the tents back at Beulah Campground, our very own unique campground in the pinewoods on our farm. Before retiring for the night, the boys search the woods for sticks and pine needles to create a smoking fire to chase mosquitoes away. Then when the fire tames down and the coals are just right, marshmallows are brought out (the coconut-covered ones are the best!) and roasted for a bedtime snack. Sometimes we'll splurge and make s'mores or mountain pies! We sleep out two or three nights at the most, and by then my soft bed in our lavender bedroom is beckoning me! When the weather is perfect, we invite our friends to enjoy a cookout supper in that lovely, quiet, secluded spot where pine needles carpet the floor. The pond, just on the edge of the woods, provides opportunity for boating with our red canoe.

When going on a hike, whether it's taking a path that leads to a misty waterfall, or the county road on the way to church some lovely Sunday morning, or just a stroll down the field lane, it is an opportunity to discuss nature. I enjoy birds, so we try to identify all the species we can. It's also interesting to observe plant life in the woods and roadside ditches.

Going fishing and being able to get a catch always gave the boys a sense of accomplishment. Sometimes we'll go as a family to the Locks and Dam to fish and then dine on a picnic lunch.

On pleasant evenings, when the outdoors beckons us, my husband and I will please the boys and join them in playing ball, pitch and catch, or riding bike down our quiet road.

For a while, our son Lewis took a notion to bow and arrow practice. One mistake he made was to stand on the porch and shoot out into the yard. He felt very deflated when an arrow pierced into the gutter along the edge of the porch roof!

It is often with relief that I send our energetic boys off to bed at night so my husband and I can enjoy peaceful, quiet moments preparing ourselves for bed. Fresh air, sunshine, and exercise soon have the boys off to dreamland in their cozy beds, and I thank God for His guardian angels keeping watch over them another day. Then as I gaze on them in peaceful slumber, I know that I would never trade my boys for anything else in this world. How rewarding it is to be a mother of boys! My prayer is that they will someday become men that God can use to build up His kingdom. Praise His name!

Do You Have Time?

MISTY NISSLEY

"**M**om, do you have time to help me with my chores?" my nine-year-old asked.

"I can't help you slop pigs, but I will sit on the skid steer and watch you. Will that work?"

"Sure!" He brightens at my suggestion.

I get on my sandals, we grab the little brothers, and out to the barnyard we go. "Let's say the books of the New Testament that's due for your Bible memory tomorrow," I suggest. "We can do it here as well as inside."

Amid the squealing, we began, "Matthew, Mark, Luke, John… Squeal!" Even more important though, we tied our hearts, and I got a little look at my boy's heart. It says, *Be with me!*

This son also comes to me on Sunday evenings. "Mom, I want to play a game with just you. Just you." He's saying, *I need your attention!*

"Yes, I think I can do that and still have some time for a game with the others." Two opportunities present themselves here. I could teach him, "No, you aren't the only fish in the pond. You must learn to share

Mom." Or "I value you, son, as a person, and I am willing to set aside time for you." Which lesson does he need to learn?

My thoughts turn to what the Bible says: *I have loved thee with an everlasting love: therefore with loving-kindness have I drawn thee* (Jer. 31:3). That doesn't sound like just another fish in the pond, does it? The Creator of heaven and earth and humankind draws us personally into close fellowship. Do you have time?

To the Mothers of Little Girls
MRS CONRAD HUBER

Your little girls are sweetness wrapped in packages of pink.
I'm sure you will agree, but I'll tell you what I think.
I'll try to say it gently now, without your feelings harming;
A little girl is sweetness, but a boy is, oh, so charming!

I can't resist the sparkle of the mischief in his eyes,
Or how he tries accomplishing things far beyond his size.
Behind the smudges on his face is a grin that's most disarming.
A little girl is sweetness, but a boy is, oh, so charming!

He's passionate 'bout simple things like water, wheels, and keys;
Or fascinated by the moon and owies on his knees;
And he can down a cookie at a speed almost alarming.
A little girl is sweetness, but a boy is, oh, so charming!

Sometimes a pang of wistfulness will creep into my heart
For tender dainty sweetness that of girlies are a part.
But all it takes to cure me is a boyish hug heartwarming.
Your little girl is sweetness, but my boy is Far More Charming!

Blessed
Abundantly
NORMA STEINER

Scene 1:

I suppose I'll be cleaning bathrooms every week for years, I mused as I scrubbed. *If only I had a daughter…*

Scene 2:

It was Saturday again and there was plenty on my to-do list. "Do you want to wash the dishes or clean the bathrooms?" I asked the boys on impulse.

"Clean the bathrooms," was the ready response as the nine-year-old eyed the counter with supper and breakfast dishes on it. I swallowed my uncertainty and jumped for it. What could it hurt to let them try? What a scrubbing and splashing I heard! I was curious but kept my distance after giving a few instructions of how and where to clean. Later I did venture to them and gave a few pointers on how to clean the floor better. They put their energies into full power, and the bathrooms got a cleaning they didn't often get. By now, cleaning the bathrooms is among their weekly chores. As their dad said, "Don't ever tell them that it is an undesired, dirty job." And I am a pleased mom who has someone to share this job with after all!

Scene 1:
I watched wistfully. Our company mom and young daughter were making their bed together. The daughter had a feminine touch that my boys just didn't have when they made a bed. The mother and daughter looked like they enjoyed working together.

Scene 2:
"What can I do for you?" my three-year-old questioned. I was folding laundry so I asked him to roll up my belts. It's a simple job, and although it's only a little help, I like the helpful, willing attitude. "I came in to roll the belts for you," he informs me, feeling very grown-up. I realize he has heard it from his older brothers, and I am grateful for all their dad has taught them by word and example.

Dad says, "There is no such thing as girls' work. We all eat, so we all work, even if it's washing dishes."

Scene 1:
Company was here again. I observed as mother and daughter sat side by side looking at our family calendar. How I wished for some feminine companionship!

Scene 2:
"Mom, what can I do for you?" Son bursts in the door. "Dad said to help you." Dad does well to send in a boy to help set the table or to bring in the wash. I think I have special time with my seven- or nine-year-old boys that I might not have if I had girls to do the girl jobs.

The boys are needed in our dairy barn over chore time, so I feel I don't get much help during school days. But they are more efficient and content in the barn, while I can accomplish more work in the house because I don't generally need to go out. So what better arrangement is there?

What about the dead sparrow in front of the microwave? Son got to carry it back out, and Mom tried to be thankful that they are equally willing to carry out the dead mouse for her.

Those things that make lots of noise: I wish for a cure-all. An eight-foot two-by-four made a good entertainer but didn't help Mom's sanity. A crib mattress made a perfect sled down the basement steps…I find we need to allow some rambunctiousness, but boys can be taught to close doors quietly and to walk—not run—in the house. Do we let them be boys or do we expect gentlemen? There is a time and a place for either one. But, oh, for wisdom to know the difference!

Maybe having all boys isn't more challenging than anyone else's life, but some do not understand the longings and experiences unique to the situation. We do enjoy our boy family very much. It is such a simple way to live—all boy clothes, all boy bedrooms. I like the photos of the boys all in a row in their Sunday best. How uniform! God has blessed us abundantly!

Explanation to Visitors

AJ RUDOLPH

A welcome to the Boy Household
Where all things age but don't get old.
Noise stays in vogue throughout the year
And only Volume changes here.

We buy the Band-Aid box in bulk
Because boys run and seldom walk.
They neither dread the depth nor height,
Nor think to calculate a flight.

Environmental substance? These:
Stones and water, grass and trees.
They take for granted mud's included.
(You didn't know? You've been deluded!)

Bugs, butterflies, and otherwise,
Whatever wiggles, swims, or flies,
Become our cherished captured guests
And, underfed… You know the rest.

You need someone to rig up wires?
Rebuild the engine, change the tires?
Clean out the furnace, fix what's breaking?
Here is a handyman-in-making!

So we mend holes and patch their pants.
Real men aren't made by merely chance,
They're built with counsel, courage, love…
And intervention from Above!

God's Lambs—
Our Boys
LUCINDA EBY

Darkness gathered at the close of another day as my husband, Kevin, stepped into the pen of squawking hens with his two-year-old son at his heels. Stephen wanted to help gather eggs. But a two-year-old dropping eggs into the basket? "Okay," Kevin answered, "but be really careful." He hovered over the youngster, half holding his breath and giving a word of caution for each egg placed into the basket.

After all twelve eggs were safely in the basket, Stephen said, "I want to take the basket."

"No, I'll carry it this time," Kevin said, thinking it too fragile for a two-year-old.

Walking back to the house in the twilight, Kevin mused about how God sees His children. We, like Stephen, sometimes feel quite capable. How must God feel about giving His tender, fragile lambs to weak parents who fail so often? Little harm is done if Stephen drops the basket of eggs. Tomorrow there will be more eggs. Not so with little boys. Carelessness on the parents' part could mean a soul lost for all eternity.

The verse, *Take heed that ye despise not one of these little ones; for I say unto you, that in heaven their angels do always behold the face of my Father which is in heaven,* reads with such tenderness toward children. Kevin could almost feel the yearning of concern with which the Father entrusts these tender lambs into the care of humanity. Yet He gives them to us with the desire that we nurture them for Him.

The Father is so patient with the imperfections of mankind. *He gently leads those that are with young* (Isaiah 40:11). *How prone we are to be impatient and reprimand our children for dropping the eggs,* Kevin considered. *The Father lovingly accepts our repentance and gives us strength to try again. Should we not much more extend that same grace to our little boys, gently giving them correction and direction? This is the way to lead them back to our heavenly Father. Only God who gave us these little lambs can empower us for the task.* The thought gave Kevin comfort and courage.

Forgotten Intention

A MOTHER OF FOUR BOYS

I was feeding the baby before suppertime. The table was only partly set when our four-year-old came in with a grasshopper and put it on *my* plate! I told him he must catch that thing and take it outside. He thought he couldn't but did get it managed. I thought to myself, *I'll get a clean plate when I'm finished feeding the baby.* A few mornings later, I happened to think about this incident and realized I'd forgotten to get a clean plate! *Gulp!*

When to Go to the ER

MEREDITH HORST

The Eternal God is thy Refuge (Deuteronomy 33:27).

For Grace

• When you find dirty fingerprints on the refrigerator door handle for the one thousandth time.

• When the mayonnaise jar is slammed onto the table causing the white substance to fly up then rain down onto the food, table, chairs, floor, and even into your hair.

• When beautiful dead birds appear at the door— "See, Mother, I killed him in the barn! Aren't his feathers shiny?"

• When in spite of your best efforts, your sons' bedroom always smells like boy.

• When they decorate the dresser top with empty bullets, deer antlers, corn kernels, dead bugs, bearing balls, rusty nails…

• When you discover special little toys that came along home from another's house in pockets.

• When the lawn mowing needs to be accomplished by popping wheelies, driving through mud holes, and mowing in odd configurations.

When curious little fingers reach under the running sweeper to see what it is like there—and return minus some skin.

When the kitchen oozes with chocolate brownie batter.

When the finger sliced in play really does need stitches.

When the ironing board gets bent out of shape from being used for vaulting.

When the eggs land on the floor and splat on clean school clothes during breakfast preparations.

When they subject their sister to endless teasing.

When you are startled to discover that you no longer need to tilt your head down to look them in the eye. (Oh, where has my little boy gone?!)

With Gratefulness

When they throw their arms around your middle and say, "You're my BEST MOTHER!"

When they poke their noses into the oven and come out shouting, "Lasagna! Mother you're SO NICE!"

When those brownies made by boys are eaten with compliments.

When you overhear one son say to another, "Mother said we are not supposed to do that."

When they sing together. (Oh, I love to hear them sing!)

When they want to fix your birthday breakfast. ("Mother, you stay in your bedroom until we say we are ready!")

When the sloppy one starts to care about his appearance.

When they voluntarily help little brother blow his nose.

When they say, "Here, Mother, let me carry that for you."

When they are dutifully protective of you, their mother, and of their only sister.

Thank you, Lord, for being a mother's **Eternal Refuge.**

Mother of Boys

AUTHOR UNKNOWN

Praise to the High One
For giving me joys
Peculiarly sweet;
I'm the mother of boys!

Mud puddles, torn blue jeans,
Toads, whistles, and worms;
The furred and the feathered
And whatever squirms;
Black knuckles, bats, arrows,
And thundering noise;
They're all in a day
For the mother of boys.

But, ah, 'tis a dear joy
To turn the blue eyes
To the manifold wonders
Of earth, sea, and skies.
And, ah, 'tis a dear joy
To watch small hands seize
The hand of his God
In the knowledge of these.

Spare me, O High One,
To praise Thee more when
This mother of boys
Is the mother of men!

All Because of Sharks

ELIZABETH LEHMAN

W hen our five-year-old twins, Brad and Brett, received a book about sharks, it was their consuming thought. Sharks. They looked at pictures of them, talked about them, dreamed about them, and even drew them. They drew great white sharks, black-tip reef sharks, whale sharks, tiger sharks, and of course, the odd-looking hammerheads.

"We should take them to the Shedd Aquarium in Chicago," I told my husband, Aaron, one day.

"Maybe that's an outing we could take with the children this summer," he agreed.

We talked it over and decided that we could take the South Shore (electric) train out of South Bend all the way to Chicago on a Friday afternoon, then visit the Willis Tower and also go to the Lego's Store and the American Girl Store. We'd eat at the Rainforest Café, then take the Blue Line Train out of the city to the O'Hare Airport and sleep at the Hilton O'Hare so the children could watch the jets land and take off. The next day we'd visit the Shedd and come home that evening. We asked Mom and Dad to go along to help with the children.

When I called the Hilton O'Hare to make sleeping reservations, there were so many automated answering machines that I barely managed to talk with a real person. When I finally had a real person on the line, he had such a strange accent that I could hardly understand him. I tried to make it clear that we wanted two rooms with a runway view. "Only one room available," he said (or I think that's what he said). I talked with him for what seemed like half an hour, and when I hung up, I wasn't sure what rooms I had reserved.

The children began to get excited as the dates approached. But my well-meaning mother-in-law was doubtful. "Surely you won't take all five children to Chicago!" she said.

I thought it over. The five-year-old twins were the main reason we had planned this, so they would go, of course. The same with seven-year-old Mackenzie. And Alex, our three-month-old baby, would have to go, of course. That left only two-year-old, barely potty-trained, little Cory. "If everyone else goes, he'll go," I reasoned. I was sure he'd be no bother.

I had a nagging bad feeling about the rooms I had reserved, so one day I called again. By the time I finally got through all their answering machines and had a real human on the line, I was quite frustrated, but was relieved that this human could talk fluent English. I gave her my confirmation numbers, and she looked up what rooms I had reserved. To my dismay, none of the rooms had a runway view. Both looked out onto the street. I told her that when I had called earlier, there had been at least one runway room available then. "Well, they're all taken up now," she said, "but I'll put you on the list, and if any open up, I'll put you in them. There's a good chance you can still have them."

Finally, the long-awaited day arrived dawning clear and beautiful. We planned that Aaron would take off work a bit early so we could take the 12:49 train out of South Bend. When I had called the driver to schedule the pickup to take us to the train station, we had debated over how much time to allow us to get there. "If I pick you up at 11:30, it would be enough time, but you wouldn't have much to spare," she said.

"Let's go with that then," I quickly said. I'm the type of person that would rather get there just in time than to go early and wait.

Friday morning I quickly got everything around, packed last-minute items, and was nearly ready when Aaron arrived home from work at 11:00. I quickly fixed sandwiches to eat on the way.

"May I wear my new flops?" Mackenzie asked.

"No, everyone shall wear their crocs," I said. "We're going to be doing a lot of walking, and I don't want your feet to get sore."

"The driver's here!" the twins cheered. They grabbed their car seats and raced for the van while I was still gathering up last minute things and the baby.

Finally, we were all loaded. We drove down to my parents to get them and then headed for the toll road. Suddenly I noticed that we weren't driving fast anymore. In fact, we kept going slower and slower. "Oh, no," I said, "we're in a traffic jam. We don't have time for this."

"Maybe we should have started off earlier," Aaron gave me a dry look.

The clock kept ticking, but the traffic barely moved! "This is disastrous!" I said. "We're gonna be late!" The clock inched closer and closer to 12:49, and we were still a few miles away, barely moving. I became hot all over. "We're gonna miss the train, and the next one isn't until 3:40!" I said. I could hardly believe it.

At 12:49, all hope left that we could still somehow make it. *Oh, why hadn't I allowed more time to get there?* "Can we go to Michigan City and try to catch up with it?" someone asked.

"There's no way I could do that," Chris said. "We can never catch up with it." She got out her cell phone and looked up the Michigan City Station. "I think there's a train that leaves at 2:40 from Michigan City," she said. "Why don't I just take you there, then you can at least leave an hour earlier than if you'd stay at South Bend."

I really wanted to get grouchy. All my carefully laid plans were destroyed. But I knew there was no way to change the circumstances, and I could choose to be happy or angry. So I chose to be happy.

"We can get ice cream while we wait at the station," Aaron said. So we settled into the ride. The children got out the activities that they had planned to do on the train and happily chattered away on the back seats.

I was amazed that everyone was still in such fine spirits. Even my parents couldn't seem to care less. "We're making memories," they said.

Around 1:30, we pulled into the Michigan City station. To our surprise, we saw that there was an electric train there, folding up their steps, getting ready to leave. Aaron quickly jumped out of the van and called out, "Where are you headed?"

"To Chicago," they said.

"Can we go along yet?" Aaron asked.

"If you hurry!" they replied.

I had barely heard their exchange, so when Aaron threw open the van doors and said, "Everyone out! Let's go!" I was rather confused. But I wasn't about to argue, even though I was thinking, *The next train goes at 2:40, so what train is this?*

By the time I gathered my purse and Baby Alex, Aaron had already put most of our luggage on the train. I didn't even have time to double check to see if we had everything. The children tumbled out of the van, and I saw that the twins were barefoot. "Get your crocs!" I quickly told them.

"Crocs?" the twins said. "We don't have any crocs. We came barefoot."

If my adrenals hadn't kicked in before, they sure did now, and I almost keeled over. "Barefoot!" I yelled. I turned to Aaron, saying, "They're barefoot!" I looked helplessly toward Chris, the driver.

"You're making memories," she said soothingly.

More like a nightmare, I thought. At least Mackenzie and Cory were wearing their crocs. Cory even had his decent crocs on instead of his oversized ones with red ribbons.

"Let's go," Aaron said. "We'll worry about it later." We ran to the train, dived on with five children and my parents, and the train lurched forward while we staggered to our seats. Everyone seemed to be laughing in exhilaration, but I didn't really know how to feel. I scrambled to help put up the luggage, but I was thinking, *How are we going to Chicago, if the twins are barefoot?*

"Which train is this?" Aaron asked the ticket agent.

"This is the 12:49 train out of South Bend," she said.

So we had somehow caught up with the train we had missed! It was nothing short of a miracle. We were actually back on schedule!

We arrived in Chicago exactly on time. "Let's head for the Willis Tower first, and maybe on the way there we can find a shoe store," Aaron said.

Where is a shoe store when you need one? We visited the tower, even went out in those glass-bottom rooms and enjoyed the view, but when we exited the tower, the twins were still barefoot.

"Surely the Water Tower Place has shoes," Aaron said. "I'll shop for some while you all go to Lego's and American Girl."

We entered the building and took the huge escalators up. Suddenly I pictured the twins' bare toes getting pinched in the steps. They were riding up front with my dad. "Pick up the twins!" I called. "They could pinch their toes!" Dad quickly grabbed a boy under each arm and lifted them up. At the top, he set them back down. Other tourists glanced at the twins, then glanced at their feet. I cringed. We kept walking; they kept walking. Thankfully!

Aaron shopped for footwear, and we went to Lego's. The children enjoyed it. We went to American Girl, then back to Lego's. Aaron still wasn't back. We waited. And waited. Finally he came back, empty-handed. The only thing he could find that was suitable for two Amish boys was overpriced Nikes. We decided to look for something on our way to the Rain Forest Café.

We had developed a routine: Aaron pushed Alex in the large stroller. I pushed Cory in the umbrella stroller. Dad pulled their little luggage on wheels (our luggage was in the strollers). Mom held each twin by the hand, their dirty bare feet slapping against the pavement. Mackenzie trotted somewhere in between. And we all kept our eyes trained for a shoe store!

Finally we came to the Rainforest Café. The children were all eyes at the impressive, lifelike animals, the sounds, and the trees. We all jumped when the giant anaconda snake dipped its head down from the ceiling and stuck its tongue out at us. We got to sit right next to the elephant. Every few minutes it would lift its head and bellow. We noticed that several other tables got a volcano cake, and they sang "Happy Birthday." Well, Mackenzie's birthday just happened to be the next day. I asked the waitress if we need to pay for the birthday cake or if it's on the house. Lo and behold, she was another person with barely passing English. I'm not sure if she really understood what I was asking, but somehow I got the drift that the cake was not free. I just told her that we'd skip the cake.

Mackenzie wanted to order a slush drink that came in a large iguana cup. It was much overpriced, but since it was her birthday, we let her. Then the waitress came out with the volcano cake. *What—? I thought I told her we'd skip it! Maybe it's on the house after all,* I thought and said nothing. We enjoyed the cake, but when she brought the bill, I wanted to throw up the cake.

The cake wasn't free, and it seemed they had charged us for the plate, too. The whole bill was so outrageous that I wished we had eaten elsewhere. We had spent so much on one meal, and there were many children in the world that had nothing to eat. I felt guilty. "Don't let it ruin your mood," Aaron murmured to me. "Now we know not to eat here again, and the children really enjoyed themselves. It was okay for once."

It was dark by the time we got out of the restaurant. We walked to the Blue Line Station and headed out towards our hotel. Somehow, I still had a bad feeling about our hotel rooms. We walked through the airport to get to the Hilton, rode escalators (picking up the twins each time), and finally got to the front desk to check in.

"Uh, no," they said at the front desk, "you don't have runway view rooms. We do have two rooms available, but they're not beside each other, and they're one hundred dollars extra."

"We can see tomorrow morning," Aaron said, and he dug into his wallet. Wearily, we found our rooms, bathed the children (scrubbed the twins' feet), and settled everyone into bed.

The next day was another beautiful day. The children woke up in a great mood. Aaron opened the curtain and looked out. While our room was facing the runway, I wouldn't have said that we had a runway view. We were too low, and there were other buildings in the way. We could only see the tops of the jets and sometimes not even that. Aaron called my parents who were several floors up from us. "Come up to us," they said. "We have a good view."

It really seemed like we should have been going for breakfast instead so we could get to the aquarium in time to be able to see everything we wanted and wouldn't miss our train home. But we had paid one hundred dollars for this, so we had to look at least a little bit. Mom and Dad did have a much better view. We even opened the window a bit to hear the rumbles of the jet engines.

Soon we decided that we'd better go eat. Eating at the hotel would save time. The breakfast was good, but by no means an Essenhaus or a Blue Gate. When the waiter brought our bill out, he discovered that we had no plane tickets. (I think you get a discount on breakfast with tickets.) Our meals were thirty dollars each, even the children's. It seemed that the waiter had pity on us, because he asked if any of the children were over five.

"Uh, yes," I said. "The twins are five, and Mackenzie turned eight today."

"She's free because it's her birthday, and the boys are free because, well, because they're twins," he said.

Why, thank you, Mr. Waiter! We only had to pay sixty dollars instead of one hundred fifty dollars.

Meanwhile, Dad and Aaron were trying to decide if it would be faster to take a taxi back into the city or the Blue Line train. We wandered outside to see if we could find a taxi. There was none around. Finally, we decided that the only way out was either a jet or the train.

We got back on the Blue Line. Aaron had forgotten to pay attention to where we got on the evening before, so he just guessed where to get off. Well, he guessed wrong. The area we got off was at a slum district, and we were far from downtown yet. "We'll just get a taxi," he said. So we started to walk and look for a taxi. We walked and walked some more. The sun was warm, and the boys' bare feet slapped against the pavement as they trotted along. (By then we had given up finding a shoe store.)

Eventually, we got close enough to downtown Chicago that we spotted a taxi. Praise the Lord! We loaded our things and enjoyed the rest of the way in air-conditioning. The taxi stopped in the second lane to let us off by the Shedd. We unloaded our things and quickly walked to the sidewalk.

"Cory!" I heard my mom yell. I turned around just in time to see Cory rush back into the traffic to the taxi that was just getting ready to pull off.

"Cory!" I yelled, my heart in my throat. Aaron quickly ran after him and grabbed him. Cory had spotted a piece of candy that had fallen from my mom's purse and had gone back to pick it up. Thankfully, the taxi hadn't moved yet, and that's what kept other cars from hitting him.

At the Shedd, the children enjoyed every minute. The boys were able to see live sharks, but they were all small. At 5:00 PM, we crawled on the South Shore train, happy and tired, ready to go home. The children played happily with their new toys. Brad and Brett each had a large shark, Mackenzie had a dolphin, and Cory had a set of small sharks, which also included a killer whale.

Around 8:00 we pulled into South Bend. "I'm going to take the children to the restroom while Aaron loads up Alex and the luggage into the van," I told Mom. "Do you want to come with me to help with the children?"

"Sure," she said. So we grabbed the four children's hands and headed in. At that moment, Mom saw someone she knew and stopped to talk. "You go on ahead," she told me.

So I took the four children on in. It seemed like everyone else from the train wanted to use the restroom too, and there was a long line.

The children were very happy, but also very hyper. Even though it was past their bedtime, they had tons of energy left. I kept trying to hush them and keep them in line as we waited.

"Look!" one twin said. "The walls of the bathrooms don't go all the way down. That way you can see if there's someone in them!" He said it as if it was the greatest thing ever, and to demonstrate, he and his twin bent down and started looking underneath the stalls. Of course, Cory followed suit and began peering underneath too.

"No!" I said, my face turning red. "Those people are using the restrooms!" I attempted to corral them back.

Just then, I saw that we were up next. My tired brain scrambled to think which would be the best way to do this. *All in one stall? No, definitely not!* I sent Mackenzie into the first stall that opened. Right then two more opened, and I sent a twin in each one. A stall opened for Cory and me, so I grabbed his hand and tried to take him into the stall with me. For some reason he kept diving back out of the stall while I kept trying to drag him back in. What was his problem?

"He dropped his toy," I overheard a woman saying to her friend.

Oh, so that was his problem. I looked, and sure enough, he had dropped his little killer whale against the wall and had been trying to retrieve it. I let him go pick it up, then turned to re-enter the stall. Just then, Brett appeared in my stall from underneath the wall, from the stall two doors down. "What are you doing?" I asked.

He beamed happily. "Look, Mom! You can crawl underneath there, and you don't even have to use the door!"

Whatever! "Is your door still locked?" I asked. I opened my stall door to peer out and see if he had even opened his stall's door. Nope, it was still shut.

"There's another one," I heard the woman say to her friend.

I turned back to Brett, and sure enough, Brad had come crawling from underneath the stall's walls from the stall beside me, just as happily as Brett had.

"They're crawling through the stalls and leaving their doors locked," I heard the woman saying.

Before I could die of embarrassment, Whoosh! The twins disappeared back underneath the stalls and went to unlock their doors. I quickly locked Cory and myself into our stall, away from the woman's disapproving looks. I'm sure she was thinking, *That Amish lady can't handle all her children.* I didn't want to tell her that there was another one yet, a baby, out in the van!

Thankfully, when Cory and I got out, the woman was gone. I made the children scrub their hands—too bad I couldn't scrub their bare feet, too!—and hustled them back to the van.

My mom was already in the van. "Where were you?!" I demanded.

"Oh," Mom said, "I stopped to talk, and when I finished I decided you could handle the children by yourself, so I just came back out. Why? Did something happen?"

Did it ever! I gave her a review, and she laughed until she had tears. I wasn't really laughing.

"Oh, Elizabeth," she said, "I am so glad I did not go with you because now we have all these good memories!"

"Memories" was correct, but whether they were all good was a matter of opinion.

The next day my mother-in-law asked about our trip. "Are you glad you took all the children along?" she asked.

"Well, yes," we said. "But next time we'd *definitely* do some things a little differently!"

one boy's touch

NAOMI CROSS

In our church, we had a widow who had a son named Gareth. He was around ten years old and very energetic. The widow worked at a Mennonite bakery to provide for herself and her son. Since she and I were good friends, I volunteered to keep Gareth after school until she got home. My husband was working away from home, and we had five children, with the oldest being eight years old. I felt like I had my hands full with our own children but wanted to help where I could. As I said, Gareth was very energetic, and his imagination ran full tilt! I soon saw that I needed to step up my imagination to keep him profitably occupied. He needed activities other than placing a two-by-four under the bedposts to make the bed sit crooked or hiding in the dryer. (He was actually a bit big for that hole. The last time he tried it, he found it difficult to get back out again. It caused a few anxious moments for us, and I don't recommend the hiding place for anyone!)

I enjoy sewing quilts, so I decided to get Gareth to sew comforter blocks together for CAM. We cut out six-inch blocks from scraps, and he arranged and sewed them together. Peace reigned in the house as he stitched away. He really enjoyed the challenge and was delighted to show his mom and others what he had accomplished! Gareth's mother appreciated that we kept him, and we were blessed to have him stay with us.

THE JOYS AND NOISE OF RAISING BOYS

NANCY MARTIN

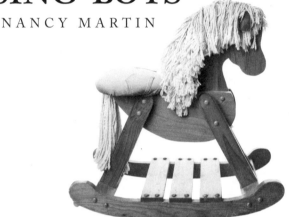

Growing up, I thought girls were nicer than boys were. I loved my brothers. Sometimes I thought they were fine men, but all three of them were older than I was, and oh, they loved to tease! I had to clean their room. They left their drawers hanging open and the beds unmade. Their room was in a constant state of untidiness. Girls were just nicer. My thoughts changed after my brothers turned out to become honorable men, and I, a mother to six boys and one girl.

Boys Are Surprising

By keeping their mother on her toes, she stays young longer! Why else would Weston sneak a small black kitten into the house and set it on the sink where I was washing dishes? I shrieked in surprise. A smile crept slowly across the twelve-year-old's face. "I just wanted to show you the kitten," he said. *Show the kitten? Indeed!*

Boys Are Entertaining

Shannon (10) came in and found his little brother in distress. Ayden (3) was coughing and crying. "You need to visit Doctor Shan," Shannon boomed. He got a broken toy arrow with a suction tip and pretended to be listening to Ayden's little heart and lungs. He peered into the gaping mouth. "There is a cough in there," Doctor Shan proclaimed.

Orange drink was poured in a cup for medicine, and chocolate chips served as pills. Ayden opened his mouth dutifully to accept the doctor's prescription. He was soon cured of both the coughing and crying.

Boys Are Inventive

The two apple trees in our yard hardly receive care. They grow and bear apples as they please. The fall that one tree was loaded with red apples, I decided they would work well for applesauce if the boys picked them. Our oldest sons hauled the ladder from the shop and picked all the apples they could reach. When they were done, there was a noticeable line around the tree. The bottom half was bare. The top half was loaded with shiny red fruit. Days went by while the apples grew riper and riper right there on the top half of the tree. Who would pick them?

One windy day, I was astonished to see the apples raining from the tree. It looked like the wind was blowing them off! *So this is how Nature unburdens an apple tree,* I mused. I went closer for a better look.

It was not the wind. It was a *boy!* Donnie (then 4) laughed down at me.

"You monkey!" I laughed up at him.

"I'm shaking the apples off the tree," he beamed. Suddenly Donnie shook those branches like a chimpanzee. "Watch out!" he shouted.

I stepped out of danger to watch. I was impressed. Never mind that they would all have a bruise from falling. The apples were coming off the tree—fast. And that is what I wanted.

Boys Are Loving

Just when a mother thinks boys are mostly tricks and noise, they show her that in their breast beats a heart of the most loving and gentle sort. I was holding our one-year-old, delighted to be the favorite of my cuddly boy, until Tristan (8) came by. Suddenly Baby Anthony stretched his chubby sweetness all the way into Brother's arms. When

I tried to take him back, he wouldn't have it! I was left there to watch as Anthony babbled in Baby Talk. "Yes," Tristan nodded, pretending to understand. Baby took a deep breath, his eyes shining like two bright chocolate drops and continued his Tale of Sweet Nothingness. Without so much as a glance at me, they disappeared out the door.

Sometimes it doesn't suit so well to be Baby's favorite. A boy is somewhat handicapped with a baby in tow.

"It takes someone special to win the heart of a child so small," I told Tristan.

His heart was touched, and so was mine when he picked up Anthony, sacrificing his freedom once more for Baby's sake.

Boys Are Little Men Growing Up

When our daughter biked to school with the boys for the first time, I was nervous. "Boys, you must watch out for her."

"We will," they said.

"You must help her look before crossing the street," I continued.

"We will, Mom. Now stop worrying," they said.

So I stopped worrying. Not many little girls are escorted to school by four big brothers.

It is an honor to have boys. Someday they will be grown, but today I will hug these boys while they're still little. I will rumple their hair. I will enjoy their rowdiness. I will place my hand on the biggest ones' shoulders, and encourage them on as they grow into honorable young men.

Smelling Pretty
MERVIN'S MOTHER

Four-year-old Mervin was helping me put jars of pumpkin on the cellar shelves. My sister had given them to me, and the box they were in smelled like soap. Mervin gave me a couple jars, then said, "M-m-m, this smells like you usually smell when you make yourself all pretty."

Cherish Your Boys

IRM

Oh, cherish the moments you have with your boys;
Their fun and their laughter, their games and their toys;
Their cute cuddly coos and giggling peek-a-boo,
The hullabaloo of "Dad, may I go too?"...
Cherish the joys of boys!

Oh, savor the moments with boys while they're small;
The puddles, the dirt, the balloons, and the ball;
Their thumps and their bumps, and occasional dumps.
Boys keep their parents and sisters 'a-jump'!
Love them from small to tall!

Oh, sing while you launder the piles of their clothes,
While sorting through socks that have holes in the toes.
While scrubbing the dirt from the pants and the shirts
With little boys clinging sometimes to your skirts.
Thank God for rows of clothes!

Oh, treasure the priv'lege of feeding your sons
With meat and potatoes, and fresh buttered buns,
Some salsa to dunk in their mountains of chips.
Get sweet boyish grins formed with their sticky lips.
Treasure the fun of sons!

Keep Both Hands on the Rail

LUCINDA EBY

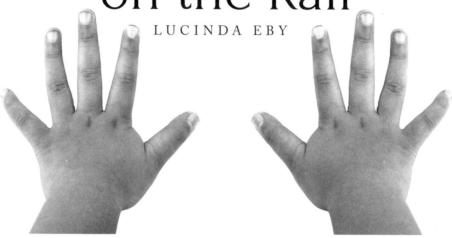

School was canceled. Everyone around the breakfast table cheered, even Mom, because Dad, the teacher, was home for the day.

Dad started the morning with a project for Mom. He was tacking material strips to the new quilting frame. Jeremy, who was nine, was assigned to hold the rail with both hands while Dad hammered the tacks in. Jeremy's heart was not in the job. "It is boring. Can someone else take a turn?" he asked sulkily. When he would get distracted or only use one hand, the rail would slide while Dad was trying to hammer.

Dad kept reminding him, "Keep both hands on the rail." He admonished Jeremy how important it is in life to learn to be simply faithful, to endure even the smallest task. "If someone asked you to hold an apple for thirty minutes," Dad said, "it is important to be faithful."

One of the next days, Dad's own words, "Keep both hands on the rail," echoed back to him as he was trying to get back into the routine of school life. He must be simply faithful in teaching the next English or math class. He must be completely faithful in the task whether it was teaching the next class or giving a student tender guidance and correction.

As he was sharing his inspiration with me, I thought how much that applies to motherhood. The responsibilities of motherhood become mundane. There are meals to fix and dishes to do three times a day. The laundry needs sorted, washed, folded, and ironed several times a week. In between all that, there are stories to read and diapers to change. Many of Mom's pressing duties are repeated each week. Other possibilities look more attractive. It may seem more exciting to make layette bundles for little babies on the other side of the ocean than to fold laundry for our own family. Maybe it becomes a drudgery to read *The Biggest Bear* to our three-year-old for the fourth time in a week. It would be more inspirational to read our own book.

Our greatest opportunity is to faithfully endure doing the work that God has called us to do, nothing more and nothing less. The truest joy and satisfaction are ours when both hands are on the rail whether we are mother, teacher, or child.

Not Wasted

M EBERSOLE

We were invited into the home of another church family for supper. Our host family consisted of mostly boys, and those of us invited had either all boys or mostly boys. After supper, the two older girls spread their card-making supplies on the table. It wasn't long until some of the younger boys, mine included, thought it looked interesting and were having fun using stamps and markers and pretty stickers. I told the host mom that I hoped they were not wasting their pretty stickers. Her reply has stuck with me. She very sweetly said, "Oh, no! They're not wasted if little boys are using them!"

Teacher's Boys

FAITH ANNE SLOTHOUR

A class of girls will sit quite still
Like flowers on the windowsill.
And like the flowers, they will bloom
And beauty bring to all the room.
But Teacher learns that different joys
Are hers when class is mostly boys.

Their feet just itch to run and race
And they can hardly keep their place.
The hardest rule to keep, of all,
Is this: "No running in the hall."
When boys line up, they often bump
And nudge and push and rush and thump,
But then their feet are awf'lly slow
When in from recess they must go.

When Teacher's class is mostly boys
At lunch they talk of things of noise
Like trucks and engines, cars and planes,
Cows and wolverines and trains;
With gestures wild and motions thick,
Words on-o-mat-o-po-et-ic

Like "Roar!" and "Hiss!" and "Growl!" and "Zoom!"
And "Rumble!" or a mighty "Vvvrrooooom!"
Till Teacher wishes wearily
That she had half their energy.

Then as they work upon a test,
They know their pencils should not rest,
But it's so *hard* to concentrate!
They dawdle till the hour is late.
All those who catch their teacher's glance
Wrinkle their foreheads—if perchance—
She'll think they were of grammar scheming
And not at all of summer dreaming.

Yes, Teacher will have different joys
When her young class is mostly boys.
There lies behind the boyish face
Some manly strength and manly ways.
They strive to do the best they can,
And soon the boy will be a man.
O Teacher! Love your class of boys!
And yours will be the richest joys!

If You're a Mother of Boys, Expect:

RACHEL ROHRER

- to dream up wildlife bedroom themes.
- to cook for a small army.
- to commit yourself to at least thirty years of baking cookies regularly.
- to have sibling grudges dropped as quickly as they started.
- to have a bedroom cleanup plan in place.
- to watch the fruit you had planned to can disappear in front of your eyes.
- to answer the question, "Gonna keep trying for a girl?" every other time your family goes to town.
- to be the only one that cares much whether the cleaning is done or not, even in the bathroom (maybe *especially* in the bathroom).
- to tell your five-year-old to watch the one-year-old, and he digs up sixteen worms while doing that.
- to hear any noise at any time.
- to check them for cleanliness *after* they bathe.
- to comment on excavating equipment yourself while driving

down the road.
- to hear "Thanks, Mom" a lot.
- to have some quiet moments while they're all with Dad.
- to provide a snack three times in one afternoon.
- to have your kitchen turn into a laboratory without warning.
- to become experienced at deciding which pants are worth patching.
- to frequently have John Deere versus Case discussions at suppertime.
- to be requested the privilege of using the new tape measure to measure your waist.
- to clean up mud and dirt, lots of it.
- to be thoroughly familiar with Cabela's and all surrounding stores within walking distance.
- to expect the unexpected.
- to have at least one of them be a comedian.
- to laugh a lot.
- to have your twelve-year-old decorate his birthday cake with CASE IH written in enormous red letters across the top.
- to fry lots of bacon.
- to have a sizable designated container for hunting magazines and tool catalogs and find them all over the house anyway.
- to be able to turn over heavy jobs even when your husband's not around.
- to feel like you're *almost* watching your husband's growing-up days.
- to pray endlessly for their purity in today's world.

WHAT ARE LITTLE BOYS MADE OF?

LUCINDA EBY

> What are little boys made of, made of?
> What are little boys made of?
> Frogs and snails
> And puppy-dogs' tails,
> That's what little boys are made of.

Have we mothers not all heard that nursery rhyme and deemed it partly true?

One winter day, my seven-year-old and I stopped to give our elderly neighbor lady a hand. She was a very fearful, demanding, and unhappy soul. Besides, she was rather set in her ways and did not handle other perspectives and suggestions well. But she became our charge day or night, so we tried to do our best and tread softly around her. Our little boys had a way of striking a tender chord in her heart, and she would cheer up when they were along. On that particular day she spun off this nursery rhyme and teasingly asked our son if he was made of "frogs and snails and puppy-dogs' tails."

He evidently had never heard Mother Goose's version of his make-up. With solemn eyes and childish simplicity, he informed her, "The Bible says we are made from dust."

Metamorphose

M EBERSOLE

The time had come.
Procrastination had gone long enough.
And yet before my mother-heart
The task looked tough.
I did not want my little son
To be a girl,
And neither should he look like one
With neck-length curl.
But…
To be a little man?
Not yet!
Please let him be the way he is,
And let me feel that baby hair of his.
Just let him be
The way he came to me!
But still the time had come.
Procrastination had gone long enough.
I bravely took the clippers
To my baby's hair.
Oh, it was tough!
And with each lock that tumbled
To the floor,
I saw my baby change…
Forevermore.
And yet with joy I knew
That time and change cannot destroy
My love so true
For this small boy!

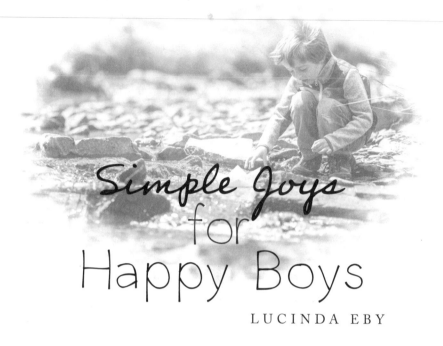

Simple Joys for Happy Boys

LUCINDA EBY

When the third boy joined our clan, the nurse at the hospital told us that boys only need three things to keep them happy: water, rocks, and trees. Ofttimes I have been amazed how true that statement was. We have woods all around us, a creek running through our property, and rocks galore.

Many happy hours on a hot summer evening have been spent splashing in the creek, and what a great splash those rocks make when thrown into the water! Trees are for what? Climbing, of course! That is one joy for boys that Mom does not share.

The boys are older now, but the refreshing creek still beckons on a hot afternoon when a break is needed from picking blueberries. Hours are spent building dams in the creek with those rocks. Trees have taken on a new joy. Boys build houses in them. Now they can drink tea, read a book, spend a night, or even chat with Mom in the tree. That seems a little safer for tree joy.

I have learned that it does not take expensive, elaborate toys for boys—just water, rocks, and trees!

Monkeys

MISTY NISSLEY

World Book says that Monkeys are "any of numerous lively mammals that rank among the most intelligent animals." (*World Book Encyclopedia 2008) Hmmm*. I gaze thoughtfully at the entry. *Wonder what you would call a boy that acts that way? I would call him a son!*

Yes, that is Silas, my third son. He was climbing ladders at nine months old and hasn't stopped. He's lanky, and his agility makes it easy for him to climb.

Case in point: We have a seventeen-foot hay barn with pole rafters. He shimmies up, wrapping his skinny legs around the pole all the way up to the rafters. "Hey, Mom, look at me!"

I cross my arms and say, "I see you, but you can't go any higher."

Then the monkey starts up the pole on the rafter and swings from the ridgepole. "Yes, I can! See, Mom!" I shake my head and laugh. He's a complete copy of his dad who spent a lot of his growing-up years in the rafters above a holding pen, playing house. It's helpful when we have hay customers that need bales pushed down. The ladies stand there, holding their breath as, *Horrors! The little boy goes up there!*

Because of my maternal fear, I could require my little monkey to wear a helmet. There are some things to restrict in life, but there are many things to let free without bodily injury. A mother of boys must often hold her breath, look the other way, and be ready with a basic knowledge of first aid or at least Band-Aids!

Monkey? No, he's not a monkey, but he acts like one. I pray for grace to be the mother he needs, not clinging, but letting him swing in the trees and clinging to him when he comes home and affectionately wraps his arms around me with, "I like you, Mommy!" (I guess monkeys do that, too!)

Boyish
Perplexity
A MARTIN

"Please cover coughs,"
And "Catch those sneezes."
"Don't pick your nose."
That quite displeases.

"Go wash your hands."
"Don't lick your fingers."
"Please use some soap
So nothing lingers."

"Don't share your germs,"
My mother teaches.
She often wipes
And sometime bleaches.

But there's one thing
That Mama misses.
Can you believe
She still gives kisses?!

For my nearly five-year-old son whose tactful response to my kiss one night revealed his opinion: "When other people kiss you, they give you their germs." Thankfully, he'll likely change his mind a few times yet before he outgrows bedtime kisses completely!

What They Need

MJH

"**M**om, Mom!" my excited five-year-old called from the open door.

With a quick fling of the rag, I hurried to hush him before he woke the baby. He paused, then asked, "Can Sis come look at the pig we caught?"

"No, not this time," I answered. "She is in the middle of washing her hair." Then on impulse, I said, "I'll come look at him."

With a light in his eyes and a quick slam of the door, he ran out into the autumn evening shouting, "Daddy, Mom is coming to look at the pig!"

With a peek at the pot of rice I had simmering on the stove, I hurried out. It was a lovely Saturday evening except for the fact that my list of duties still loomed too large for comfort.

My husband and three young sons were busy in the pasture trying to catch our pig (while his pen was mud-free), to move him to a better place. I had heard the sounds of squealing, shrieking boys and concluded their job was proving to be a challenge. With a quick prayer for their safety, my mind had gone on to other cares until it was interrupted by my son's enthused voice.

I found the jolly crew still in excitement. It was amusing to hear the lively tales, embellished with gestures, of the thrilling catch. "See the pigs' new pen, Mom? Do you like it?"

But what thrilled my heart was the smile on Daddy's face and the sight of three happy boys. It made the evening perfect.

This was not the first time I was rewarded for giving of my time. *Why don't I do it more?* I mused as I returned to the house. My boys weren't asking for $100, only for Mom's interest in their achievements. Some things mean much to our growing sons. They want Mom to rejoice with them about the animal they caught in their trap, the big hole they dug in the garden, the ball they hit, or the picture they drew. Someday, too soon, these moments will be over, and they will remember whether Mom took an interest in their lives or not. Only for a few short years will I be the most important woman in their lives. Someday I might wish they were begging for my attention.

Today and every day, I'll pray for help from above to be a better mom, for cheerful patience to accept the fact that clean floors and windows won't be spotless for long, for a calm firmness when calling them from their monkey perch on the truck roof. And when my boys come in the door extremely dirty by midday, I need to remind myself that it only costs a shower and a clean set of clothes. Boys need to play in the dirt and to be outside even when the weather isn't perfect.

Most importantly, I feel an ever-present urge to pray for the souls of our dear sons. This world is dark and needs faithful men, but first a praying mom!

Boys Will Be Boys

MARILYN WEAVER

We have been given
A family of boys.
We've so many trials
Yet so many joys.
Shoes in the corner
And clothes on the floor,
Teaching them manners
Is, oh, what a chore!
The toilet lid's up,
There's mud on the wall,
Their clothes are all filthy;
They don't mind at all.
Some dirt never hurt,
So why do I fret?
When they are all grown,
These days I'll forget.
The noise gets so tiring,
The talk gets so old,
But what would I do
With no small boys to hold?
They play truck in the morning,
Digger at noon,

Dozer at naptime,
And then all too soon,
The day's almost over,
But still they aren't done.
They've tractors to play with;
They're having such fun.
Popping wheelies with bikes,
Riding through puddles,
They are on the brakes,
And then on the throttles.
They harass the cats,
Make friends with the dogs,
They dream of some ponies,
Some chickens, some hogs.
What is a pocket
With nothing in it?
Imagination,
The sky is the limit.
Boys will be boys,
Or that's what they say,
But, Lord, help us raise them
To be men some day!

Buckets of Blessings

MD

My sister-in-law has a saying on her refrigerator that goes like this: Boy—*A noise with dirt on it.* All mothers who see it nod their heads with agreement. Those seven words say it all.

We have four boys. The oldest is five. One son walks through the door, and there is a big rip in his shirt. You gasp, "What happened?"

He looks down with surprise and says, "Oh! I don't know. I didn't even know it was there." More nods. More agreement. We all have one boy like that.

You notice the flower planter is lying askew by the sidewalk. Upon further inspection, you see there are some flowers lying on the ground beside a small pile of dirt. You ask the boys, "What happened?"

One pipes up, "Nothing."

The other agrees, "Yes. Nothing. We were just having rides on the wagon, and 'round the corner we flew, and then we looked back, and the flower pot was lying on the ground." *You see, nothing happened.*

Yes. Nothing happens to the ripped-off suspender, to the hole in the screen, and to the broken flyswatter. I have learned not to be attached to things that can be replaced and that have no eternal value. We have rules in our household, common rules most people have: No yelling. No kicking. No throwing.

Boys tussle. Soon the tussling turns to kicking which leads to throwing. You watch the ball sail through the air and land on the vase you just bought a couple of weeks ago for an amazing price at a Goodwill.

You almost cry as you pick up the pieces and realize it's beyond Super Glue repair. You feel ashamed that you cry because probably no other grown woman cries over such a thing. And it's just a thing, but a thing that needn't have happened if there wouldn't have been any throwing. Or kicking. Or tussling. For two seconds you are tempted to yell. But one look at their wide, frightened eyes, and you realize that is exactly what they expect you'll do. More shame. You calmly tell them to go outside while your mind tries to figure out a proper punishment with a better perspective.

My mother-in-law has nine sons. She enjoys nothing more than to get together with her now married sons. She wants to know details about each of their lives. I learn a lot from her. She would rather be with her sons than our group of ladies at a family get-together. I am not offended at all, for they are her sons! She fed them, raised them, and gave one of them to me. Let's each be thankful to our mother-in-law and show our appreciation by visiting her faithfully and letting our husbands do things for her. God will bless us for it.

I know that my blessing bucket will be truly overflowing the day I am surrounded by my grown sons, and I say something, and they guffaw, "Oh, Mom," and shake their heads and laugh and laugh. For I know that is their manly way of saying, "I still love you, Mother, and I have many fond memories of being your son." May all our buckets be running over with such blessings.

Thou therefore, my son, be strong in the grace that is in Christ Jesus.
II Timothy 2:1

All in a Lifetime of Growing Boys

A MOTHER OF FIVE BOYS

• A three-year-old innocently questioning, "How many fingers was I when I came to Daddy and Mother?"

• Seeking to comfort a little boy when his favorite pet kittens got into the mouse bait. Finding your own eyes damp, not because you miss the kittens that were always underfoot, but because it hurts to see your son so sad and weeping.

• Young son taping up birthday cards—#11…12…13…and feeling sorry for his daddy who gets three at the most. "Don't grown men send birthday cards?" he wonders.

• Coming in from outside and finding an unassigned task completed by your baby (the baby is seven).

• Watching the cleaning happen in half the time it takes you to do it—when the boys are at it!

• Managing three boys baking bars (all new recipes) while their daddy is at a meeting.

• Realizing your pre-teenager came to the table with his haystack tamed instead of you needing to dismiss him to comb his hair.

• Giving a boy the choice of jobs: washing dishes or sweeping floors, washing dishes or hanging laundry, washing dishes or cleaning the bathrooms—and always it is the choice other than washing dishes!

• Watching a boy become a man—when asked to wash dishes, he replies, "Sure!"

• Giving a teenager the job of slicing homemade bread, and when the platter of bread appears at the table the bread is arranged in a fancy swirl.

• Seeing energy in a young man who gets out of bed before his parents to work on his hobby.

• Experiencing the joy of a young man asking for help to find salvation.

• Giving your son a mini-lecture on the major subject of forgiveness, or trust, or greater yet, surrender; and then feeling defeated because how is an eleven-year-old to master the depth of such doctrines when you are still lacking in those areas yourself? Then feeling hope when you remember the advice of the ancient prophet, *For precept must be upon precept, precept upon precept; line upon line, line upon line; here a little, and there a little...*

Haircutting Time

JUDITH MARTIN

When I gave my oldest sons their haircuts, they would say, "Don't cut my sideburns! Don't cut my sideburns!" (Sorry, I always did.)

Anthony was only three or four when he copied them and said, "Don't cut my sideburns!"

I told him, "You don't have any!"

He was so surprised. "I don't?"

Growing Pains

ONE WHO'S BEEN THERE

As two happily married twenty-year-olds, my husband and I eagerly welcomed our first baby—a boy! Happiness complete! Daddy, Mommy, and baby make three… and that is a very cozy little triangle! We remained a cozy triangle for all of three months until I discovered we would be exchanging our triangle for a square…*oh, my. A square just isn't quite as an adorable shape as a triangle…but then, a square gives you four cute little corners instead of just three…*

We happily welcomed an adorable little girl! A million-dollar family!…for four months. *Oh. My.*

After a record-breaking hot summer, I was overjoyed to welcome baby number three—another boy! We soon found out this was not just any boy either—not your regular run-of-the-mill boy. This was a B.O.Y. with all the regular, typical boyishness times two, and all of it at high speed! He wasn't very old until his name, Michael, just didn't seem complete without "motorcycle" tacked onto the end. He wasn't hyper; he was just active. He wasn't mean; he was just impulsive. He was always "oh-so-sorry." He didn't stop to think that you could actually KILL a froggie by squirting it with very hot water!

Baby number four arrived when number three was one-and-a-half years old. I felt so thankful for the break between those two babies. Half a year longer than the other times! (Never mind that there was a surgery thrown in for good measure!) I felt revived and ready to welcome this new baby—another boy! This one was everything number three was not. He was big for his age and easily intimidated. He could see danger when it stared him straight in the eyes, which was something number three never could. I lovingly called number four my gentle giant. I was so grateful that he was more slow natured, and usually the only trouble or danger he got into was a direct result of his older brother's influence!

Trouble and danger were plentiful wherever those two went! Despite my vigilant, near-paranoid watchfulness along with my husband's help, those boys managed to pull some terrific stunts! I begged God daily to *please* help me keep my precious little ones alive, and I truly believe it was by the grace of God alone that they survived childhood. Three different times I called my mom in tears and begged her to please take Michael and raise him for us. I was so afraid he would kill himself, or himself and his brother, before he was old enough to see danger. My dear mother always reassured me, "Just do your best. That's all anyone can do. Then leave the rest to God."

I wavered between loving my hectic life filled with love, children, happiness, and health, and nearly despairing of keeping those four little ones safe from day to day. I thanked God each time all four were tucked safely into their beds at the end of one more busy day.

Two years after our fourth child was born, we were thrilled to welcome another girl. Now we had five children, and the oldest was almost six. Life stepped up a pace, and my husband and I were kept on a gallop trying to stay one step ahead of the pack! Life was interesting and full…and exhausting…but we were happy!

When number five was almost a year old, we learned our family would expand yet again…and we soon had reasons to wonder if perhaps we would be welcoming *two* little ones?!?! An ultrasound confirmed our suspicions. Meanwhile, I tried to keep my tribe clothed and fed…and safe. And I waited. And dreamed. And waited.

Finally, the day arrived to meet our two little ones! We were so happy to have reached this momentous, long-awaited day… But what a shock! What a mixture of feelings, to finally be holding our two little sons in our arms—the one alive and breathing, the other one silent and…gone! Such a terrible blow! We discovered a truth we did not want to know—joy and sorrow can live in the same heart.

Sadly, we went home from the hospital with our two car seats, but only one baby. I knew I was blessed, and I knew God was good to have allowed us to have one baby to love and cuddle. My arms weren't empty, but still there was a baby-sized, baby-shaped hole in my heart. Life went on, and when I missed my little stillborn baby, I held my other babies a little closer. We healed, slowly…but we healed.

When our little twinny baby was half a year old, the thing that I had feared all those years came to pass. Our dear little busybody, Michael, now five years old, was in an accident. For a time his life hung in the balance. Prayers ascended to heaven. Thanks to God, our son's life was spared, but he lost his one foot and severely injured the other one. Once again, we went through grief…and so did our son. Did you know five-year-olds can become depressed? For a while, he chose to deal with his loss by denying it. He refused to look at the place where his foot should have been. He would hold a pillow in front of his face when wound care was done on his foot. The hospital made us promise to get counseling for him. Thankfully, just being home for a while surrounded by his brothers and sisters was enough to boost his mood. We only took him to one counseling appointment, and the counselor felt he was coping well enough that we didn't need to continue. Life went on. Not the same…but it went on.

And it still goes on! We were blessed with three more baby boys, bringing the total to seven living boys and two girls. There were many days, amid the noise, the dirt, and the boyish stunts that the thought of the little boy we lost helped me appreciate the seven that were still with us. It helped me keep a proper perspective. DIRT means alive!

Our youngest is five, and our oldest twenty. It is almost shocking to me. *What happened to all the little ones? How could it have changed so fast? One day I was dealing with burp diapers, diaper rash, potty training...and suddenly one day was the last day there was a sleeper in the laundry, or a baby blanket flapping on the line...and I never saw it coming!* In the midst of it, it seemed like it would always be that way. But it wasn't. I MISS the babies! Yes, there are times I look at a mouthy sixth grader and think longingly of the days he couldn't say much other than "Mama"!

This is a good time too! It's so easy now to say, "Shall we have a hot dog roast for supper?" The next thing you know a fire is crackling away merrily, and hot dogs are thawing. The cupboard door is wide open where one little boy got matches, the office door is standing open where another boy grabbed some of his dad's (hopefully) old newspapers, and the washhouse door stands wide open. Smile. Go along and shut those doors. Enjoy the roasted hot dog. Remember, this too shall pass!

I never did appreciate hearing older mothers say they are busier now than they were when the children were young. To me that always felt depressing. *You mean it will only get worse?!* I would like to tell all young, busy, nearly overwhelmed mothers, "It does get easier!" Trust me, there is a reason forty- to fifty-year-old moms are carrying more weight around than young moms! Sure, in one way, your brain is busier with older children, but now I can be in the bathroom for more than five minutes without a little darling having to "go potty *right now!*" Also, I can actually take a bath during the day if I want to, instead of waiting until the children are in bed. By that time I was so tired I often fell asleep in the tub and awoke to cold water.

I wish to tell every young parent to teach your children prompt, cheerful obedience while they are still young. If you cannot make Junior listen at six, do you think you will be able to make him listen at sixteen? Some of the happiest children I have known were the ones who knew that only cheerful, immediate obedience would be acceptable. Similarly, the most miserable children I have known were the ones who knew they did not have to obey. When our children didn't want to obey or submit, we had a rule that they must say, "Yes, Mom," or "Yes, Dad." If they were not willing to say that, we would punish them until they gave up and were willing to say it, and say it nicely.

We are still learning. Sometimes we're not sure if we did anything right. We hope so. All we can do is to keep on doing the best we can and enjoy those boys while they are still young. We have tea parties with the girls, and all sorts of interesting, noisy experiences with the boys. But now I think I'll go for a nice, hot soak in the tub!

Disgraced

JUDITH MARTIN

Our second son, Philip, was in the lower grades in school when I took cream cheese-filled cupcakes to school for his birthday treat. I had not frosted them. I thought the filling baked in the middle was their sweetness. When he came home that day, he said, "Mom, why didn't you frost those cupcakes? They looked like we were some poor people!"

The Joys
OF BOYS

B Z

Life with children is definitely amazing, inspiring, overwhelming sometimes, humbling, and a gift of God. Why else do we laugh when we wish to cry? Or tears come pushing on a joyous occasion such as the first day of school for our first grader, or the decision to trust God as their personal Saviour?

I am an outdoor person, and I always wished for a family of boys. (Maybe I should have wished for girls to do the housework so I could be outdoors more.) We were richly blessed with four sons and one daughter. Although natured differently, there are definitely two things that all our boys have in common. That is the need to burn off energy outdoors and the enjoyment of eating.

Our boys all take an interest in helping in the kitchen. Some enjoy baking; some like making breakfast food. Our youngest son is an early riser. I awoke one morning to hear him, at the age of two, making breakfast! He was nearly through cracking two dozen eggs. Perhaps half a dozen of those had made it into the pan; the rest were in a slithery puddle on the countertop and down the side of the range. He was so delighted to serve breakfast to his siblings.

We live in the woods, and gardening isn't my specialty, so we have few flowerbeds. What excitement though when the mulch truck arrives with beautiful, fresh mulch! Shovels, buckets, and the wagon are brought out, and mulch is soon flying. The wagon engine revs, and the tires peel rubber, and work is in progress. I usually give some pointers on mulching, then retreat to the kitchen where I can watch as I go about my housework. Eventually when enthusiasm fades and a knock on the window to correct some errant deed is no longer sufficient, I join them to finish. Ice cream treats when the job is done make it all worthwhile in a boy's eyes.

I chuckled one day when I saw Little Sister, at eighteen months, receiving hanging-up-wash lessons from big brother who is anxious to pass on the job. Another day I heard a frightened yell from the same brother. I hurried outside to find him suspended in midair on the pulley line. His older brother had convinced him it would be a thrilling ride. The brother on the line was not impressed at big brother's laughter. He muttered, "That wasn't funny!"

Shopping is something I never enjoyed very much, and one shopping trip with the boys stands out to me as unforgettable. The three oldest boys were five, three, and one. Since we were at Wal-Mart, I had them all in the cart to keep them together. The oldest son had a coco flower basket liner upside down on top of his head to be Farmer Ben. The second son had a hose nozzle and was quietly shooting targets at whatever we were passing. Baby managed to squash the bread (much to the horror of the cashier) while my attention was elsewhere. But squashed bread can be eaten too, and we went home to expand our borders beyond the size of a shopping cart!

Our boys love to read. Did you ever try reading books while standing on your head? Boys seem to enjoy that kind of thing. First, place a stack of books upon the sofa, do a headstand, wrap your legs over the back of the sofa, and you are all set!

A highlight of theirs is hunting season and going along to Grandpa's to be included in the excitement. Now that three of them are old enough to hunt, there is quite a collection of gear in the laundry and on the wash line to air. It is so enjoyable to see their excitement over a successful hunt.

There is no end to things boys can dream up to do. *We are fearfully and wonderfully made* (Ps. 139:14). Let's keep on raising our children in the fear of the Lord.

"Hey, Mom!"

MISTY NISSLEY

Isaac is loud. No, let me repeat that. Isaac is very loud! He is so loud that at times I have questioned if he is deaf.

He's not.

He's only eleven years old, going on twenty-two, and thinks he needs to live aloud to get his point across. Does having six younger siblings make that worse? Or being the oldest? Or maybe just being Isaac? Does that have any sway?

Sometime, and maybe even ten times a day, everyone will need my attention simultaneously. Guaranteed. Then I will need to answer questions in order and without partiality.

Then comes a time when everyone is gone, and Isaac and I are alone in the house.

"Hey, Mom," comes a low confidential voice, "is it right for _____ to do that?"

"Hey, Mom, did you know what happened in school today?"

"Hey, Mom, did you ever…?"

It's his I-really-want-to-talk voice, and my mother-heart answers, "Here am I." This voice is not so loud. I attune my ears for soul glimpses and know if I don't listen *now* the opportunity will come less and less. "Hey, Mom" will change to "Hey, friend," "Hey, phone," "Hey, job."

It is my goal to listen to my boys so that when I hear, "Hey, Mom," it will give both of us joy.

No Place for *Boys*

AUTHOR UNKNOWN

What can a boy do, and where can a boy stay
If he's always told to get out of the way?
He cannot sit here, and he must not stand there;
The cushions that cover that fine rocking chair
Were put there, of course, to be seen and admired;
A boy has no business to ever be tired.
The beautiful roses and flowers that bloom
On the floor of the darkened and delicate room
Are not made to walk on—at least not by boys;
The house is no place, anyway, for their noise.

Yet boys must walk somewhere; and what if their feet
Sent out of our houses, sent into the street,
Should stop 'round the corner and pause at the door
Where other boys' feet have paused oft before;
Should pass through the gateway of glittering light,
Where jokes that are merry and songs that are bright

Ring a warm welcome with flattering voice,
And temptingly say, "Here's a place for the boys"?
Oh, what if they should! What if your boy or mine
Should cross o'er the threshold which marks out the line
'Twixt virtue and vice, 'twixt pureness and sin,
And leave all his innocent boyhood within!

Oh, what if they should, because you and I,
While the days and the months and the years hurry by,
Are too busy with cares and with life's fleeting joys
To make 'round our hearthstone a place for our boys!
There's a place for the boys. They'll find it somewhere;
And if our own homes are too daintily fair
For the touch of their fingers, the tread of their feet,
They'll find it, and find it, alas, in the street
'Mid the gildings of sin and the glitter of vice.
And with heartaches and longings we pay a dear price
For the getting of gain that our lifetime employs
If we fail to provide a good place for the boys.

Communicate!

A MOTHER OF TEN

Keep the lines of communication open with your boys. When they become teens and don't like talking, write a note and place it in their rooms. Explain about a problem or attitude you are concerned about. Don't forget to include something positive about them for which you are thankful. Tell them you're praying for them. Boys are: Energy— rough and tumble. But also a lot of joy and blessing. Communicate!

Heart Exercise

MRS KUHNS

When I read about boys, hear about boys, and see boys, it strikes a chord in my heart. You see, I am a mom of four boys (though some days it sounds and feels like eight boys!). Boys are near and dear to my heart.

Speaking of my heart, I do wonder if other moms of boys feel like their heart gets daily exercise from their adventure-seeking, daring, energetic, shirt-and-pants-clad humans?! My heart races as I dive for the tower of dishes that is growing with every piece that Son wipes dry. My heart skips a beat when a tennis ball comes flying through the living room narrowly missing the clock (the same clock that has long since given up its glass face). My heart stops as I call for my son outside, and he answers from twenty feet up the tree. "But, Mom, I won't fall," comes the reply as I stand at the bottom, hands on my hips, spouting wisdom about broken bones and being paralyzed never to walk again while watching those bare toes reaching down limb to limb till he's safe on the ground. I silently thank the Lord for keeping him safe once again.

It reminded me of the episode we had when my son insisted he was stuck up in the tree. I brought the stepladder, but that was too short. I was ready to go find the extension ladder when Son figured out how to become un-stuck. He made his way down to a disgruntled mom who tried to explain that it's easier to get up than back down!

Our third son started his young life so accident-prone. Anytime he was out of sight and I heard him cry, I panicked and assumed the worst. (Talk about heart exercise!) At eighteen months, a two-drawer stand tipped over and cut his eyeball. (I know, it makes me cringe just to think of it!) I learned you can actually get stitches in the eye! We had a wonderful eye specialist who performed the surgery. The recovery was simple except that an eighteen-month-old does not understand that eye drops three times a day are for his benefit! Once the cut healed, the doctor put him to sleep again to remove the stitches. The after effect is a pupil that no longer dilates.

A mere five months later, this same son and I were sitting in yet another specialist's office. It was an ear/nose/throat doctor this time where I heard the words, "Bring him in tomorrow morning, and we will put him to sleep a bit to perform the procedure." You're wondering, *What procedure?* The little fellow stuck a Lego up his nose! So far up that Dad and Mom couldn't get it out. So far up that all you could see was a faint blue shine when using a bright pen light. So far up that the local doctor couldn't get it out. (The other patients likely wondered what was happening in that room when they heard the screams!) So far up that the specialists didn't even try to get it, which brought the words that they would need to put him to sleep.

If you've never had to put your small one in a tiny hospital gown and hand him to the nurses, be thankful—it's heart wrenching. Once he was asleep and holding still, it took less than fifteen minutes. Afterwards, the doctor came into the waiting room and handed me a small clear cup holding the offending little round blue Lego. That Lego is taped in a certain little boy's baby book among more than one hospital wristband. Is there any wonder his uncle suggested putting earmuffs on the little fellow because those might be next?!

If I hear someone declaring that girls are so much more expensive than boys are, I chuckle and reply that it all depends how often the boys hurt themselves! We've had a broken arm to add to our injury list, but who's counting?

Our boys have taught me simplicity: as long as there are cookies in the cupboard, balls to play with, and their favorite pants can be worn to school no matter how often or how many others are in the closet, they're happy! Yet my oldest is only ten, so you veterans with teenagers and beyond could teach me a lot, I'm sure.

Since I grew up with only one brother six years older than I, I'll admit there are days that all the boyness gets to me, and I wonder if I'm some stranger in the land of men. My advice: Don't forget to keep a few corners of your own. Do you need a new tablet? Buy a bright pink one. Does your toothbrush blend in with all the blues and greens? Have a purple or bright yellow. Decorate with bright flowers. Their cheerfulness is always in season. (Also, flowers are nature, so they go well with the deer mount or antlers that might be residing on the wall!)

I have yet to figure out the right response when well-meaning folks say, "Oh, don't give up. We had four boys before our girl," or "I imagine you are really hoping for a girl." I guess I feel a little defensive. We are not waiting on a girl. Neither do we feel slighted that we have all boys. They might be all boys, but their personalities are very different! One son can make candy disappear before you can ask how many pieces he ate. The other son is still eating Christmas candy at Easter. One son loves to work in the kitchen and is getting good at making egg sandwiches for lunch. I love that!

It's a challenge sometimes to keep the boys busy with their daddy working six and one-half days a week. However, the Lord tells us not to worry, so I try to leave it all to Him when I feel overwhelmed with the parenting process. And be it boys or girls, parenting can be overwhelming when we think of the responsibility of each small blessing. Each day is different, some smooth and happy, some bumpy and grumpy. We each must learn from the bumps and choose happiness! It is good for the heart!

When Little Boys Wash Dishes

LMY

They have a creek with rushing falls,
A pool that's calm and clear.
They have a pond with whipped-up suds
On which great waves appear.
The knives become the wiggly fish
That swim and dive below.
The forks are spears to spear them with
As through the pond they go.

The spoons—the swiftest little boats
That dart and dash about.
The plates are huge, enormous ships
That sail an ocean route.
The tumblers are such helpful things
To view the ocean floor,
And can be filled quite easily
To make a rushing roar.

"Oops, Mom! I really didn't mean
To splash up all the windowpane;
But see, my pond is pretty clean;
I'll use this towel I used before;
I'll wipe those drops, like so.
It's not as bad as when the falls
Had missed the creek, you know!"

And Mommy sighs, 'tis true of course,
The drips are minor things,
As are the spills and dripping clothes,
For all the joy it brings.
For when I'm old with boys all grown,
I'll think of happy days
When dirty pots and pans were washed
In splashing, boyish ways.

Little Overalls

AUTHOR UNKNOWN

Funny little overalls… Blue you were—now spots. I am putting you away… in the attic—in that box… Where my keepsakes all must stay… Their work finished for alway… Tiny, little overalls… Faded almost white in spots… Faded patches on each knee… One suspender tied in knots… Great big worn-through patch in back… Pockets empty, hanging slack… Dear, dear little overalls… I just can't throw you away… I must keep you, just because… Memories bring you back today…Once worn by my baby son… I saw you jump and climb and run… Funny, small patched overalls… Do you know you make me cry?… Thinking of the years gone by… Nevermore that little man… Will hold, so tight, his mommy's hand… Ne'er forgotten overalls… I am putting you away… Keep for me those memories sweet… Of my little boy at play… Of him, tiny, sleepy lad…Toddling in, overall clad… Work all finished, overalls… Take the rest that you deserve… Here with dresses, booties small… There's a place for you reserved… I must hold you close once more… then go out and shut the door.

Mom: "Son, tuck your shirt in. We're almost ready for church."

Son: "But, Mom, I don't like how it feels. It makes my pants so full!"

BOYS IN THE KITCHEN

MARTHA BEILER

"Mamas love hugs, and Mamas love kisses;
But what Mamas really LOVE is help with the dishes!"
Boys bring so much life to the kitchen! Even though some of them groan at the thought of doing dishes (AGAIN!), they use all manner of imagination to keep it interesting. They use soapsuds and pretend they have white-haired beards. They build bridges with utensils. On the drying mats, they sort glasses and jars by teams. They sort utensils in the drying rack pretending to have football teams. They often auction each item as they clear the table or put the dishes away. Auctioneering takes time, of course, and gets to be a bit hair-raising, especially when the nine-year-old holds a pitcher full of grape juice on top of his head. You can only imagine what happened next!

Our second son has always dreaded the dishwashing job the most, and for a long time he wished for twin girls to join our family to relieve him of his job. Little did he seem to realize that twin girls would make his mama busier than ever, and he would have even more dishes to wash!

It can be such a riot when boys wash dishes! Depending on who is washing, somehow there are always puddles on the floor. Some boys stack dishes neatly, and some slap them helter-skelter in the dish rack or chuck them in the corner after they dry them. We've used many different methods in taking turns to do dishes. If we didn't have a regular system, the same thing happened after each meal—

"It's not my turn," says Boy #1.

"I just did it the last time," says Boy #2.

"Mom, you always make me wash dishes!" says Boy #3.

And Boy #4 wilts in despair just at the sight of the kitchen sink.

Sound familiar? Sometimes we took turns by days or by weeks, but they really tire of washing dishes every day for a whole week. We enjoy our latest system the best. Each meal the boys are available to help, they take turns with washing, rinsing, and drying. It helps to break the monotony of the same procedure repeated. I like to motivate them by promising that I'll wash the pots and pans if they are finished with the other things in a certain amount of time. Nothing looks more overwhelming to a child than when there is a whole sink FULL of dirty dishes, and it's their turn to wash. At times like that I like to treat them by telling them I'll do their dishes and perhaps give them another job to do. I'm always rewarded with a grateful response! Sometimes their daddy helps which makes it fun. He challenges them to clean the stove and put *all* the dishes away. Not just some of them, leaving the rest for Mom.

Today I have a choice. I can choose to be grateful for all their help or feel exasperated by their lack of neatness. I choose to be grateful (even amidst the moments of exasperation!). Someday when I am a gray-haired grandma, I will think back fondly to the busy days with five little boys in the kitchen. I'll probably smile in remembering puddles on the floor and soapsud beards on their faces.

Josh's favorite riddle: Why did the man drive over the cliff?

Answer: He wanted to test his air brakes!

D Rose Weaver

Mother of Boys

MOM OF NINE BOYS

Her days are brimful of wonders and joys,
Explorers' discov'ries—she's a mother of boys.
The dirt that tracks in, her soul not annoys;
She knows it will wash—she's a mother of boys.
Trades of the future she sees in the toys
That lie on the floor—she's a mother of boys.
Clatter and clamor that others call noise,
Is music to her—she's a mother of boys.
She always is baking; it's one of her joys
To fill hungry stomachs—she's a mother of boys.
Hobbies can't draw her, nor other employs,
From her post of duty—she's a mother of boys.
She's firm as a rock, yet never destroys
A child's tender trust—she's a mother of boys.
She's shaping the future that's hid 'round the bend
For these carefree boys—she's a mother of men!
They'll soon be strong pillars, the truth to defend,
Still led by her teaching—she's a mother of men!
God bless this mother, on Him she'll depend
For wisdom and strength—she's a mother of men!

✝ My Prayer

BETHANY BRUBACHER

Dear Lord,

I thank You for the most precious gifts that You have blessed my husband and me with—that of our three dear sons.

Our hearts were torn with pain when our firstborn, a son, died shortly after his premature birth. Three and one-half years later, we still miss him. However, I thank You that we have the faith that he will spend eternity with You. There is peace in the thought that we have a family started in heaven.

Our hearts were filled with joy and thankfulness when thirteen months later You blessed us with a healthy full-term son. Our cup was full... and running over when eighteen months later, another baby boy joined our little family.

Lord, I praise You for blessing us with a little boy to keep after losing one, and I am filled with gratitude toward You for also giving that son a living brother. I feel as though my dream of being a mother of sons is fulfilled. I like little boys! Perhaps the one reason that I enjoy having a son who has a brother is because I had only one brother. His four older sisters supplied him with four brothers-in-law, but it is not the same as growing up with a brother.

And now, Lord, I have these two little boys to love, care for, and train. So often I am weary with keeping after my active pair. I know so little about this assignment You have given me. I've wished that I could ask my mother-in-law for her tips on raising sons since she raised five in the very house in which my family and I live, but I can't because You called her home before I got to know her.

I pray that my sons will learn to be obedient, honest, and kind. I pray that they will grow up to be men of faith and courage. I pray that they will resist the enemy and evil. I pray that they will grow up to be useful, hardworking men. And Lord, I pray if it is Your will, that someday they will find Christian girls of virtue to be their wives. Oh, Lord, help my sons to protect the purity of those girls until the day they take them for their wives.

Lord, I pray for the father of my sons. I thank You that he is exclusively mine. Give him the grace and guidance to train up his sons in the way that they should go. I think of the wintry day when I hurried out the sidewalk after my husband and sons. There was a light dusting of snow on the sidewalk. My husband's large footprints were all the way down the walk, and beside them were the smaller ones of our two-year-old son's. As my husband held the hand of our toddler with one hand and the infant car seat in the other hand, our infant son reached up and held his daddy's hand. Lord, I pray that my husband will be able to hold his sons' hands for a while, and more importantly hold their hearts forever. I hope they will follow in their daddy's footsteps.

And... I wonder... Will I pray for a daughter someday? Will I feel as though I'm missing out if I never give birth to at least one daughter? Yes, I think in some ways I will, and yet... When I think of my friends who have never borne children and maybe never will, or when I think of the baby I buried—I wonder if I may even dare to feel that way!

And so, oh Lord, as I'm here wondering how to finish my prayer, the words "helpmeet," "respect," and "love" whirl through my brain in a perhaps unorganized fashion. It becomes evident that once again I'm thinking of the father of my sons, the head of our family. He has his ideals of how he wants me to play my part in the raising of our sons. It is his responsibility to see that they are trained and taught according to Your Word. I am his helpmeet in this. It has been said that the best thing a father can do for his children is to love their mother. Likewise, it could be said that the best thing a mother can do for her children is to respect their father.

So help me, Lord!

In Jesus' Name,

Amen.

Mothering My Messy Man

ANONYMOUS

My thoughtful gaze swept the rolling hills outside my kitchen window. The little boys had eagerly skipped out the door with their daddy this morning, and a rare quiet pervaded the house while the wee one napped. My spirits should have soared with the birds in the glorious splendor of spring sunshine, but they didn't. Even the belated amaryllis at my window was opening up a regal display of loveliness. That bulb itself was an illustration of my nature, often a day or days late (who else had a blooming amaryllis in mid-April?) and sometimes a dozen eggs short. The latter is what it was this morning. Perhaps that started Greg and me out on the wrong foot.

My husband, Darrell, had needed to fetch us more eggs from the neighboring farm before breakfast. Then Greg made himself the chef while I combed Lori's hair for school. Ordinarily, I hover anxiously when my seven-year-old son cracks eggs, but for once I stayed away, occupied in brushing Lori's thick, wavy hair. Greg had gotten to the whisking step when I glimpsed him leaning over the sink. I looked again. A school shirt clad elbow was emerging, dripping wet, from the soapy water I had left there. That's when I opened my mouth. I shouldn't have. My words ended with several exclamation points and a big question mark.

"I didn't know there was some egg spilled on the counter, and I got my sleeve in it," Greg replied lamely as he hastily rubbed a towel over the soaked sleeve.

I moved to get the eggs frying, warning him that there were to be *no* eggs spilled outside the pan. Just as I wrapped a band around the end of Lori's second braid, Greg turned off the burner and pronounced the eggs done. "There's some dripped on the stove," he reported anxiously. "But I don't know how it got there. I didn't see *any* spill out." Emphatically, he left the kitchen.

"Hmm…so you think they just jumped out." I pulled the undone eggs back onto the burner.

The rest of the family was gathering for family worship when Lori gasped, "There's egg all over the back of Greg's pants!"

Her exaggeration sounded rebukingly familiar to my ears, but I ignored it. The rebuke, that is. Setting the pan of eggs on a hot pad, I reached for a dishcloth, vainly attempting to squelch my rising exasperation. *Couldn't he ever keep his clothes clean?!* "You almost should be punished for being so careless," I reprimanded heartlessly as I scrubbed the spot of egg white off the side of his pants. "It must have rubbed off your elbow," I guessed.

"Well, I rested my arm on the counter, and here it was sticky," he explained regretfully.

My voice softened several degrees. "Was your arm tired from whisking?"

"Yeah."

We sat down and strains of "He Owns the Cattle on a Thousand Hills" wafted to the heavens at Greg's suggestion. His voice rang out lustily, "I know that He will care for me."

Minutes later, we rose from our knees and a hubbub ensued as our lively troop vied for a turn to kiss the baby or jostled for their places at the table, each trying to tell their stories or plans. We divided the scrambled eggs and filled tumblers amid cautions and directions. Egg chunks dangled from the four-year-old's mouth.

"Conner, that's the way dogs eat," Darrell reproved, prompting a series of chuckles.

I cringed at the stream that trickled from Jalyn's nose to his chomping mouth until Darrell's ever-faithful handkerchief came to the rescue. *Oh well, you can't expect a two-year-old to wipe his own nose.*

All three of our sons were winsome fellows to my motherly partiality but also very prone to messiness. Greg was chief. Just now, he was reaching for the jug of apple juice. "No, Greg, you may not pour your own," I stated, stopping him firmly.

The bottle was two inches empty. *A wise mother learns to prevent disasters,* I told myself, only half aware that my energetic son was now lunging for the honey bear on the back of the stove. He plopped it onto the table at the same moment I realized he had not asked for permission to leave his place. *How has that uncivilized habit become so entrenched?* To his dismay, we forbade him to use the honey on his cereal.

We passed the sucanat. Greg spooned a generous heap, then seized by some strange whim (which only boys can comprehend), he leaned down and puffed at his sucanat-coated cream of wheat. His face registered surprised embarrassment as his sister exclaimed over the grit that had flown. I sighed and sent another string of rebuking words Greg's way. He repented dutifully and commenced to fill his hungry stomach. When Greg asked for seconds of cereal, Lori obligingly passed the kettle. Greg-style, he spun it around, causing the handle to collide with Lori's half-full cup of apple juice. The liquid and the girlish shriek poured out simultaneously.

"Grab a rag, Lori," I ordered wearily. *Is it only 7:35?*

I exchanged glances with my husband. He sat, composed and unruffled, by my side, a strong, steady rock in contrast to my escalating emotions. While he inserted calm direction to the children, his eyes spoke volumes to mine. Was I reading, *Relax, honey, it'll be okay...?*

But, how? I wondered. Since Greg was serving himself cereal, I handed over the spatula. I spooned warm cereal into Daisy's eager mouth while I kept a wary eye on the proceedings opposite me. Cream of wheat strung over the sides of the pan. "Greg, be careful," I warned.

Cereal splattered onto the table close to his elbows. My frustration mounted. "Look, you dripped it!" Cream of wheat smeared onto unskilled hands. "Don't get it on your shirt!" My thoughts churned, *Must you be so clumsy and careless?*

"Whew!" Lori breathed. "I feel like leaving the table. I'm getting tired of Mother needing to tell Greg things!" (I wondered uneasily who was most wearisome.)

Finally, Greg deemed the kettle empty, and Darrell asked him to wipe the table. Under my critical eyes, he swiped the dishcloth across the smears. When he returned to his seat, I noticed a bit of cereal clinging to the front of his pants. Frowning, I pointed it out. "Please clean it off."

Barely glancing down, he brushed his pants, catching the grains of damp cereal… and slid his hands into his pocket. If only I could have pocketed my irritation as smoothly. It simmered ominously, and I pursed my lips for a moment. Greg waited, his expression unreadable.

Desperately trying to keep my voice level, I said, "You smeared the cereal on your hand, and now it's probably in your pocket!"

With a brief glance at his hand, Greg slid onto the bench to devour his interrupted breakfast.

We finished our meal, and everyone scattered to prepare for the day. I inspected Greg for breakfast remains (checking pockets!). The clock was chiming 8:15 when he shrugged into his jacket. I smiled at his shining face, smoothed-down locks, and somewhat clean clothes. He stumbled out the door with his sister. Cheery good-byes and "have-a-good-day" floated after them. *I did TRY to be a sweet mother, didn't I?*

With Daisy tucked in for her morning nap, I finished cleaning up the kitchen. The reprieve of the unusual stillness prompted a playback of the day's beginning. My precious family had enthusiastically eaten their breakfast at this now polished table. What kind of breakfast had I served them? *It was tasty and nourishing, wasn't it?* Yet something seemed lacking. Pleasantness? Cheerfulness? *But it's Greg,* I excused myself. *If only he wouldn't be so uncouth…*

Greg was natured so differently from me. I thrived on neatness and spotlessness—perfection. Greg? He just enjoyed each moment to the fullest, often heedless of proper etiquette. I worked carefully and methodically. He whirled from one thing to the next with speed and gusto and a singular goal of completion, like Darrell's family. When I became one of the Shrocks, I learned quickly that efficiency was a priority and neatness sometimes became secondary. However, they were generally on time, too. (Mom's amaryllises had bloomed weeks ago.) Darrell, I often rejoiced fondly, was one of the most careful of the clan, balancing efficiency and tidiness almost perfectly. The Shrocks were all busy, happy people, unafraid of dirt and hard work. I loved them for it.

I loved my children, too. I tucked away memories of smiling into each of my babies' charming faces with their sparkling blue eyes, inherited from their daddy. Greg, especially, had big round eyes like blueberries! I loved my children growing up, too, with each bit of maturity the months and years added. Or did I? I squirmed.

The age-old song my children could sing snatches of as soon as they could talk flitted through my mind. "Jesus loves me when I'm good, when I do the things I should. Jesus loves me when I'm bad…" Had Greg meant to be bad when he was making messes, or was he simply an awkward gentleman-in-the-making?

And then the scales fell off my eyes. As crystal clear as the blue sky that stretched above the hills, I saw myself as God saw me. I wasn't so different from Greg after all. I was clumsy and careless. Worse than spilling food and smudging clothes (such easily remedied problems!), I was spilling harsh words and dampening feelings and hearts with unkindness. The hearts of these little ones Jesus loves. The implications were so much more far-reaching. I was the bad one, yet Jesus still loved me. He would forgive me. He would extend another chance to me. With relief, I realized that the problems I caused could be remedied too: by wiping away the harsh words with sincere apologies, by brightening hearts and feelings with kindness and forbearance, by serving love.

That is what boys need most. And my boys are so needy. Every day I settle countless squabbles, scrub numberless shirts and pants, serve endless dishes of food, and clean up just as many messes. I try to teach my sons how to be gentlemen. In all those daily details, too often I forget that boys need lots of love. I could do all those things perfectly, yet what does 1 Corinthians 13 say? If I have not charity, God's love in me, I am—an imperfect mother? I AM NOTHING! However, add love, then we have excellence. Everything else is put into proper perspective. Love will teach her sons how to be gentlemen. Yet she will delight in the spontaneity of her boyish gifts from God, chuckling at the clever way of washing a shirtsleeve, perhaps. Love will smile as she wipes away spots and spills. She will gently remind the careless one of his responsibility to be careful. Or she will patiently take the spatula and show him how.

My thoughtful gaze again swept the rolling hills outside my kitchen window. I will not be clumsy with God's little boys. I will serve love. For "the greatest of these is charity."

Battered-Up Boys

MARY ANN MARTIN

Scrapes and burns,
Bumps and bruises,
Scratches on the arm,
Or where the cat chooses.

Bites and stings
From bugs and bees,
A gash in the leg
And skinned-up knees.

Abrasion on the elbow,
Lump on his head,

Big black and blue spot,
"Right here," he said.

One black eye
And a boo-boo too,
All scraped up
They come to you.

Go get the Band-Aids,
Put on some salve;
It's life with boys,
And this you'll have!

A Few Moments of
JOY

MARTHA BEILER

A beautiful rain watered the world as I sat down to feed my baby. Almost immediately, my two little boys brought their storybooks. "Mommy, read a story," they begged.

With a nine-month-old baby, story time and feeding-the-baby time needed to be separated. It was much too interesting for the baby to eat when he wanted to listen and see the pictures, too! "When I am finished, I'll read to you," I promised, and soon I was engrossed in an old copy of *Ladies' Journal* magazine.

"Coming Over!" I tore my mind from the magazine, and out of the corner of my eye, I saw five-year-old Isaiah throw a ball over the loveseat.

I opened my mouth to say, "No, Isaiah, not in the living room!" Instead, my reprimand turned to chuckles when two-year-old Josiah's wee little voice replied from behind the loveseat, "Piggy slop."

Oh! A game of Coming Over, I thought. *This is too cute!* Just then, as the ball was thrown back to Isaiah, I realized their ball was a plastic toy tomato. I watched in total amusement as the game continued. Throwing their ball back and forth, calling "Coming Over" and laughing—they were definitely having a grand time! The next thing I knew, Josiah was running out from behind the loveseat trying to tag Isaiah and saying, "I'm going to catch you!"

Their game lasted for probably a total of ten minutes before they moved on to some other entertainment. I had to smile and was so glad I had not stopped their game (even in the living room!), for surely I would have missed a few moments of joy with little boys!

Of Boys

JENNY GOOD

I heard someone say that boys will be boys
With all of their antics and all of their noise.
I thought it was true, you see, we have four
That troop through the house and bounce out the door!

First, they were babies, so innocent, sweet;
They soon pattered 'round on inquisitive feet.
So soon comes the day that a hammer's "the thing,"
And screwdrivers, wire, wood, pieces of string.

Trucks, tractors, equipment (the real ones or toys)
Hold much fascination for all growing boys.
They long to know all about many things,
Like how monarch worms grow butterfly wings.

They lick off the beaters and help sweep the floor.
The sweeper's a combine, the dishes—a bore!
The bikes and the trikes go many a mile;
The lawn-mowing job is done with a smile.

The blue jeans are filthy, worn through at the knees
From work in the garden and climbing the trees.
The day usually comes they want to earn money.
Complete inventory? Each boy has a bunny!

Plans get hatched out in little boy huddles
And mud rearranged in magnetic mud puddles!
No weeds in our sandbox, few dolls with the toys—
It's all in the life of the parents of boys!

When comes the night and they're all tucked in bed,
I sink to my pillow with whirling head.
We settled the fights, and we doctored the bumps—
Is all of their lives full of hops, skips, and jumps?!

Someone once said some words worthy of mention,
Thus showing a vision that grabs my attention:
"These boys, yes, they're boys, but so soon they'll be men;
So therefore, be wise, drive foolishness from them."

We need Solomon's wisdom, the patience of Job,
The vision of Hannah and Mary of old.
We must water the noble and weed out the bad;
Soon a man will be made from each little lad.

God help us raise Daniels and Noahs and Pauls,
Men who say, "Yes, Lord," when their Saviour calls.
Men who will steadfastly stand for the right
Will someday live in the mansions of light.

My Neighbor Boy

LINDA S NOLT

He is all boy, tough and rough. He kicks our dog to show he is not scared of him but is reduced to quivering fear when the dog turns on him and barks.

When I open the door to his knock, he bursts in, talking about everything from caterpillars to hot air balloons. I cannot doubt that he is an expert on every subject.

He has an undisputed right to my food, my books, and my lap. Every time he comes, I must read *The Cat in the Hat* to him and the story about Pierre hiding in the pot of soup.

Today he is here for a meal. My husband, Melvin, asks him if he likes olives.

"Yes, yes, I like olives, and Daddy likes olives, too," he replies. But when Melvin offers him some olives, he says, "No, I don't like olives, but Daddy likes olives."

He spills pudding on his little chair, and I give him a rag to wipe it up. What I learn is that small boys don't wipe up spills; they smear them around. "I'll sit on it," he offers.

I love this boy. He is not mine, but in a sense he is, this neighbor boy who comes to my house and is in my care for a few hours of his life. He is not mine, but because he loves me as well, a bit of my influence may stay with him forever.

Mind Over Matter

LJW

"**M**om!" his eager summons reached me in the bedroom. "There's corn growing around our tree! Come look!"

I smiled to myself as I heeded his call. "No, son, it's not corn. It's daylilies coming up," I corrected him. "It's too early for corn to be growing, and we don't usually plant corn around the tree, do we?"

As my son returned to his exploration of the spring-like day, I pondered how ironic his excitement was over this simple finding of green things growing that reminded him of corn plants. Not too many weeks ago when a seed catalog appeared in our mailbox, my children pored over the lovely pictures. They offered comments about which flower caught their eye or what vegetable appeared tasty. Sonny has not yet developed a taste for tomatoes, and green vegetables naturally cause him alarm, so it was the page loaded with perfect roasting ears that he brought to my attention. "I can't wait till we grow corncobs in the garden," he said. And indeed, last summer he was as excited as any of us when we harvested the first roasting ears for lunch. One ear was not sufficient for him either after he had gnawed the first one into the cob.

The irony on which I was pondering was that this same small son caused much disturbance at the table about this very vegetable. How can he despise creamed corn on his plate, cut-off corn in casseroles or soup, and foolishly complain that he only likes corn on the cob? How can he gag on our favorite Dairy Casserole or yummy Taco Soup simply because he sees those corn kernels staring at him? The rest of us sigh in exasperation because corn is such a favorite with us. It makes no sense to us that someone who likes to chew corn off a cob could stubbornly refuse to eat it off his plate. (So simple, so mess-free that way.) It seems evident that we are dealing with a head problem.

This dilemma makes me sigh. Our son struggles to eat any dish that has any vegetable in it. I never thought I'd allow my children to be this way. I never would have dreamed that I'd change my way of cooking just for one choosy child. I simply don't make big batches of these vegetable-laden meals anymore to stock my freezer for handy suppers. It makes it difficult to know what to keep on hand for suppers that must prepare themselves while I am at the barn. Moreover, if we are to have a balanced meal that includes a vegetable, I need to fix that separately after I come in. This results in more time and more dirty dishes to wash.

How did I gravitate to this standard? I guess I grew so weary of the constant battle at the table. No, we didn't just give in and let him get by. We made him take a little; we made him do without dessert; we heated it up again at the next meal. We endured gagging; we ignored tears; we tried punishments. We began to dread dinner and supper, the meals where vegetables are served.

All the time his big sister calmly ate her share of greens without complaint. Peas, limas, salad, tomatoes—whatever we gave her, she ate. I struggled to understand how two siblings could be so different. I thought boys were the eaters, the ones who wolfed down their dinners and held out their plates for more. But not my boy. The presence of any offending food causes his first course to move very slowly into his stomach. One small bite, containing one small pea, circles around and around in his mouth and painfully goes down. The remaining bites grow frosty on his plate. Even at breakfast, where the food choices tend to agree with him better, he chews slowly and dawdles between bites.

I should have been more prepared for this behavior. I had warning about his sensitive palate when he was quite young. At nine months, he suddenly determined that he had outgrown Mom's milk and took heartily to table food. (Veggies were well ground and well hidden then!) I was disturbed by his lack of milk consumption. After all, he was still a baby, and all babies must drink some kind of milk. Formula repulsed him, and I was fast losing interest in trying to nurse him because he was balking and biting. I offered him cows' milk even though I thought he was too young for that. (In this family, we are milk drinkers. We would drink milk at every meal if we didn't have self-control. Nevertheless, absolutely, we drink milk from our cups at breakfast. Who could tolerate water with their pancakes and gravy or egg omelet?) However, this small son refused milk. I tried and tried, but he would not accept it. Once again, I thought this had to be a matter of the mind. *This baby would learn to drink milk!* But this same son who has grown out of babyhood has never learned to enjoy plain milk. He accepts any other form of dairy product hungrily, and begs for chocolate milk or hot chocolate. He eats granola with milk. However, he tolerates water in his cup at breakfast. He actually requests it! He drinks water with his scrambled eggs or blueberry coffee cake.

It seems like I need to offer some kind of hope for other moms who are dealing with finicky little boys, but we certainly are not at the end of this matter. All we can do is keep encouraging him to eat what is set before him even if he doesn't exactly care for it. I hope we can have wisdom to know when to allow him to have his own set of preferences and when he needs to eat a helping for his health's sake. It is encouraging to see a little progress sometimes. I try to have faith that some day when he is no longer a little boy and is eating supper at a Disaster Response volunteer kitchen, he will dip willingly into the pot of Taco Soup and will not need help to clean up his plate.

Sunday School
AN AMUSED MOM

After our oldest son started attending Sunday School, he told me one Sunday afternoon, "I liked that story about the fire chief and the humble man."

It took a few minutes to click. Then I decided he was talking about the Pharisee and the publican going to the temple to pray!

THE SHACKS

EVELYN FISHER

O ur boys thought it was fun to build houses. Sometimes it was a blanket house under the table. Once I had actually sewed material together to drape over the table. There were doors and windows. Of course, a house needs a light, so the boys would round up a lamp and run an extension cord. Naptime was more exciting in that kind of house than in their bed!

Sometimes for their house, they would use the cardboard box that appliances came in. With the box turned upside down, doors and windows that opened and shut could be cut into it. Maybe their house was a shelter they enlarged under the low-hanging branches of the trumpet vine or under the sheet they put across the clothesline for their teepee or under the tablecloths draped across two clotheslines to dry. One time it was the old shack out back by the garden. It had been an old corncrib, but they set up a playhouse complete with the (girlish) touch of a guestbook!

As the boys got older, they watched how Daddy built a barn. They were thrilled to be able to help in their own way, and then they used the scraps and built their own shack. They dug holes and set up poles, used a header, and nailed up plywood walls. They used an old door to give their house a more finished look. Sometimes they climbed up on the plywood roof and used it for their deer stand; sometimes they put ears of corn up there for the squirrels.

To make the neighborhood more complete, they began to build a house in the mulberry tree. Although it might never have been completely finished, it boasted a tin roof. These two houses were built at opposite ends of the lily patch. The lily patch was the common orange daylilies that were beautiful in June. I was flabbergasted when I discovered my sons had made a bike trail right through my lily bed to connect the houses. I had a real struggle when I saw what had happened to the lilies in their path until I remembered I was a mother of boys. The memories they were making was worth more than a perfect bed of lilies. I don't know that I ever walked the bike trail, and it wasn't until later years that I found out they had gone to great work to make the trail, even using stone left over from the barn-building project. They also built a unique bridge over the gully that ran through the lily bed.

Then there was the house built by the little boys. They used ten-foot plastic shelves that had been used for all kinds of boys' projects before. This time they set four shelves on end with the two walls meeting at the top to form a teepee-type structure. They tied the shelves together with baler twine. Next, they took four more shelves to close up the two ends. The six-foot house was very simply built yet strong enough for boys to climb all over. In the spring when one of the little boys planted his garden, he began to take down the house walls to put up a garden fence. Another boy stopped him, exclaiming, "We still want our house!" There was a compromise. A couple of the plastic shelves went into a fence, and the house still stood.

Those houses were built by little boys. The one that was my style was built in the lower branches of the black walnut tree. It was built by boys who had a better understanding of basic building skills. They had strength to accomplish the big project. It looked like a real tree house with a ladder built up to the porch. The children dug a ditch from the shop to the tree house, and with Daddy overseeing the project, they ran electricity to their cute little house.

There was also the little tin shack built with steel left over from Daddy's building projects. Some of the tin had gone through a shop fire, but it was good enough for the young carpenter. The shack was tucked snugly in between the bridal wreath bush and the quince tree out in the back corner of our little property. The builder made it homier by digging up flowerbeds around his house and planting irises. Like so many of the houses before, the owner lost interest as he went on to other projects, and the shack eventually came down to give more room for other interests.

Out in the lily bed stands an old shack hidden behind the lilac bushes. It is under the mulberry tree, and if the tree could tell stories, it would have many stories about shacks and tree climbing and boyish dreams of the past twenty-five years! This house is put together with all kinds of scraps and has a bit of a tumbledown look. Eventually the young owners will say, "Let us tear down this house," and maybe they will add, "Let's build a better one."

Some of these boyish shacks have been a little bit of an eyesore for me. I dream of a perfectly manicured landscape. Yet over the years, I have tried to remember my boys are learning carpentry skills from their own little building projects. When they are busy dreaming and planning together how to make do with the materials on hand, it prepares them for bigger projects in the future. More than that, they are occupied in a profitable way. It is like the motto my son recently gave me:

> **Pardon the mess,**
> **But my children**
> **are making memories.**

Boys & Toys

MARLENE BEILER

It was February, cold and drab. Those winter humdrums were settling in when two-year-old Isaiah discovered the play food in the
basement. He was intrigued. Appealing morsels found their way up
the steps and scattered across the floor: scoops of ice cream, chocolate
cookies, french-fries, and cheesy pepperoni pizza.

Maybe, I pondered, *it's time to bring the play kitchen set up from the
basement. Perhaps Isaiah and five-year-old Malachi would enjoy pretend
cooking and feasting as much as their siblings, Jethro and Hanna, did
when they were younger. Maybe.*

So at my request, Jethro lugged the kitchen and accessories up from
the basement. I handed wipes to the younger boys and set them to
work cleaning their kitchen. Meanwhile, I envisioned newly enter-
tained preschoolers. It didn't take long for them to discover that the
top half of the play kitchen could be removed. That piece could even
be separated in two pieces. Thus began moving day and they hauled
the pieces hither and thither. The next thing I knew there was a noisy

auction underway—a kitchen set auction. Sold!

As I sat feeding and rocking our newborn son during the following weeks, I was fascinated as I watched the boys' play. They never did play kitchen, even though I showed them how. However, they played *with* the kitchen! One day they were cabinet men. They loaded it onto their truck, which in reality was the fireplace. They spent lots of time strapping it securely with jump ropes to take out to their job to install.

Once more, the kitchen was sold to the highest bidder.

There was a thrilling game of football in the dining room. It was a close game as Malachi (the only real player) blocked and tackled his opponents and threw the imaginary ball for a deep pass. Exhausted, he settled himself in the stadium, the kitchen set, to cheer for the next game. Touchdown!

The kitchen was auctioned off. Again.

Bang! Bang! Pow! Malachi and Isaiah trudge through the woods. Ah! Finally, they reached their tree stand and up they clamber. This happens to be the bottom of the kitchen set pushed against the sofa. (I believe the top was sold.) They sat on the sofa back with their feet resting on the kitchen set. Perched comfortably in the tree stand, they eagerly scanned the woods for deer or perhaps even a bear. Bang!

"Two dollars, now three, SOLD!"

OF BEASTS

and Boys

MRS NM

I know the falsehood, crime, and shame
Of evolution's theory.
The Bible plainly proves it wrong;
My teachers taught that clearly.
And yet, I see within my sons
Some things that make me wonder;
Sometimes they act like animals,
And then I have to ponder...

The other day I heard the sound
Of cats. And they were fighting!
In boyish tones they snarled and spat,
And then they started biting.
I hustled to the battleground,
And spanked each hissing kitten.
The one had scratches on his cheek;
The other's thumb was bitten.

At bedtime, if I sit beneath
The boys' bedroom flooring,

I hear a herd of elephants—
Vibrations, thumping, roaring.
Or just inside the door, I'll spy
An empty shrunken "snakeskin."
The boy who had been wearing it
Has fled. (Or I'm mistaken.)

I watch for beastly tendencies
When seated at the table.
We are not piglets at the trough,
Or cattle in the stable.
If someone spills his water cup,
Don't holler like a monkey.
If someone tells a funny tale,
Don't hee-haw like a donkey.

Please tell me how to teach my sons,
"Don't clear your throat like mooses.
And when it's time to blow your nose,
Don't honk like ducks or gooses.
When drinking, don't slurp like a cow;
Don't belch and spit like llamas.
Don't push and shove like baby goats
Who think they need their mamas."

Lord, help me tame the trumpeting,
The sniffing, snarling, snorting,
The horsing, hooting, hollering,
The kicking and cavorting.
Bless me with grace each day, dear Lord,
To help each little laddie
Lay down the traits of animals;
Be *manly* like his daddy!

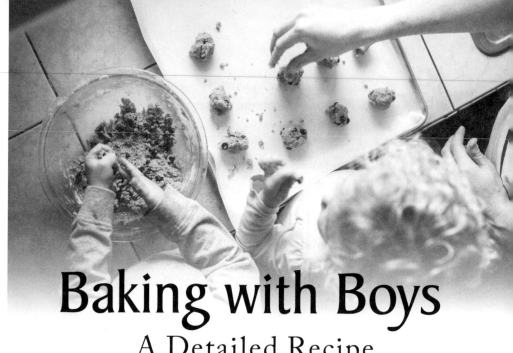

Baking with Boys
A Detailed Recipe
CRYSTAL FAUS

Uncle Joel's Birthday Cherry Swirl Coffee Bars
First, gather three excited boys who all want to help make a birthday gift for Uncle Joel. Small Son (eleven months) sits on the counter on one side of the mixer. Give him a wooden spoon to wave, bang, or chew. Oldest Son (six) and Middle Son (four) attempt to share a chair.

Send Oldest Son to the basement for a quart of cherry pie filling. Sigh, but smile, when he comes up with two quarts and asks to make a double batch. Explain that you will not give the whole pan away. You will eat the leftovers.

Help Middle Son dump **1½ cups of sugar** into the mixing bowl.

Give Oldest Son **1 stick of butter** and a table knife. Instruct him not to shave the butter but use two hands to chunk it, and then throw the chunks into the mixing bowl.

Meanwhile, Middle Son scrapes in **½ cup of lard**.

Small Son delights in sliding the switch to turn the mixer on. Today we can make use of his ability. The faster the mixer whirls, the more rapidly his little toes twirl.

Turn off mixer before Middle Son dumps in ½ **teaspoon baking powder.**

Attempt to add **1 teaspoon vanilla.** When Small Son grabs your arm, add ¼ teaspoon to the counter instead. Grin at the older two as they sample vanilla and discuss how yummy it smells and how yucky it tastes.

Small Son slides that switch again. Grab the wooden spoon away from the beater. Pick the chair up off the floor. Assist Oldest Son to upright position. After searching for injuries and finding nothing serious, add ½ **teaspoon almond flavoring.**

Admonish the older two sons to stop dipping and licking batter so we will have some left to bake. Grab the wooden spoon back several more times.

Ask Oldest Son to bring **4 eggs** from the refrigerator. Inform him that you will be the one cracking the eggs, and then proceed to crack two eggs into a small bowl. Instruct Oldest Son not to pop the yolks with the butter-cutting knife but to dump them into the mixing bowl after you have slowed the mixer from high speed. Crack two more eggs into the bowl. Once more Small Son has the mixer whipping at high speed. Slow it down to low speed before Middle Son adds those two eggs. Now it's permissible for Small Son to slide the switch to high speed to whip these ingredients for 2 minutes.

Again, turn mixer down to low speed before adding **3 cups of flour.** Give the first cupful to Oldest Son to dump in, the second cupful to Middle Son, and you dump in the last cupful of flour.

Stop mixer and remove bowl to scrape down sides. Be sure to unplug mixer as well to avoid Small Son sliding the switch and whirling batter from the beater. Replace bowl and plug mixer back in. Mix a bit more before calling the batter finished.

Push back all the dipping fingers and go to a different counter to spread ⅔ of batter into a 10"x15" pan.

When you hear a smack, Small Son's cry, and Middle Son saying, "That's just what you get," question Middle Son. When he informs you that Small Son was hindering him, remind Middle Son that it's not his job to punish and that in the future he shall talk to you about Small Son's misdeeds.

Spread **1 quart of cherry pie filling** on top of batter and tell Oldest Son we really do not know how many bars we will give away and how many we will keep. And he needs to be okay with that because we aren't deciding right now. Spoon remaining batter on top of cherries. Send older sons off to play and take a picture of Small Son emptying the crock of utensils.

Bake the bars at 350° for 35-40 minutes. Meanwhile, put Small Son down for a nap.

Put utensils back into crock and wipe counter.

Make glaze by whisking **1 heaping cup of 10-x sugar** with **2 table-spoons of milk**. Drizzle over bars while they are warm. Sample warm bars with Oldest Son and give Middle Son some chips to snack on since he does not like cherries. Frown when Oldest Son complains that the glaze is too sugary and take another sample.

Stop Middle Son from sneaking pieces without cherries.

Cut the bars when sons are napping. Arrange bars on a plate for the birthday gift. Put the remaining bars in a container. Adjust the puzzle pieces in the refrigerator to accommodate both.

Wash the baking dishes with the dinner dishes. When the pan slips from the overflowing dish drainer and crashes to the floor, comfort Small Son.

You are done! And you have: a gift to give—homemade with lots of personal touches—memories made in the kitchen, another gray hair, a few bars for hungry little sons.

Anyone without access to three small sons who would like to try this recipe may check into borrowing some. The bars will not turn out the same without them. ☼

The Mechanic

EVELYN FISHER

I was awestruck one day as my nine-year-old son, who was a mechanic at heart, began to tell me how to fix the mower problem. I was left in the dust as his skills continued to develop, and his daddy taught him things I didn't even begin to comprehend. Today his daddy has set up his own mechanic shop, and our fifth son is dreaming of his own shop. "I will put a lift in," he says.

It is interesting to watch the boys' skills spread beyond the simple mechanics as they take after their daddy. In the first years of our marriage, my husband fixed up old vehicles to resell and painted vehicles for others. As the years rolled by, accidents happened. Once a car ran into the back of our old pickup and totaled it. My husband bought an old scrap pickup to fix up the totaled one. The boys got hold of the old scrap vehicle and said, "This is too good to junk." They made a flatbed for it, and farm-use tags sufficed for a time until it was licensed for real! Then we had two vehicles. The same thing happened with a couple of cars. One car we have is really two totaled cars put together to produce one good car.

A number of our sons bought older pickups or cars, even a tractor, and fixed and painted them. Our less than two-acre property looks like a vehicle lot at times. Our one son especially took an interest in old vehicles and bought cheap ones. Through his hands-on college education (as we call the learning of a trade by the trial and error method of self-teaching), he prepared vehicles for reselling. His cousin exclaimed over the fact that he must have a lot of money floating around to buy so many vehicles. With quick calculation, it was discovered that his cousin paid more for his one car than our son paid for the six vehicles he was in the process of fixing up.

Outside my kitchen window, parked in front of the shop, is an interesting looking Ford Crown Victoria. It was a police car that was crunched from both ends. Sometimes my son stands at the kitchen window smiling and dreaming. He plans to turn the car into a cute little pickup.

The same son bought a police car to fix up. It was in good shape, and he repainted it and claimed it as his very own car to keep. He wanted to take it out and surprise his brother who was teaching school a distance from home. The trip out went well except they had no heat. When I got off the phone from talking to my son and told the family about it, my husband looked up from his book long enough to go over a short list of things that could have happened. I grabbed up a paper and quickly wrote down the list. (I like to pretend I know a few mechanical terms and have a little bit of knowledge.) I called my son back, and of course, he could not see the paper I held in my hand as I shared with him that "I was thinking…" As I went down over the list, he said, "No, it can't be that," "I checked that," "No, not that either." I got to the end of what I had written, and he had said, "No," to the whole short list my mechanic husband had very quickly offered. I had gotten almost to the end of what I had to offer. "Guess it must be the bearings in the water line!" We both chuckled.

Boys are full of vehicle thoughts. One evening our young son needed to stop his play to come get his haircut. He was not very eager to sit for a haircut. They were having so much fun tumbling down the steps with the beanbag. He was telling me all about it and said, "I want to go Peterbiltin' down the steps again."

One day my sons came in from a project they had excitedly been working on for days. "Mother, come see the bucket seat."

Bucket seat? I pictured a vehicle where the driver and passengers each had their own soft bucket seats. I burst out laughing when I saw their project, and they joined right in. It was a bucket seat all right. They had made a three-wheeled thing with a wooden frame. It has a bicycle wheel in the front and two smaller wheels in the rear. It sits kind of low with its true bucket seat. They took a five-gallon bucket and cut the one side out, using the cutout to make two curved fenders for the back wheels. They fastened the bucket to the wooden frame; there they sit in the bucket with the bucket fitting nicely around them on three sides. To run the apparatus, they either have someone push; or they tie a rope to it, and someone pulls. The driver steers with the bike handlebars they had rigged up.

They made another gizmo by using a bicycle frame. Daddy got two bearings to use where the back wheel had been. They put a sprocket on an axle, slid the axle through the bearing, and put an old tiller wheel on each end. They used the steering wheel from the scrapped Honda and had a unique tricycle for the big folks. They found the wheels were very small, so they exchanged them for bicycle wheels. When the one back wheel came off, they didn't bother putting it back on right away. "Mother, you ought to try it. It's fun!" said my son, and he rode off balancing himself on the two-wheeled contraption. "It's not hard," he shouted as I watched the antic. A wheel in the front, the good left wheel, and a lively rider; to me it looked like a serious case of doggie tracking!

God Wants the Boys

MOTHER OF SIX SONS AND ONE DAUGHTER

What is a better way to enjoy the first welcome rays of the sun on a new day than to sit on the rocker holding two sons? Their golden-haired heads, warm and soft, rest against my neck, and the sunshine fills our hearts. I listen to my husband and older sons read the Bible. I have taken turns reading too, until my lap becomes too full of freshly awakened sons. I lay my Bible aside and listen to the story of the sufferings of our Lord, how He was beaten, falsely accused, and then crucified like a sinner when He was so perfect and so pure. Being a mother and raising our children to live for Him is so little I can do for Him compared to the cruelty He suffered for me. I hold my sons tightly. They are so innocent. Today, God is giving me another opportunity to teach them godly virtues, which will produce honest, pure, faithful young men.

I hope I'll never forget the way one of our sons came home from school one day. My thoughts were not overly positive at the moment with a mother's work on every side. An ever-growing mending pile was weighing down the sewing machine. A dirty, cluttered floor stared at me. An unhappy baby son was riding along on my arm.

My ears caught the welcome sound of the four scholars coming home. I paused to figure out what they were chanting. The door opened, and I heard it loudly and clearly:

"God wants the boys, the merry, merry boys,

The noisy boys, the funny boys, the thoughtless boys.
God wants the boys with all their joys
That He as gold may make them pure
And teach them trials to endure.
His heroes brave He'd have them be
Fighting for truth and purity,
God wants the boys!"

Jason had learned their new program verse! Like usual, he chanted it repeatedly. We heard snatches of it all evening and more evenings following. Surprisingly, I did not get tired of hearing it. Rather, it gave me fresh courage, a reminder of what a great blessing it is to be a mother of boys. How high and honorable the calling is! God wants the boys!

Who has a greater opportunity to teach our boys to live for God, than I do, their mother? The task is large, and there is no time to lose. God wants the boys! What does it matter if the house is not new, the pants are patched, and the coats are ragged? There are boys to love and to teach. And God wants them.

Secret to an Exciting Life
JUST ANOTHER MOTHER

When we were expecting our sixth child, nearly every time I went to town with our five boys, I could expect some shopper to say, "I sure hope this one's a girl!"

"We love our boys," I would say. "Life at our house is exciting!"

One day at the checkout, someone said something to one of the boys about hoping the new baby is a girl.

"Oh, my mom wants a boy," Son replied. "She thinks she has an exciting life!"

Making
MOUNTAINS OUT
OF COAT HILLS
ANONYMOUS

I gave a tired sigh within my soul as I hurried through the coat porch en route from dishpan to washing machine. There IT lay as usual. A jumbled heap in the corner: a tassel cap, a sweater, and a pair of coveralls. They were my son Leon's barn clothes. This was one of his besetting faults. Almost every morning he hustled in from the barn, walked *past* his coat hooks (I had assigned the most convenient hooks to him) and over to the corner. There he hastily shed his clothes into The Heap. What's the rush? A HUNGRY thirteen-year-old boy at 7:30 in the morning after helping milk a hundred cows! Therefore, unless his daddy or I happened to see him shedding and reminded him *once more* to hang up his clothes, there lay The Heap until evening. Now that Leon had entered his teens, there were other issues: teacher issues, peer issues, sibling issues, and yes, even some parent issues he grappled with.

God grant us wisdom, I murmured to myself and then whispered a prayer for my son, this boy-almost-man. Was it even right to haggle over such small issues as The Heap when there were larger issues that needed addressed? In addition, how could we show our son that we wanted to be his rock, the ones he could lean on in these rippling years of teenhood? So often we seemed to be his enemies, throwing stones of rebuke, criticism, and perpetual nagging.

Later that day, I once again passed by The Heap and noticed a little piece of torn paper lying in plain sight on top. I stopped for a closer look and read:

Dear Mommy,
     Though my clothes are in a heap,
     You taught me: Those who sow will reap,
     When I become a man, I will
     Remember your love, and keep it, still!
                    Love,
                    Your son, Leon

It was written in my husband's handwriting. I chuckled and went on my way, wondering what Leon would say when he discovered it.

That evening at barn time, after his snack, Leon strolled into the room where I was looking at Richard's first grade papers. He was wearing a sheepish look on his face and carrying a crumpled piece of paper. At my snippy look he exclaimed, "You!" and tossed the paper at me. He was laughing as he went out, and I knew that he recognized his father's handwriting. The paper had been well received.

The next morning, as I set the eggs on the breakfast table, I saw Leon hustle through the porch. Straight past the hook, straight to The Corner. Off came his hat, off came his coat, and then just as he dropped it, a look of remembrance flashed across his face. He stopped, picked up his clothes, walked back to his hook, and *hung them up!*

I gave a thankful sigh within my soul. Thank God for giving us a daddy with the wisdom to peacefully rectify even the little unsightly quirks in his son's character!

Inventors

EVELYN FISHER

"Mother, may I have an ice cream bucket?" my nine-year-old son asked. With unruly cowlick and shirttail askew, he came bounding to my side where I was busy sewing. I looked up, wondering what he was up to this time. "I want to make a welder," he said, his eyes sparkling. His hands fluttered over the dish of pins. Grabbing the scissors, he opened and closed them a couple times as I digested his request.

"How do you intend to do that?" I asked puzzled. I am a mother. I am feminine. I don't think like a boy. I use my ice cream buckets for many things like filling with food or storing patches for my comfort, or maybe for a cleaning bucket, but I never thought of making a welder!

My son stood there hopping from one foot to the other as he went into great descriptions of his plan. It sounded like it was not too risky, so I gave consent and told him to look for one that the lip is beginning to break. (I knew when he used the bucket, I would never get it back!)

It wasn't long until he came to my side again, this time with his welder. He had taken a 6-volt lantern battery, hooked some wires up to it, and ran the wires through the holes he had poked in the side of the bucket. As he touched the two wires together, the welder purred.

"Hear the welder!" he exclaimed while the sparks flew. "See me welding!" He had connected the power through a horn that he had rescued from a vehicle that was destined for the junkyard.

One day this same boy called the family together to watch his bomb go off. He wanted to make sure Mother was right there to see the happenings. I felt a little apprehensive as everyone stood back to watch this bomb. It is hard to know what to expect with some of these boyish experiments. The bomb consisted of a tin can with some hair spray. He dropped a burning match in, and we waited... but nothing happened!

This same inventor made what he calls an "annoyer," and it actually was a good name for it when it was new. (Now it sits, quiet and somewhat forgotten.) It is a little box with a handle, which is cranked to make a cog inside go around. As the cog makes its round, the teeth hit a piece of hard plastic—"clink-clink-clink-clink." It truly did get annoying as he ran around cranking the handle. It is very similar to the noise from the credit card that is taped securely to the bike frame. As the wheel goes around, the spokes sing a song. But those songs coming from the bike are sung outside instead of in the confines of a room as the annoyer was used.

Years before, an older brother invented ways to make cruise control on the mower by fastening a wooden block to the pedal; then there was no need to keep your foot always on the pedal. The problem was the catastrophe when there was no way to stop quickly!

Speaking of inventions, one day I quickly turned the water on at the kitchen sink and suddenly was sprayed in the face. Someone had fastened down the handle on the handheld sprayer behind the sink. It had to be a boy's invention of showering in the kitchen!

Grateful to Husk

MRS ALLAN MARTIN

"Oh, hello, Rhoda," I greeted my neighbor. Cradling the phone receiver against my ear, I shifted the baby, Boy #5, to the other arm.

"Does your family like corn on the cob?" Rhoda wondered.

"Well, yes," I answered. "But our corn patch is finished for this year."

"I planted a later kind for fresh eating, but it's more than we can eat," Rhoda explained. "And I already have enough in the freezer. I figured with your row of boys, you could help us out!"

How generous of her, I thought as I hung up the phone a bit later. *Fresh corn will be a treat again. We haven't had any for several weeks.*

On our way home from town that afternoon, I turned in the lane at Rhoda's to get corn for supper. "What are we doing here?" Junior wondered.

"Rhoda offered that we may fetch some corn for supper," I explained.

"Corn on the cob?" Junior asked excitedly. "Oh, yummy!"

As I drove up to the house, I saw a five-gallon pail of corn sitting at the end of the sidewalk. *Bless her heart,* I mused. *Not only is she giving us corn, she even has it all ready for us. With all the rain we've had lately, I'm glad I don't need to go into the garden with my good shoes.*

Apparently, Junior's thoughts were different from mine. Spying the pail of corn, he said disappointedly, "You mean we have to husk it ourselves?"

I wasn't sure whether to laugh or scold! Rhoda would not have had to share her corn nor take it off the stalk for us, but she did. How dare my son complain about having to husk it before he could enjoy the treat! I was appalled at Junior's ingratitude.

Yet as I thought about it, I began wondering if I really do so much better than my son does. I could think of instances when God blessed me with good things and I only saw the negative.

God gives a gentle rain on a Monday morning, and instead of thanking Him for watering the garden, I think, *What about all my laundry?* Instead of being grateful that my children can hear and talk, I wonder why they quarrel so much. Hubby has a great workplace and enjoys his job, and instead of being appreciative, I just wish he would be more prompt for supper. I get a closet housecleaned, and rather than feeling satisfaction at the tidy space, I am out of sorts that there wasn't time to do the whole room. The more I think about it, the more appalled I am at *my* ingratitude. What makes me think I deserve *husked* corn on the cob?

My son's stomach is hungry about every thirty minutes. I have found a peanut butter and jelly sandwich is a great snack. We have many apples, popcorn, and usually something baked in the house. It's amazing how much can go into his belly!
MARTHA SCHMUCKER

Refining Flaws

or

Accepting the Boy

THANKING GOD FOR ALL MY BOY BLESSINGS

"*God grant me the serenity to accept the boy in my son, the courage to refine the flaws in his character, and the wisdom to know the difference.*" After finding this saying in a Pathway publication, I immediately tacked it on my fridge. That's exactly my prayer as a mother of boys. May we never let an incident slide by, using "boys will be boys" as an excuse to not discipline when necessary. But, oh, for the wisdom to know the difference!

When Son complains that doing dishes is girls' work, his character needs refined; when he gives in and does the job willingly but never notices the puddles left on the counter, that's the boy in my son. When brothers get into a fight and fists start to fly, we need to refine flaws; if they enjoy a wrestling match, that's the boys in my sons. If Son complains about eating salad again, his character needs refined; if his first question when he barges in the door at mealtime is always, "What's for supper?," that's the boy in my son.

Some incidents are easy to discern; others require more wisdom. When Dad buys his son a truck to drive to work and Son complains that it is an old relic without any bells or whistles, his character needs refined. If Son drives the truck, that was replaced with a newer one, onto the cement pad and burns all the rubber off the tires because "it's a shame to take good tires to the junkyard," is that the boy in my son? What about the time the boys offered to take me shopping? That was a very rare occasion, and I had warm circles around my heart, until... "No offense intended, but you may have the back seat, and remember, I know how to drive." The warm circles had a way of quickly disappearing after a few S turns were taken just a *little* fast to see if I would scream. Please help me define that one!

Another area we need to be careful in saying "boys will be boys" is in personal hygiene. It varies in boys, but it seems, overall, we need to remind them often, "Comb your hair," "Tuck in your shirt"... We do want them to grow up to be respectful men! Another area of respect is learning to avoid or clean up any mishaps in the bathroom. (Any mother of boys knows what I'm referring to!) If taught young with many reminders, we can refine that flaw!

Not all of us mothers are able to raise our boys on farms alongside their dads, but if possible, I think it's important that boys have some animals to raise. It teaches them responsibility. Even though it takes up some of our time in supervising and helping, it's worth every minute! Our boys have enjoyed many types of animals over the years. I also have many fond memories, and hope to make more, of working with my boys in our vegetable garden and flowerbeds.

They say the way to a boy's heart is through his stomach. That might explain why I spend so much time in the kitchen! I find making them their favorite pie an excellent reward for a special job they have done for me. I like to encourage healthful eating, but I find it hard to motivate teenage boys to do a job by promising carrot sticks!

Sometimes I feel left out when Dad and all his boys are restoring a tractor or having one of those conversations only men understand, but Dad does not stand a chance when the boys are sick or hurt. Then Mom is the person of choice! I'm enjoying my title as the only Queen of the palace. I know there might come a time in my boys' lives when I will be dethroned.

BEWARE!

DONNA J PETRE

If you your lips would keep from slips,
Five things observe with care:
Of whom you speak, to whom you speak,
And how, and when, and where...

My mother penned these words in my autograph book. What sage advice for a twelve-year-old only sister sandwiched between two brothers!

Tomorrows became todays, and I became a wife. Two small sons later, we moved to a house on the hill above my husband's workplace.

Our new family room was filled with loveseat, chairs, and sewing cabinet. We placed the rolltop desk and baby-changing table in the long, narrow laundry room. This arrangement worked well. If my husband needed solitude when studying, he could close the door. When I was dressing or changing the baby, the washer and laundry sink were conveniently behind me. The bathroom was three steps away.

Babies' bubbles, toddlers' tumbles, school schedules, and suddenly we were parents of a teenager!

One Sunday evening as I was dressing our youngest son, a man's voice approached, and my husband's shadow walked toward the desk. Without turning, I asked, "Do you want to take Little Man in church tonight, or shall I?"

A surprised pause, then an amused, "Sure! He can sit with me!"

Puzzled, I turned toward the voice, and behold, I gazed at the face of our fourteen-year-old.

BRING ON THE
Boys

MRS ZEE

I am writing the rough draft of this article with a turkey feather pen. It's over a foot long and waves grandly above my paper, a beauty to look at. If you like wild turkey feathers, that is. For myself, I never paid much attention to those creatures until I became a mother of boys. My sons have taught me so many things, even how to get excited by a wild turkey that Daddy shot and deposited in the front lawn for butchering. Instantly, the hapless fowl was surrounded by eager boys and their tomboy sisters, each vying to pluck the choicest quills to add to their treasure stash. I found some of these feathers a few days later on my basement table. By that time, they smelled rather overpowering; not the feathers themselves, but the chunk of decaying meat to which they were fastened. Can you believe what I did? I gingerly plucked the nicest feathers and scrubbed the quills all nice and clean in my laundry water! What a mother won't stoop to do for the love of her children!

However, I didn't fare so well with frozen muskrats. "Do something with those muskrats in my freezer!" I huffed to my son. "I was rummaging around looking for donut sugar and found myself holding a clear plastic bag with this ratty creature inside looking at me!"

As I said, they teach me many things.

It's been brought to my attention that families containing all, or mostly, boys tend to be laid-back. Now being laid-back is not all that bad. We all know there are character traits that are much worse. If sons keep me from becoming too high-minded, then bring on the boys! (Daughters have their own ways of keeping one humble. My own mother raised eight daughters, and she is one of the most humble people I know, but we'll save that story for later.)

I believe in every mother's heart there is a yearning for daughters. When our latest son joined his four brothers and two sisters, I entered the following in my diary: *Was Mama disappointed that this wasn't girl number three instead of boy number five? Good question. True, I had stirring hopes for another daughter, but I can say very confidently that just because he is a boy doesn't say I love him less. He is already so dear to my heart, and I love to hold him close while he sleeps so peacefully. Welcome, Son, welcome!* Now this son is a year old already. He sits on the floor beside the desk where I'm writing, gurgling contentedly in baby language while trying his pearly whites on a stray crayon. "E-w-w, Josiah!" I say, and hearing his name, he raises his brown eyes and charms me with a toothy, crayon-flecked grin. I cannot imagine how I would even want to replace him with a daughter.

Nearly fourteen years ago, when we discovered we would be parents for the first time, I was secretly hoping for a son, partly because I liked our boy's choice of name better, but mostly for my husband's sake who grew up surrounded by sisters. Don't get me wrong; they are all lovely, and he enjoys being with them, but he was ten years old when he got his first brother. "I used to feel sorry for him," Mom-in-law remarked. "He'd be roaming outside all alone while my kitchen teemed with girls." (She didn't waste a lot of pity on him though. He could handle his own end quite comfortably.) Thus, you can imagine how thrilled we were to welcome our firstborn son into our world. Nearly two years later, Philip crowed with his parents as we examined his new brother, Gerald, in delight.

"These boys!" Daddy said, shaking his head. Nevertheless, he was not able to keep the huge grin from his face. Eleven years later, we're still saying, "These boys!" —with or without the grin.

Our two oldest are quite different in nature, but in spite of that (or maybe, because?) they stick up for each other so much that their sister complains about it. This does not mean they never disagree! Oh, my, no! I had to separate chubby, flailing fists at age one and two already, to my consternation. Nevertheless, they are quick to make up in typical happy-go-lucky boy fashion. About the only thing they hold in common is their thirst for books. Once I was reading to Philip and he started whining insistently, "I wanna go *inside* that book, Mom!" Apparently, life outside that book was drab in comparison.

As Philip grew, his interests fanned out into more and bigger dreams: trapping, hunting, starting up his own business—the sky's the limit!

Our second son dreams as well, but mainly about books and more books. If you enter my kitchen and hear a tap-tapping sound above your head, don't be alarmed. That would be Gerald, flat on his stomach up in the library, absentmindedly thunking his toes against the floor. It didn't take us long to discover that if we want to know anything from Old Testament history to the names of WWII generals, just ask Gerald. If he doesn't know the answer right off, he knows where to find it. Take the time he was supposed to be washing dishes, and at the other end of my long kitchen, Daddy was reading this riddle to me from a magazine: "A man and his son were in a car accident. Both survived, but while the father was being extricated from the car, the son was rushed to the hospital. When he arrived, the surgeon said, 'I can't operate on this boy; he is my son.' How is this possible?"

We both knew there was an easy answer to this riddle, but we just couldn't get it. Reading it over slowly and deliberately, examining it from all angles, we were shaking our heads in defeat when my dishwasher boy ambled over from where he had been perking his ears at the sink. Sticking his nine-year-old head among our thirty-three-year-old ones, he said so unassumingly, "Was the surgeon a woman?" Daddy and I broke into guffaws, and Gerald went back to his dishes with an abashed but pleased look on his face.

When our first daughter joined our family, my cup of happiness overflowed. Daughters don't need to be very old until they can connect with their mother's feminine side in a way sons can't. In other ways, I've always felt that God intended sons to share healthy bonds with their mothers, as well as daughters with their fathers.

There might be a reason why our first daughter inherited a saucy tinge to her nature, for she was soon followed by her third brother. Benny's voice nearly woke up the whole household when he drew his first breath, and he has been keeping it exercised ever since. Yesterday evening, his legs waved in the air from the headrest of the recliner, as he lay upside down lost in a storybook. Being in first grade, he is turning into a bookworm like the rest of us!

Boys in the Kitchen…Hang onto Your Hat!

My boys were excited when I decided they were old enough to bake something without my help. (More so than I, I confess!) They have discovered new recipe favorites and have proved themselves quite handy if I don't mind sugared hands wiped on pant legs or globs of grease on my cookbook from a mixer turned prematurely on high. Their enthusiasm draws the little ones who hope for a good view and possible handouts. Perching on chairs as close as they dare, they watch in awe as big brother industriously measures and mixes and loudly defends his territory.

"Where's my measuring cup?" he demands as he noisily jangles the set of nickel-plated measuring spoons. "Help! I lost my cup!"

Help! I'm losing my mind! I echo wryly, but not audibly.

No, it's never dull with a boy-chef. He thinks stirring white sauce is dull though. "Mom, your oven hood should have a set of built-in beaters. You could just pull them down, like this," he demonstrated. "Then I wouldn't need to stand here stirring on and on." *Indeed, never thought of that! Make sure you put a patent on that, Sonny.*

Making Memories...and a Little Cash

A few summers ago, I helped my boys plant a small patch of gourds at the edge of Daddy's cornfield. We've been dreaming bigger every summer, although we've learned a few things by now. Like not to plant snake gourds again! Those greedy vines smothered any other plants within reach and yielded pale, flabby "snakes" that sold for hardly anything at our local produce auction. We've also learned not to leave a prize orange pumpkin outside overnight where a new puppy might use it for a scratching post. Nevertheless, our venture has turned into a project all of the children enjoy, although it's mainly the oldest boys' responsibility. They revel in poring over seed catalogs in search of the wartiest or most colorful varieties. However, when it comes down to laying plastic or hoeing weeds? Let's just say Mom steps in sometimes and directs affairs her way, though the boys grumble if I help *too* much because that means I get more of their produce check!

I love to watch my brood bring in the fruit of their labor. The wagon is piled high with colorful gourds and disheveled, grinning youngsters, all towed by big brother on the riding mower.

Even though I hardly have time to juggle more duties, I always find myself taken up with helping them wash, sort, and finally admire the rows of boxes ready to take to the produce auction. Then I straighten my tired back and return to my babies, relieved to be finished with that task for another season. Is there a project anywhere that occupies children resourcefully without creating more work for Mom or Dad? If there is, I would like to know about it!

A Boy's Best Friend... (and Mom's Worst Enemy?)

"When are we going to get a dog again?" The question was picking up momentum after our farm had been dogless for nearly a year.

Over the years, we had acquired various mongrels, only to bid farewell to them in less than pleasant ways. There was Teddy—he disappeared mysteriously after Daddy's futile attempts of keeping him from roaming with the neighbor's dogs and eating from their dish. Trixie wandered out on the road once too often and was killed by a car in plain view of five-year-old Benny, who cried heartbrokenly. In addition, Roxy, the one we liked best, met her death in the haybine.

Would we try another dog again? (Not as in *would* we, but how *soon* can we?) I could easily live without one, but the children thought they couldn't. It seems their schoolmate's new batch of puppies had something to do with it. Every day when the school van drove in their lane, these Shibas would poke their inquisitive little heads out of the barn and act cute.

Finally, we allowed Philip and Gerald to bike over and choose a new puppy. (Even though Daddy predicted that we might as well tear a hundred dollar bill in pieces rather than spend it on yet another accident-prone canine.) When the boys arrived with Bella, as they dubbed her on the way home, we couldn't help but adore the blond puppy nosing her way out of the box strapped on Philip's bike.

Bella grew in stature but not in wisdom. Surrounded by doting puppy lovers, she became spoiled and aggressively friendly. We are still trying, nearly one year later, to break her from the bad habit of jumping all over anyone arriving at our place whether it's immaculately dressed salespersons or frail grandmas. When I graciously open the door to answer the knock, that annoying dog lunges between us, jealous for attention, and slobbers all over *me*, seeming to take advantage of the fact that I won't be giving her a free-for-all right at the moment. (Not unlike the way my children act when I'm on the phone.)

Then one day, Bella killed a bantam hen. The boys weren't too happy, but since we had more hens, they did not make a big fuss. Having acquired a thirst for blood, our dog wasn't satisfied with one slaughter. The next time it was the boys' only prize rooster. This was too much. "Let's get rid of that worthless dog and buy us a real one!" Philip fumed.

We persuaded him to give Bella another chance. "Try attaching the dead rooster to her collar," I suggested. "See if dragging that around won't cure her."

So that is what he did. At first Bella was a true picture of shame and contrition. However, as the days went by, she got used to her encumbrance and was back to her old self again. A shop customer did a double take when he was greeted by an overjoyed dog, dragging a rotting, dismembered rooster. "Chicken-killin' dog," Daddy explained dryly.

The following morning my peaceful contemplations were interrupted when I heard the basement door slam, and Philip came dashing upstairs. Barely pausing to remove his chore boots, he hurried over to the washbowl where I was combing myself and sprang up on the vanity top right in front of me.

"Now what?" I grumped to his back as he rooted around in the medicine cabinet gathering a stash of gauze, ointment, and first-aid tape. "Come on, you're blocking my mirror."

"Bella hurt her foot," he answered over his shoulder, leaving chaff and disorder in his wake. "It looks as if she completely ripped off one of the pads from the bottom of her paw."

"Yip!" came an affirming reply from below me.

"What?! You brought her inside?" Following him downstairs, I met up with Bella favoring a bloody paw, but not being deterred from galumphing all over my basement, still dragging that detestable rooster.

"Now sit, Bella, and let me bandage your foot. Mom won't appreciate that rooster on her floor," Philip instructed. (Credit him for that!)

I stood at the steps, watching, and wondered, *Is this the same son who had threatened to disown his dog?* What an excellent Norman Rockwell painting they would have made (minus the rooster, of course!): a kneeling boy bent compassionately over his dog who was obediently holding up her paw to be bandaged.

This was not without raising a fuss though. Bella was acting for all the world like a pain-intolerant child. "Bella!" scolded her master. "Stop being such a wimp. Every time I nearly manage to wrap this tape around your foot, you jerk it or lick my fingers away!"

In reply, Bella opened her mouth wide and chomped down on Philip's hand as if threatening to swallow it whole. "E-er-row!" she yelped louder and squirmed all over, thumping her tail against the concrete.

Even though her paw was hurting, I could see she loved being babied. "I wouldn't go to all that bother," I advised. "She's going to tear off that bandage anyway, as soon as you let her go."

"I know, Mom. I thought of that too. In one of our Animal Ark books, they fit a lampshade on their dog's head. That way she could still eat, but she couldn't reach her foot."

Since we did not have a spare lampshade, Philip used an empty ice cream bucket. With a hole cut here and a bit of string there, he soon had Bella's head snugly encased. Giggles erupted from the growing audience who had been wakened by the ruckus and one by one had clambered downstairs to join the fun. I couldn't keep myself from joining in the laughter at the comical sight. "She looks like she's wearing a bonnet!" my daughter shrieked.

As I sped back to my breakfast preparations, I caught a glimpse through the sink window of Philip striding back to the barn. In his arms, he carried his coddled dog, who was tossing her bonneted head in dislike, her tattered rooster dangling. Another day had begun...

Bring My Children In...

The days steal into years, and just as steadily, my children are growing. I yearn to hold them back to savor more fully these tender years when my sons' main concerns include slipping out of washing dishes or wondering whether their bantam eggs will hatch. When they derive simple joys from bringing home their newest first grade reading book or snuggling beside Mom on the recliner sucking on two middle fingers after waking from a nap. Or tasting crayons.

"Raising a family is like experiencing a thunderstorm," my friend's mom remarked once. "It's a real commotion while it lasts, but so soon it's over and gone."

I often think of her words amidst the cheerful roar in my house. Sometimes I feel utterly inadequate to instill anything beneficial into my children during this short "squall." It's enough to bring me to my knees, and that is where I need to keep returning. I'm only now beginning to realize the burden we unknowingly placed on our parents. A burden now rests on our generation's shoulders—that of being entrusted with never-dying souls. We dare not lose touch of this burden among the ever-mushrooming distractions this world has to offer.

When this earthly tempest, by the will of God, is lulled into eternal calm, we will have no greater joy than to hear the Master's voice, "Bring in my boys."

Help for the Howl

DONNA J PETRE

It was a delightful song for boys. My aunt learned it in third grade memory work. She, with the help of her sister, composed a haunting melody for it when they were schoolgirls. Our boys learned about "The Wolf Song" from their cousins.

Singing lessens the drudgery of dishwashing for our sons. Repeatedly, the house rang with "The Wolf Song." Soon my husband and I had memorized snatches:

"…So he sits with his long, lean face to the sky,
Watching the ragged clouds go by.
There in the woods alone, apart,
Singing the song of his lone, wild heart.
Far away on the world's dark rim,
He H-O-W-L-S, and it seems to comfort him…"
Georgia R. Durston

Then the earthquake erupted. "On a scale of 1 to 5, with 1 being no suspicion to 5 being 95% sure it's cancer, I'd rate what I am seeing as a 5," Dr. Harston's calm voice entered my barely comprehending ears. That one little sentence, and I along with my family spun into the stressful swirl of a cancer journey.

Surgery came first with four weeks to recuperate before starting chemo treatments. The Sunday night before chemo began, we planned to cut off my hair so it could be used in making my hairpiece. Our thoughts dripped with dread as we faced the formidable future. How would baldness, sickness, and fatigue affect our marriage? Our children?

"I feel somewhat like 'The Wolf Song,'" my husband shared. "He H-O-W-L-S and it seems to comfort him..."

Wordlessly, I nodded. Reaching for the envelopes that had come in our mailbox that day, I opened a card from yet another someone in our big, caring brotherhood. But what was this? I could hardly believe what I was seeing! In the card was a poem titled, "Leave the HOW with Jesus." We laughed. We cried. We were comforted.

Our boys' song. Our friends' card. Perfect timing. It had to be OUR GOD!

Missing the Point

MARTHA SCHMUCKER

The other day we were sitting at the table eating vegetable soup with noodles. Our son is not so fond of that fare and wanted to grumble. I said, "Mike, there are a lot of hungry children in this world who don't have anything to eat."

He replied, "Well, Mom, I really think we should give all this soup to them."

THE COLLECTOR

FONDA HEGE

Do you have a son at your house who is a collector? Our third son collects anything from A-Z! It may be pretty stones, bird feathers, parts from little motors, old pieces of chalk, business cards, stickers, stamps, plastic clips off bread bags, pens, flashlight parts… You name it; he may have it!

His bedroom door even has this carefully made sign hanging on it: "HEGE'S COLLECTION STORE." It became a bit frustrating to know what to do with all his treasures, but my husband encouraged me not to stop his collection, instead help him organize it. He said, "You never know what he may come up with to make or do with his things!"

My husband salvaged a little set of shelves, and our son had so much fun stacking things on it. For his seventh birthday, we gave him one of those plastic organizers. This one had eighteen small drawers and sits nicely on a table in his room. He was overjoyed and spent so much time filling it up, then emptying it out and rearranging it a different way. Of course, Mother was pleased with an orderly way to store a little boy's treasures.

Evidently, all his possessions were becoming a bit overwhelming to him also because at housecleaning time he helped me go through his drawers, his nightstand, his shelves, *and* under his bed. We decided what to save and what to pitch. We organized the things that he wanted to save. It really tickled me when we got finished, and he said heartily, "Thank you so much for helping me. I didn't know what to do with everything!"

Her Name Is Mother

I can feel her cringe at the Philistine's curse;
I can see her packing the shepherd's purse;
I can hear her heart overflowing with verse;
    But I never read her name.
Though she slew no Goliath, no lion, no bear;
Though she penned no psalms, yet her name is there.
And I know that she faithfully played her part,
For she fashioned a man after God's own heart.

    I can feel her wince at the dulcimer beats;
    I can see her shunning the royal meats;
    I can hear her pray over Babylon's streets;
        But I never read her name.
    Though she walked no palace, no lions' lair,
    Though she opened no dreams, yet her name is there.
    And I know she faithfully filled her role,
    For she fashioned a son with an excellent soul.

I can feel her thrill to the words Christ said;
I can see her baking the fisherman's bread;
I can hear her weep when the Master bled;
    But I never read her name.
Though she healed no cripple and walked no wave,
Though she never looked into the conquered grave,
Yet her name is there, for her lot she filled,
And she nurtured a son who Christ's church would build.

    I can feel the hope of her pulsing heart;
    I can see her sculptures of ageless art;
    I can hear her doctrines in home or mart;
        And I daily read her name.
    For her children arise and call her blest,
    Her name is "Mother," end here thy quest
    For a woman of virtue. She shapes in clay
    And polishes stones for God's palace today.

INTERRUPTED
Inspiration

DONNA J PETRE

*B*ut the fruit of the Spirit is... JOY, I printed at the top of my journal. Paging through the topical Bible, I found a large list of references to joy. The first one was Deut. 12:18. Interesting! I had not remembered there was a command like this. I began to copy it: *Thou shalt rejoice before the Lord...*

"Mo-o-o-ther-r-r-r," our caboose's distressed call came from the doorway. "I'm trying to make a snowman, but the second ball just keeps falling apart!" His siblings were in school, so that left me to come to his aid.

I swallowed a sigh. If I would have had my devotions earlier... before the children awoke... But I was experiencing post-chemo fatigue. Sometimes it was best to make use of the quiet morning moments after the school children were out the door.

I pulled on a coat, shoved my feet into boots, exited the house, and then remembered I would need gloves. Outside again, I began packing snow into a ball. It fell apart. I tried the second time. No success. *Hmmm, those storybooks with perfectly molded snowmen should be outlawed,* I muttered mentally. *Making a snowman is tricky!*

Finally a second ball was formed! Then the whole process needed to be repeated for Mr. Snowman's head. We could not forget the nose! I fetched a carrot and gingerly inserted it, hoping the snowman's pate would not explode. Little Man went off to find stones for eyes, mouth, and buttons.

The crisp winter air chased the fuming from my brain. I returned to the warmth of JOY meditations. Blinking, I reread the verse I'd started writing earlier: *...rejoice before the Lord thy God in all that thou puttest thine hands unto.*

Boys About the House

ELSIE KUHNS

I continue to be amazed...
the signs of boys about the house—
—tractors in the bathroom
—boats in the sink
—arrows clinging to the window
—a cow beneath the table
—cookie crumb trails
—soapsud mustaches
—balls too many to count
flying through the air,
bouncing off the floor,
rolling between my feet.
—tools hanging from their waists
—forts beside the sofa
—a game of balloon volleyball
in the middle of the living room.
So if you step into our home,
you won't ever need to wonder
if there are boys
about the house!

Boys' Quilts

EVELYN FISHER

Our first four children are every other one—a girl, a boy, a girl, and then another boy that begins the string of four boys and a girl with four more boys to finish the family. Mothering nine boys affects my thinking when I go shopping, when I choose bed sheets, and even when I do a sewing project such as making quilts for my sons.

I enjoy making quilts and comforts from start to finish, and my children enjoy helping in their own way. When the older children were quite young, they liked to quilt. Their quilting sometimes consisted of putting real stitches in real quilts. Depending on the age and ability, the stitches sometimes came back out after the quilter left to play. All my boys have put stitches in quilts. Some of the children's first quiltings consisted of sitting on the floor, around the rebounder, with a small blanket spread out in front of them, jabbing away with toothpicks. What jolly quiltings those were! Perhaps it was a sister's idea, but the boys enjoyed the quiltings too!

One project the boys were excited about starting as three- or four-year-olds were the nine-patch comforts. I helped them pick out matching patches—four light-colored patches and five dark-colored patches. By hand, they stitched up the three strips. Then the exciting part was to be able to push the pedal to sew the three strips into the finished square. It took several years to sew up their forty-two patches to make the comfort top. As the boys got older, it was a challenge to find enough boyish patches to please them. They liked patches that had tractors, patches with waterfowl, patches with animals, and patches with candy and boyish colors. When they neared completion of sewing the patches together, we went to the fabric store, and they picked out the material they wanted for their comfort backs.

I also embroidered for my boys. Some had more boyish designs like a dog with a border of bones, or with butterflies, but some are more girlish designs like flowers or bows. One thing that makes the boys' quilts stand out from the girls' is the color. The boys have red, green, and blue, orange and brown, even yellow and lavender, but none are pink!

I had a huge stack of worn-out jeans—blue jeans, black jeans, faded jeans, and little boys' odd-colored green, blue, and brown jeans. The stack was growing bigger and bigger. I had dreams of cutting the good parts into strips and making rugs someday, but it did not seem to be working out. Then one of my daughters suggested making rag quilts with the jeans. The idea became reality as I cut up the immense pile. Ten-inch squares from the upper leg of the big pants, eight-inch squares, seven-inch squares, and then from the smaller pants I cut six-inch strips. While sewing each patch together, I sewed with loving thoughts of my boys who had worn holes into the knees of their pants. The colors I used on the back of the jean quilts were boyish. After I put quilt batting between the two layers of material, I sewed in the middle of the patches with not only simple flowers and hearts, but also fish, ducks, ponies, and stick boys. However, the patch I liked the best was this one.

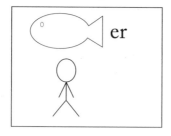

It is perfect for my nine Fisher boys!

Where Has My Boy Gone?

M EBERSOLE

Oh, where, oh, where has my little boy gone?
Oh, where, oh, where can he be?
With his hair cut short and his pants cut long—
Oh, where, oh, where did he flee?

Oh, where, oh, where has my little boy gone?
Oh, please, would someone tell me—
He has bright blue eyes and a winning smile;
His shirttail likely hangs free.

Oh, where, oh, where has my little boy gone?
Oh, please bring him back to me.
I'll hold him close with his blanket so soft,
Play ride-a-horse on my knee.

Oh, where, oh, where has my little boy gone?
Oh, there they've found him for me!
With his hair too long, and his pants too short,
His eyes still blue as can be.

Oh, where, oh, where has my little boy gone?
He's gone to school and left me.
No longer he begs for stories be read—
He's reading stories to me!

Meaningful THINGS

MJH

A helpless, little pansy plant appeared in my kitchen one February afternoon. Our dirt-loving son had uprooted, potted, and watered it to the best of his boyish ability. It boasted one bloom, but in his eyes it was very special. "I want to take this to my teacher tomorrow," he explained.

To me, this pitiful pansy plant seemed nothing beautiful. I expected it to last only a day or two. It was definitely not a special gift for his dear teacher, but I resolved to hold my tongue. "We'll ask Daddy," I replied, wanting to prolong an answer and secretly hoping Son would give up his idea.

Daddy didn't have the heart to say "no" to Son's good intentions either. "Let's give it some time to be sure this wild plant will live inside," we told him.

Next morning, the plant stayed on the kitchen counter with the excuse that Mom needed to fix a cover for the drab green pot. *Perhaps there's still hope that Son will relinquish his gift idea,* I thought. *Or maybe I should offer to buy his teacher a new plant.*

But no, the next morning came, and we "cheerfully" sent that little plant to school. I trusted that the teacher would understand.

The plant surprisingly thrived in the classroom window. Now more than a month later, it has over twenty little blooms, and we have a very happy son! Each time I peek at this plant, which is often because my son wants to prove that his plant is special, I remember my previous qualms. *Did God make this plant thrive to teach me?* I believe He did!

Why not cheerfully share the enthusiasm and enjoy the meaningful things in my sons' lives? Why not delight in the feathers and stones on display in their bedroom? Why not value the sticky pumpkin and watermelon seeds they stored from last year? Why not smile and give them good memories of a mom who calmly tolerated their trivial treasures?

I am learning things that I wouldn't have learned without my sons. My sons. My teachers. I love them!

For the Love of a Son

MRS ALLAN MARTIN

I did not grow up in a family that hunts. We considered guns scary and dangerous. While the man I married isn't a hunter, his dad and brothers are, and this hunting blood was passed down to our son. Already as a preschooler, he got excited for deer season. He would put on an orange vest and play hunting all week.

Finally, the day came that he was old enough to go out and hunt for real. Two hours into the season, he had shot a deer. Even a non-hunting mother, who is not that fond of venison, can rejoice with her son when a lifelong dream comes true.

My son said to me, "It's a nice-sized buck. Too bad it has such a small rack—only 6 points."

I replied, "What does that matter? You don't eat the antlers anyway." (Isn't it a good thing I didn't marry a hunter? But really, I do know better.)

Now those antlers, complete with the deer skull, hang in my (er, I mean our) house! In a basement bedroom, at least, but still! Oh, the stretching and maturing a mom does right along with her growing children! When I was a teenager, and even for quite a few years beyond, I couldn't have imagined letting that pass as acceptable for a house. But the love of a mother for her son does unexpected things.

Protecting My Son's Purity

"CAROLE"

God began our family with a precious little girl. I reveled in the duties of motherhood. Our life as "two become one" took on a new dimension as I nursed, bathed, rocked, and cuddled. Being an avid do-it-yourselfer, I also tackled endless projects at the sewing machine to clothe our little one. Nighties for a little girl were such fun. I had found a small piece of fabric at a thrift store that really caught my eye. Covered with large lovely tulips, the lightweight fabric was ideal for a little girl's summer nightgown—or so I thought.

It was a satisfying feeling to see our lithe little girl tripping upstairs in her spring blooms outfit. With time though, she outgrew it, and it was packed away into storage.

Our second child was a son. The cycle of mothering resumed. Again I took delight in sewing little garments to clothe the new life in our care.

Our third child was another daughter. By now, there was much less time for extra sewing, and I was glad to reuse what I had. The garments that I had sewed with such delight for our oldest daughter were retrieved from storage with equal satisfaction to serve their second term. Out came the tulip-spangled nightgown.

I recognized that the already lightweight fabric was now faded and worn, but it wasn't worn out. I didn't give it much thought until one evening my son, now five years old, spoke to me. In quiet, shy tones akin with his nature, he said to me, "Mom, I wish you'd make a nightgown for her that we can't see through."

I was smitten that my innocent preschool son should need to teach me to clothe my daughters modestly! Yet I recognized it as a red-light signal.

My thrift instincts cried out within me as I snipped the flimsy gown to rags. Out of storage came a second gown of that size. It was less used, less attractive, and less see-through. My thrift instincts suffered a blow, but my maternal instincts were at rest.

Don't ask them
TO LIVE IN YOUR WORLD...
visit theirs instead!

Submitted by Marilyn Weaver

Not for the Faint of Heart

IRENE S RAMER

Motherhood is not for the faint of heart!

Now, why would she say that? you may think in surprise. *Isn't motherhood just playing doll, except ever-so-much-more-so?*

Why yes, I hasten to assure you, motherhood is ever so much more than playing doll! Those sweet little babies are not very old until it is evident that they each have a mind and a personality of their own, and sometimes it is a mind and a personality that is quite at odds with your own. Perhaps it is even a mind and a personality that you are unable to understand.

When our second son was born, he looked so much like my dad that I automatically allotted him my dad's personality. Quiet. Calm. Cautious.

But Lyndon was not very old until I realized he is not quiet. With his face red and unhappy, he cried and fussed and fretted about needs that I could not begin to understand and could not fulfill. Sometimes I rocked serenely while he vented his feelings, and sometimes I vented mine too.

As Lyndon grew older, I realized he is not calm either. He did not sit on the floor and play with toys as my dolls used to. In fact, he rarely played with toys. But he cleaned out my cupboards and played with my pots and pans. He dug through the trash can and played with greasy mayonnaise jars and discarded lengths of dental floss. He threw brand-new soap bars into the toilet and flushed it. And he did all this with a lot of noise.

As Lyndon grew older, he did not grow more quiet or calm. Even when he was sick, it was hard to keep him rested and still so that he could get well. One winter day as he was recovering from a bout of bronchitis, he half sat, half lay on his daddy's easy chair. "I am charged!" he announced to all who would listen, and every time someone came within his reach, he would touch them and yell, "Zap!" It was especially fun when it was one of his just-older sisters that came too close. "I am full of electricity," he told them grandly, "and every time I touch you, you are shocked! Z-A-P! Gotcha!"

Girlish shrieks of protest ensued, and I was forced to intervene.

And then one fine summer day, I accepted the fact that neither is Lyndon cautious. Grandmother and I sat on the porch, snapping beans and visiting contentedly.

Along came Lyndon. As usual, his pants needed patching, and his shirt was grimy though it had been fresh from the drawer just a few hours earlier. His straw hat was tattered, and his face smudged, but his grin was happy, and his dark eyes sparkled as he held his hands behind his back.

"Mom, can you guess what I have?" he asked. Then, not waiting for my reply, he stuck both fisted hands into my face. "Look!" he said excitedly, slowly opening his hands.

I looked. And I looked again. Why, that treasure in his grimy hands looked like some kind of teeth. Could it be—small animal teeth?

"These are teeth," he stated, answering my unspoken question. "I got them off that old cat behind the barn."

Stunned, I gazed in horrified silence at him and his grubby little hands holding that stash of cat teeth, .

"Oh, Mom," he said quickly, misinterpreting my horror and my silence. "It was a dead cat."

A Boys' WORLD

MABEL REIFF

"Some call it chaos—we call it family," reads the plaque my husband noticed last spring when he picked up a prescription at Royer's Pharmacy. We needed that. He knew it belonged in our kitchen.

"Do other homes have this much noise—this much action at the table?" he lamented after a particularly boisterous meal.

I knew what he meant. We are a noisy bunch. Most boys cannot tell a story without a wide range of motions accompanied by all the sound effects imaginable; ours are no exception.

"And when he took off at the stop sign, smoke poured out the back, tires screeched…errrch!" Lucas spun his hands in short vicious circles to give us the full effect of the car he had seen after school—and hit his soup plate, dumping it on his lap. His screech faded into an "Oops."

I kept eating. He scooped up the worst of it and scampered off to change and get a rag.

It's a rule. Accident or not, if you spill it, you clean it up. Even our three-year-old knows this. But I am a woman; their best doesn't meet my expectations, and I am not above going over a few spots with a rag after they leave the kitchen.

Not only do they make noise, their engines and equipment meet the same requirements.

"Did you hear the mower?" Jethro asked, his eyes sparkling.

I heard. Loud and clear. I wouldn't have expected that sound to be a riding mower, not even an old one that hadn't been used for mowing in years.

"I couldn't take out those screws." Javan pointed to the offending area in answer to Dad's question. "That's why I had to use the Saws-All."

Had to? When Ivan invested in a Saws-All to fix irrigation pipes more efficiently, we had no idea what else that Saws-All could be used to do. It certainly sawed all—garden tractor muffler included.

It could be welded. At eleven years old, Javan could do it himself. His dad had taught him young. At eleven years old, he knew better, too, and that alone bore consequences.

We have noise. We have action. We've never been bored. Caleb would see to that if no one else did; he manages to be the one who clogs the commode. It would clog for me, too, if I used as much paper as he does. We often catch it before it overflows, and for this I am happy. When I have to throw towel after towel on the river flowing out the hall toward the laundry room, I am…upset.

Last week I wiped up such a mess. The floor looked nice and shiny; I don't often wash floors with toilet bowl water, but it did improve appearances.

Caleb didn't follow me out of the bathroom. I didn't even notice until I heard the toilet flush—again.

"What are you doing?" I called from the snuggly chair where I had settled to feed baby Josiah.

"Getting a drink."

"From where?" I hollered.

"From a cup."

Caleb. The one with no qualms about drinking from the fish tank. On Sunday morning, I caught him drinking from a water-filled barn boot. Most people use boots in the water, not water in the boots.

I need not have worried. In typical Caleb-fashion, he had moved faster than I had thought possible; he got his water at the utility tub in the laundry room.

Chaos. It describes moments we experience, not normal life. On second thought, those moments might happen more than I realize; I might be immune to them by now.

We have boys, and we're raising them as boys. We don't want them to be ladylike; we do expect them to be mannerly and respectful.

No belching or other rude noises at mealtimes—unless you want to wash dishes. Boots stay out of the kitchen, and when driving the pony, you don't pelt the backside with BB's. Be reverent during devotions, pick up after yourself, and never play ball or build snow forts on the shop roof.

We are raising a future generation full of life, love, and respect for God and their fellowman (and woman) while enjoying the journey to adulthood. In the process, there are many things to learn—one of them being: NEVER SAW OFF A MUFFLER.

A Fun Wall Motto for a Boy Household

Cut a scrapbook sheet with a boyish theme on it, 8 x 10 inches. A piece of blue Bristol board works too. Scrapbook this verse on it—Ps. 133:1: *Behold, how good and how pleasant it is for brethren to dwell together in unity!* Now add a 4 x 6 inch photo of your boys—the more the better. Frame it. Every time you add a new boy to the family, be sure to update the photo!

Fighting the Brotherly Battles

CRYSTAL FAUS

I was combing my hair when I heard it. An attack followed by a war whoop. I knew a fight would soon be in full swing. Determination set in. We were not going to spend the day warring. I would let them know first thing this morning that I meant business; halt the combat and order a truce.

Revival week had been inspiring, but by Saturday morning, a week of late bedtimes was beginning to tell on us. Sleeping in had seemed appropriate to this exhausted mother, but not so to my six- and four-year-old sons. In fact, Roger and Terry seemed extra energetic because they began the day with a battle.

So I administered the first spanking with hanging hair. I returned to my combing and mentally went over my day—prepare supper for the evangelist and make the five pies I had agreed to take for lunch at church the next day. I wasn't sure my late start to this day would leave time for much else. I hoped the feuds were over.

My hair wasn't yet in place when the next uprising occurred. Well, I couldn't let this pass, but I would feel better equipped fully combed.

So I sent the brothers to the couch. I would come soon and talk peace with them. I added another project to my mental list for the day—train the boys to think of others first. It was important to me. I would *make* time.

Hair finally combed and Bible in hand, I headed to the couch. Alas, though the boys sat, they sat arguing. I spanked them both and read some fitting Bible verses. I explained and expounded on the Golden Rule. The Bible way to peace is to prefer others before ourselves. I thought they understood that the hostility and conflict must cease. Training session over, they wanted to go outside and rake leaves. Yes, fresh air and wide-open space would be conducive to ending wars.

They bundled up and were headed through the garage when I heard a scream. Screams do not sound like peace. So I investigated. Roger put his cold hands on Terry's back. *Oh. Now what?*

I was serious about them thinking of others first. I was also convinced we did not need to sound a war cry over small discomforts. So off came the coats and boots. The brothers sat on their chairs at the table until they could sing a song together. They were not impressed with this new form of punishment. It took all of fifteen minutes until they finally chimed out, "Jesus Loves Me."

Now they were ready to try going outside again. This time they made it outside and out of hearing distance. I was busy rolling pie dough and had already spent too much of my day disciplining. But just because the boys were out of sight did not mean they were out of mind. Was the concord continuing? I decided to desert my pies for a bit and check on them. I stood at the garage door and watched and wondered why my disciplining had so little effect. Another skirmish was developing. Roger wanted to rake leaves onto separate piles. Terry wanted to rake leaves onto one big pile. Terry raked Roger's leaves away from him. Roger moved on to another spot. Terry followed and raked those away.

I decided pies or no pies, company or no company, I needed to go out. I asked the boys how things were going, and they both said, "Good!"

I told them that it did not *sound* good. I lectured and instructed and wondered again what I was doing wrong. How could I *make* them think of others before themselves?

Then God sent an answer to my pleas for peace between brothers. He did not tell me what I was doing wrong, but He gave me an idea to try instead. I would *show* them how! My boys would come before my five pies. I would sacrifice my impressive company menu for some quality moments with my sons. "Shall we play single base?" I asked Roger and Terry.

"Sure," came the ready answer.

I'm a far cry from an athlete, and I'm glad I couldn't observe our game from the sidelines. But the boys loved having Mom racing around the yard with them, scurrying around trees and darting around the garden shed. They chased and dodged and rolled and slid. But they did not battle. They had forgotten the brotherly war.

I discovered it was *me* who was in need of admonition that day— **Mother, you can persuade and preach, talk and teach all you want about thinking of others first. But the lesson caught most quickly is the lesson that you demonstrate.** ☼

"Thank you, Son!"

ANONYMOUS

The oldest boy in a family proved his manliness one day when he saw the disaster zone one of his younger brothers had left behind in the bathroom. He took a Sharpie and wrote on the bathroom mirror, *Clean up after yourself even if your mom does work here.* ☼

Times Change

MRS ALLAN MARTIN

I was ready to start housecleaning my little laundry corner. Armed with a pail of hot, soapy water, the wall mop, a broom, and the vacuum cleaner, I set to work. No sooner had I begun than my preschool boys, wanting to help, surrounded me. They took my rag, so I fetched more. I tried to act patient, but I would much rather have worked alone. It seemed that one of the boys was always ready for whatever I needed. When I wanted the mop, they needed it too. Same with the broom and the vacuum cleaner. I stepped back and took a deep breath. If I wanted them to help me for real someday, I needed to let them help now. The oldest looked over at me, standing there, doing nothing.

"Soon we'll be able to do all the work ourselves," he said with enthusiasm. "What are you going to do then?"

Ten years later: I was housecleaning in the storeroom with our oldest son. What a breeze! All I had to do was point and say, "I want that box moved there and that one over here…" and the work was done. (Mind you, I did help too!) Time brings changes—large and small!

A Boy and His Anger

ANONYMOUS FOR THE SAKE OF MY SONS

"Whack! Thump! Smack!" The ceiling above my head vibrated. Loud voices reverberated down the stairs.

They were at it again! Those two boys! They were supposed to be changing their clothes, but it sounded like they were into another of those Big Fights. I groaned inwardly. *Why can't they just get along? Don't I teach them to be kind and love each other?*

Loud wails shot down the stairs. "M-O-M! He hit me with his belt!"

With a sigh, I headed up the steps. I opened the bedroom door and faced the boys. They hadn't even started changing their clothes. For a brief moment, I felt utterly helpless. All my parenting ideals and tricks of the trade seemed to have taken wings! What was I to do with these ten- and thirteen-year-olds glaring at each other with fire dancing in their eyes? I took a deep breath and exhaled a silent prayer. Then I said, "Boys, this is totally uncalled for! You will be changed in two minutes and get out the door for your chores! But first there will be apologies."

The boys' glare loosened, and they said the right words, but I was not convinced their apologies were genuine.

It seemed that recently Sanford was restless. He often initiated these scraps with his younger brother. At thirteen, Sanford was fast entering into the world of young adulthood. He was stretching up, resulting in outgrown clothes. His voice was changing. He thrilled to the feel of a shaver in his hand. He could lift those things that caused him a struggle before. He liked running his hands over those rippling muscles in his arms. It gave him the feeling of becoming a MAN! It spelled "power" to him and that meant control. In his mind, he was not a little boy anymore. Thus, when his younger brother irked him, he could handle it! All he needed to do was to twist David's arms behind his back in one swift motion. In addition, he could pinch hard enough to leave a bruise. The feeling of control felt good at the time, but Sanford felt bad afterward. He didn't always understand the surges of anger that swept over him. One day he felt like a man; the next day he felt like a little boy.

I pondered these outbursts as I headed back to the kitchen. I recalled stories of grown men who never learned to control their anger, and their family suffered because of this monster. I trembled to think of our son turning out like that! Today was my day of opportunity. I needed to think about it some more and talk with my husband. God cared too, and He promised wisdom if I asked.

That evening I prepared an assignment for Sanford:

Write seventy-five words minimum for each question. This must be done neatly on notebook paper and laid on Daddy's dresser by tomorrow evening.

1. What causes me to get angry, and how do I feel when I'm angry?

2. What can I do to overcome getting angry?

3. Write five Bible verses on kindness or being gentle.

I did not see Sanford working at his assignment, but by the following evening, there was a neatly folded sheet of paper lying on the dresser in our bedroom. I read:

1. I get angry because I want to get even with David for what he did

to me. I don't stop and think what would happen to him if I hurt him. I don't try hard enough to be kind to him. I feel miserable and wish I would never have done what I did. I would like to put more effort forth in controlling my anger and not letting it come out on other people and harming them.

2. I can overcome my anger by praying to God and asking for help in controlling my anger. When I am tempted to get angry, I must do something else to prevent myself from getting angry. I can overcome by not letting my thoughts run wild and keeping them on good ideas and not wishing to get even if I am mistreated. I am sorry for my anger and will try to do better.

3. *And be ye kind one to another, tenderhearted, forgiving one another, even as God for Christ's sake has forgiven you* (Eph. 4:32).

Thou shalt not avenge, nor bear any grudge against the children of thy people, but thou shalt love thy neighbor as thyself... (Lev. 19:18).

This is my commandment, that ye love one another, as I have loved you (John 15:12).

And the servant of the Lord must not strive; but be gentle unto all men, apt to teach, patient (II Tim. 2:24).

To speak evil of no man, to be no brawlers, but gentle, shewing all meekness unto all men (Titus 3:2).

My heart was touched to read Sanford's answers. Inside this macho boy was a tender spirit that needed guidance and nurturing. It seemed like an overwhelming task! It was not mastered in a few weeks or months, but I could see signs of improvement in my soon-to-be-angry teenage son.

Today, I realize it is by God's grace that Sanford has turned into a kindhearted, gentle young man.

Rid me, and deliver me from the hand of strange children, whose mouth speaketh vanity, and their right hand is a right hand of falsehood: that our sons may be as plants grown up in their youth...

Happy is that people, that is in such a case: yea, happy is that people, whose God is the Lord (Psalm 144:11,12a,15).

HERE A LITTLE,
There a Little
ANONYMOUS

It was such a simple question from my husband, "Do you know where my truck keys are?"

Our son Clement dropped the *Hoard's Dairyman* magazine, rolled his eyes far up under his eyelids, and let out an exaggerated puff of steam. "How would I know? If you'd put them where they belong, you wouldn't always have to hunt for them." The words were mumbled, the shoulders pulled upward and then let fall like Dad was a hopeless case.

Mark glanced at me, cocking one black eyebrow up, with a *Wow! What's eating him?* expression. "I'm sorry for asking," Mark said aloud to our son. "I just thought perhaps you saw them…"

Clement tossed the magazine in a frustrated heap on the couch and stood up. "I'm going to bed. I didn't see your old keys anywhere. Nobody around here puts anything where it belongs." His words sputtered out through partially closed lips. On his way to the kitchen for a drink, he stumbled over Cleophas' farm set. No words this time, only steam, then he trudged upstairs with hands jammed into his pockets.

As I watched, I remembered the stack of clean laundry I had intended to send along up with him. I didn't call him back. He was liable to huff off something about that being a good job for Cleophas. I didn't want to see a full-blown eruption.

"What's come over him?" Mark wondered as soon as the bedroom door upstairs clicked shut. "He acts like we are two old cracked nuts."

I shook my head. "Maybe we are. But that doesn't give him reason to talk disrespectfully to you. I thought he knew better."

Now it was Mark's turn to let out one long discouraged sigh of steam. "I know. I guess I will have to talk to him again. I thought he was doing so well…and all of a sudden he almost explodes like this…"

This morning Clement had bounded in from chores, shoved the farm set aside with one smooth push, and sat down to breakfast with a whistle of delight. "Pancakes and gravy! My favorite! Thanks, Mom." His smile had been genuine, and his mood contagious as he discussed milk prices with Mark between shovelfuls of breakfast.

We were baffled. What would cause a boy's moods to be so changeable? The twins' moods had been more predictable—generally happy, not easily ruffled. I threw out my hands in frustration. "Raising Carlin and Carson was a dish of ice cream compared to Clement!"

"What?" Mark looked startled. "Don't you remember how we had to spoon feed them till they were two and tied their shoes till they were eight? And when it was time for any sort of work, we had to poke and prod and plead till we were exhausted?" Mark shook his head. "I wouldn't say they were ice cream at any rate."

"I guess I forgot about that," I admitted. "Clement always does work with a will, doesn't he?"

"Sure does. I can hardly stay ahead of him. Since the twins are married, he has taken on more responsibility with the cows. I'm impressed, really." Mark frowned. "Impressed, except for how he tries to micromanage the younger boys. Cletus and Cleophas can't do anything good enough for Clement."

Thinking about our youngest sons made me even more disheartened. "I don't have a good report from Cletus' school teacher."

"What now?"

"Sister Ethel called this evening and asked how she can help Cletus. He has such a sloppy desk and cannot find his assignments promptly. When he does locate them, he often has missed several answers. She has tried several incentive programs, but they all failed. She says he simply doesn't seem to care."

Mark ruffled his hair into a scare. "Did she say anything about Cleophas? I may as well get all the bad news at once and get it over with."

"Yes, unfortunately. He is not totally obedient. He obeys her no-talking-in-class rule, but he makes eye contact with the other boys and manages to communicate that way. She said he has this little trick of being able to humor his classmates to the point of distraction, yet he always appears sober and obedient."

I watched Mark pull his ear lobes. He had no clue how ridiculous he was making himself look, especially with his nose wrinkled up. "So what did you tell Sister Ethel?"

I allowed myself to grin. "I told her I would tell you about it. You would figure out something, then we would get back with her."

"Oh, no," Mark groaned. He smoothed out his hair, straightened his nose, and leaned back into the couch. "So Clement has bad moods." He held up one rough finger. "Cletus is sloppy and doesn't care." The second finger went up. "Cleophas distracts his classmates." There went the third finger. Mark wiggled the standing fingers. "We have at least three big problems to figure out solutions for besides half a dozen smaller problems." He shook his head. "We didn't know what problems were when we were changing diapers and filling milk bottles, did we?"

"Now that is true," I agreed. "Colic and RSV and umbilical hernias look simple now."

"Simple?"

"Well, maybe not simple, but the consequences are not so..."

"...far reaching," Mark finished.

"That's the word."

We sat silently in the lamplight thinking. Thinking backward. Thinking forward. I wondered once again why God trusted imperfect parents with the grave responsibility of guiding souls—boys' souls at that—back to His fold. I wondered how Mark and I could do this. I wondered how other parents did it.

I looked at Mark. "Ronald and Jeanette's row of boys seem so respectful and obedient. How do you think they do it? Can you imagine their Randall ever talking to Ronald as Clement did to you this evening? What's their secret? Or do you think some boys are easier to train than others are?"

Mark's black eyes searched my own. "I don't know. Maybe you should ask Jeanette. Tell her what our boys are up to and ask her advice."

I almost panicked. Jeanette was…well, unapproachable. "Mark! You wouldn't make me do that, would you?" I nudged his arm. "We are discussing boys, after all. Maybe you should discuss it with Ronald!"

Humor lurked at the corners of Mark's lips. "I thought I would get a rise out of you." He smiled, then sobered. "Really, it wouldn't hurt to talk to Ronald; he's easy to talk to. I might get a chance tomorrow at church."

"Cletus! You are being one sloppy pig!" Clement slid his chair well beyond Cletus' reach. "You're getting milk all over my Sunday shirt. Why don't you go outside to eat your breakfast in the pigpen with your relatives?"

"But Cleophas is kicking me! I can't help it if I slosh milk when someone is ramming his hoof into my foot every other second. Dad! Make Cleophas stop kicking me!" Cletus wailed.

"Cleophas. Behave yourself." I could hear the frustration just under Mark's reprimand.

"What am I even doing wrong?" Cleophas asked. "I'm just sittin' here eatin', and Cletus gets mad at me out of the clear blue. I don't know nothin' about kickin' his ole foot." He looked innocently offended.

"You were kicking my chair leg, then," Cletus insisted. He looked ready to jab his fork into his brother rather than his waffle.

I didn't feel like finishing my own glass of milk and waffle. What kind of dysfunctional parents were we if our three teenage sons couldn't even eat a Sunday morning breakfast in peace? I could imagine Ronald's family discussing the Sunday school lesson and chuckling about the weather in goodwill, calmly looking forward to the worship service. What was their secret? I sure hoped they would share it, whatever it was.

"Well! I saw you talking to Ronald this morning at church. Any advice?" We had enjoyed a dinner invitation and afternoon of visiting friends after services. Now Mark and I were ready to relax while the boys did the chores.

Mark rolled down his socks, slid them over his heels, and tossed them neatly onto the back of Cleophas' dump truck. "There. That feels better." He stretched out his feet, looked at me, and grinned. "Ronald didn't have any secrets. No answers either. He just asked me a bunch of questions."

"What?"

"Yes. I simply asked him for the secret formula to raising a row of obedient, respectful boys like he has, and you should have heard him interrogate me." Mark chuckled. "He spouted off so fast I couldn't keep up. He asked me what we do for a twelve-year-old pouter. And how do we cure an eight-year-old of telling lies? And what do we do for any age of slowpokes? And what type of discipline do we use on a grumpy seventeen-year-old? And how do our boys even get ready for church in the same room without ripping each other's shirt buttons off? And how do we ever leave home when five boys are standing there fighting over the favorite seat in the van?"

I felt something funny creep up my throat, and before I could stop it, a little giggle popped out. "Do you really mean their boys act like that?"

Mark nodded. "They sure do, according to Ronald. And they aren't the only ones. He said his brother Raymond's boys were at each other's throats so bad one day that Raymond finally told them they wouldn't be getting any more meals until they act civil."

I pictured Raymond and Vera's dark-haired, quiet boys. At each other's throats though? I couldn't imagine that. "Did Raymond's remedy work?"

"Sure. Like other punishments, it helped for one day. Raymond gave up that idea; he hadn't intended to starve his sons to death."

"Are you saying there are no answers? Everybody's boys are acting the same, so we just all wait and hope they grow up and behave after a while? Are we making mountains out of molehills?"

"No, no," Mark said. He pulled the lever back on his recliner, and the footrest popped out. "Problems never go away while we look the other direction. It just doesn't work that way. Actually, Uncle Elam came partway through our conversation, and he listened in. Ronald asked him if he had any advice for us. Uncle Elam said there is only one way to raise a family of boys or girls."

"How's that?"

"He quoted, 'Precept upon precept. Line upon line. Here a little and there a little.' He reminded us that America was not settled in a day, and a boy will not become a man in one day either. There were days when he wondered if it was worth settling one more quarrel or punishing one more bad attitude in his children. But after weeks and months of perseverance and prayer, he noticed a few positive moves in the right direction. And after several years of toil and sweat, his children actually hold civil conversations most of the time."

I leaned back in my glider and shut my eyes. "So we just have to keep on and keep on and keep on and..." Depressing. I wanted to see at least a few results right now.

"Yes, Dear." Mark put down his footrest and sat up. "Most of life's problems have no quick fix. Child training is no exception." He came over and put his hand on my shoulder. "Don't look so dejected," he said.

"How do you know what I look like? I have my eyes shut."

"Your posture gives you all away." He pecked my cheek. "Lighten up. Our boys aren't total failures. Think of all the times they do obey.

Think about their humor and their exciting ideas and… Well, Uncle Elam said we can't dwell on our sons' failures any more than we would want someone to dwell on our failures."

I opened my eyes and met Mark's. "Now that is a thought," I admitted. "I wouldn't want you keeping track of all the times I feel grouchy."

Mark grinned. "And please don't start adding up the times I don't put my things away." He walked over and fetched his balled-up socks out of the dump truck with a sheepish face. "Actually, if I had put my truck keys on the hook as soon as I came home from the bank yesterday, I wouldn't have had to hunt for them last evening."

"Did you find them, then?"

"Uh-huh. They were on my desk under the checkbook."

"Oh." I got up and stretched. "I think I am going to make a bowl of popcorn for the boys to eat when they get finished with the chores."

"Sounds good." Mark headed for the laundry to deposit his socks.

I got out my biggest kettle, dumped canola oil in, and turned the burner on high. I watched as the oil formed little bubbles and chased each other around in the pan. Just like our boys, I thought. *Always chasing each other around—with words, if they aren't carrying sticks. And what are we going to do about the way Clement talked to Mark last evening? And how are we ever going to fix Cletus' and Cleophas' problems at school?*

The oil steamed, hot and ready. I measured one cup of corn kernels, dumped them in, and clapped on the lid. I shook the kettle fast, back and forth across the hot burner, listening for the first light "pop, pop, pop." My thoughts darted with the kettle. *Why did God give us five boys when Mark and I are such imperfect parents? But we wanted these boys! We love them! Why can't we train them? How are there other families who have such good boys? Oh, that's right. Mark said Ronald's boys have problems. And Raymond's boys are naughty. Maybe…maybe our boys are… normal? Mark said I should focus on our boys' good points.*

The popping came faster and louder, and I could hear the corn rising up and up and up in the kettle until it pushed the lid gently from the pan. I thought of the evening last week when my dentist appointment ran late. I came home to find that Cleophas and Cletus had hurried with their chores, then came into the house, cleaned up the kitchen, and made potato soup for supper. "Because we know you like hot soup when you are tired," they had informed me with smiles.

And our boys were all good with our two grandchildren. Last week when I babysat the twins' children, Clement had helped Carlin's little Lelin hook up his tractor, chopper, and wagon, then ran the chopper for a few minutes before going out after lunch. Cletus and Cleophas had condescended to hold Carson's Brenda's doll when she asked them to. I chuckled, remembering how Cleophas had told her the doll had pinkeye, and he needed to put eye drops in to make her well.

Normal. Maybe our boys are normal. When our boys quarrel, we immediately think of Cain and Abel, and we are grieved in our hearts. But maybe…maybe our boys can quarrel and make up like Jacob and Esau. When our boys are disrespectful, our minds linger on Absalom, and we think we must see swift and sure change. But maybe…maybe boys can fail at times, and still turn out to be Davids.

The popping slowed to an occasional "pop…pop…pop." Then silence. I turned off the burner, lifted the lid, and dumped the whole pile of fluff into my big metal bowl. Mark appeared and grabbed the first handful before I even salted it.

"Maybe our boys are just normal," I said. I opened the spice cupboard for the saltshaker. "You know, we focus on their failures, and we want results right now, but maybe that is how it is for families of normal children." I dumped all my thoughts from the past five minutes onto Mark. "Our boys are kind and respectful some of the time. And they are a pile of fun most of the time. Here, put the salt on this popcorn, will you? I always get too much or not enough."

Mark took the little pink saltshaker. "I think you are right," he said. He sprinkled salt, then shook the bowl letting the salt filter all down through the popcorn. "There are children who are not normal, and their parents need more answers. But for our family, I think we need to just keep on keeping on. And being open to the counsel of those with experience. Uncle Elam remarked this morning that there is an old saying, 'It takes a whole village to raise a child.' He said he likes to think instead that it takes a whole church to raise a child. We don't have all the answers ourselves. And we need each other for encouragement to keep on." He ate another handful of popcorn. "I forgot to tell you, Clement apologized to me this morning in the milking parlor for the way he talked last evening."

"Really?" I was surprised in a way. Yet, when I thought about it, Clement usually did repent when he showed bad attitudes.

"Yes. He has his failures, but he has an open heart. That means a lot. We had quite a discussion out of his apology." Mark looked at me. "You know, we have a lot to be thankful for. Not every child is as open to correction and instruction as our boys are. I believe Uncle Elam is right. It takes a continual here a little and there a little." Mark shook more salt on the popcorn.

A sudden thundering through the kitchen door interrupted him. "Cletus! You pushed me!"

"I did not! You kicked me!"

"Did not."

"Did so."

"M-m-m, popcorn! Thanks, Mom! It smells delicious," Clement praised. "Hey! What are you boys doing? Watch it! You're spilling half my dish. Dad! Make these boys straighten up. They've been at each other's throats the whole time we were doing chores, and they don't need to start on mine."

At each other's throats? Where had I heard that before today? I sighed. Yes, our boys were normal. And it would take the normal prayer and perseverance and patience to train them. Each day our sons were growing older, and someday they would be further out of our reach. Someday, despite our best efforts they might even make choices that grieve us. (Forbid it, Lord!) But for now…now while they are still in our care and under our authority, we are responsible to be a pattern of good works for them to follow and to keep on sowing seeds of truth and right. Precept upon precept. Precept upon precept. Line upon line. Line upon line. Here a little, and there a little.

Go in Peace

MRS ALLAN MARTIN

When I became a mother, I did not anticipate the increased opportunities to worry. I discovered it from the start. As soon as Caleb was born, the nurses whisked our firstborn off to the Special Care nursery because of meconium in the amniotic fluid. After that crisis, we struggled for weeks to get him back to birth weight. In those days, I naively expected it would get better as he got older.

Caleb is now sixteen. This fall he got his learners' permit to drive a vehicle and began a carpentry job. He is with the youth group. He lives in a world of technology that didn't exist when his parents were that age. Fewer worries? I think not. Oh, how I pray for that boy! (Along with all of our other children, of course.)

"It wasn't the greatest day at work," Caleb might state casually. "Because of the snow, the roof we were working on was kind of slippery."

And I keep praying. A firm belief that God is in control is what keeps me going.

Last Tuesday morning found us following our typical weekday morning routine. I made Caleb's lunch and ate breakfast with my husband and son. Allan went out to start the van and came back inside stamping the snow from his boots. Here in Canada, we were experiencing typical December weather—cold and snowy.

"It's rather blustery out there," Allan remarked to me. "I'm glad you're not planning to go away."

What about you? I wondered, silently breathing a prayer for their protection. Allan would chauffeur Caleb to work, about a twenty-minute drive, and then take the van back to his own job.

The men were off. I poured another cup of coffee and settled down with a magazine. About fifteen minutes later, the phone rang. *Caleb's number. Did he forget something?*

It was my husband's voice, not my son's. "How're ya now?" Allan asked cheerfully.

"Almost done with my coffee."

"We're in the ditch!"

"Oh! Shall I bring the other van?"

"Sure," Allan replied. "You'll find us just before Melvin's driveway. Maybe you can take Caleb on to work."

I hope they're both all right, I thought as I hung up. *I didn't even ask.*

I scrawled a note for our five children who were still slumbering. Then I bundled up, my mind racing. *They were gone for fifteen minutes, and they are only at Melvin's? Must be they were trying to push the van out. I'd better take a couple shovels along.* I was pleased that I had thought of it. Allan would be surprised.

Once on the road, I discovered it was indeed a blustery morning. The swirling snow in the darkness made visibility poor. The road was all white too, with no indication of where the road ended and the ditch began.

No wonder Caleb drove into the ditch! I thought. *He should hardly have been driving in such bad weather! But I guess he may as well get practice with winter driving with his daddy beside him.*

I stopped at the stop sign and turned left onto the highway. I strained my eyes for a vehicle in the ditch as I neared Melvin's lane. What if I missed seeing them in the storm?

Then I saw it. Not a van standing where it had slid into the right-hand ditch as I was expecting. Instead, I saw the roof of our Mazda.

It lay on the driver's side in the opposite ditch!

"Oh, my poor, dear son!" I gasped aloud. I had rolled a van on snowy roads many years earlier, and I knew the horror of it. I was so sorry that Caleb had to have such an experience.

"Are you both okay?" I asked anxiously as I approached the overturned van. Caleb was crawling around inside, trying to reassemble his lunch containers. Allan stood outside, taking the contents and repacking them in the lunch box.

"We're fine," Allan assured me. "Caleb wasn't going fast, and the snow made a soft landing. It all kind of happened in slow motion."

I'm a mother of boys, and I've learned a thing or two in my day, so I didn't fuss. At least not out loud. Inside, I was praising God for sparing these two very precious men. That highway is full of big trucks. How easily the Mazda could have collided with one! Our family could be planning a funeral right now...or two.

I took Caleb on to work while Allan waited with the van until the tow truck came. We planned that I would go to John's Towing on my way back through town so I could pick Allan up.

Although Caleb said he wanted to go to work, I felt all torn up as I watched my boy stride manfully to the shop. Traumatized though he was, Caleb was grown up enough to push forward, going on with the day. I had to let him.

As I drove back to town, I pondered some things. Just how was a mother to do it? How could she cope with letting go of her son, given all the possibilities for physical and moral danger? How did she survive it without having a nervous breakdown? I was thankful that this accident wasn't worse, yes, but what would the future hold? I hadn't come up with a conclusive answer as I pulled in at John's Towing and waited for the arrival of our van.

When the tow truck arrived, I walked over to the Mazda. Allan joined me. Jerking open the driver's door, I saw dirt everywhere! "I guess all the dirt from the floor of a work van has been redistributed to the dash and seats," I remarked.

"Not quite all of it is on the seats," Allan corrected. "Some of it is in my hair." He ran a hand gingerly over his head.

"The Bible must have flown out of the cubbyhole," I said, picking it up from the floor.

Allan was rummaging around in the middle seats. "Here's a page from Judges that tore out."

I looked at the page he held up. Surely, a lone page torn from the Bible in an accident must carry a special message! "Can I look at that?"

I scanned the page eagerly. Judges 18. It didn't look very promising, but then my eyes came across verse six. ... *Go in peace. The presence of the Lord be with you on your way.*

I loved it! "Thank You, God," I murmured. These were the very words a mother needed every time her son went out the door. ... *Go in peace. The presence of the Lord be with you on your way.*

That page from Judges is on my desk in our bedroom. Verse 6 is highlighted in pink, and as I walk by, I ponder the words often. ... *Go in peace. The presence of the Lord be with you on your way.*

It does not promise that nothing heartbreaking will happen. It does not promise that we'll always be kept from harm. But the promise of peace and the Lord's presence...what more could a mother ask for? I'm planning that this verse—my special message from God that morning—will become my life motto as we go on from here.

You see, I have four more boys coming along. -ゝ◎ゝ

Boys in the Sewing Room
FONDA HEGE

Do they like to sew? Our one son has cut out and sewn his own (and his daddy's) pajamas. Who sees if they are not perfect? They are so much more fun to wear if the boy made them himself! Pillowcases are another easy thing to sew, especially if you get cute material with monkeys or tools on them. -ゝ◎ゝ

After Many Days

J ANN

C *ast thy bread upon the waters…*

It was 4:30, Monday morning. I flipped the light switch on in the kitchen of our old farmhouse. Shuffling in my slippers and bathrobe, I shook my head and stretched, trying to clear my night fog. I had been up with little Russell almost every hour. How my head ached.

As I opened the refrigerator and started gathering things to make a sandwich, I heard Derrick lustily singing in the shower. He was preparing for his day. He was nineteen and a teacher. He would come home Friday evening after school and drive the hour and one-half back to Crosspoints on Monday morning.

I finished the sandwich and placed the rest of the things in the lunch box. As I snapped it shut, Derrick walked into the kitchen. "Good morning, Mom," he said with a smile as he pulled out a chair.

I placed a mug of coffee beside the lunch box as Derrick slipped his shoes on and tied them. "How was your date last night?" I asked.

"I like Charlotte more all the time!" Derrick's eyes shone with the thought of her.

"I'm glad it's going well for you!" I smiled at my son.

"Well, I really should be going." Derrick pushed the chair in at the table and grabbed his lunch box and coffee.

"Have a good week!" I encouraged as I followed him across the kitchen. Standing at the front door, I watched as Derrick backed his car out of the garage. Then I ran to the kitchen window and waved. I wondered if the kitchen window loved this ritual as much as I did! Derrick tooted the horn and blinked the lights on his car.

"Dear Lord," I pleaded, "keep our dear son safe as he travels, and bless his work in the classroom as he serves You there." I watched Derrick's headlights disappear into the horizon before I pulled myself from the window.

"You know," my husband whispered as we passed each other on the stairs, "you could pack Derrick's lunch on Sunday evening. On the other hand, Derrick could just get it himself on Monday morning. I feel sorry for you getting up so early after not getting your rest at night."

"No," I ventured, "I really want to do it. Derrick may not always live at home. He is still my little boy!" Smiling, I continued up the steps.

"I understand," my good-natured husband replied.

...for thou shalt find it after many days (Eccl. 11:1).

Ten years later—

I believe that is Derrick's pickup coming, I mused to myself as I drove down the last little stretch toward home. It didn't take long for a confirmation. Derrick's long arm shot out the open window and pumped up and down. I waved in a motherly fashion and smiled as I passed my son. My eyes scanned the cab. No little hands were along waving this morning.

A lovely spring breeze blew in the window as I washed the breakfast dishes. I paused as I heard a pickup roll in the lane. "Oh, it's Derrick," I murmured. Soapsuds fell from my hand as I waved from the window.

Derrick leaned out the open truck window and waved. Something seemed strangely familiar. I chuckled as I remembered, and my heart felt warmed. After so many years, my adult son still loved waving to me.

A Man's Best Friend

MWR

In the sheer joy of finding ourselves still intact at the end of the doctor's examination, my sons and I had a quiet snuggle. Murray was there for an eighteen-month checkup, and Jordan needed his preschool shot. Jordan was doctor-phobic so I had scheduled his visit secretly, and he came along just to watch Murray get his shots. I sneaked a little stick-it note onto his chart to tell the nurse to play him through the weighing and measuring along with his brother, and she had done a first-prize job.

The doctor was considerately brief with the exam. She entered the new information on the computer while I helped the boys into as many clothes as they could have before the upcoming shots. The boys were delighted to have the doctor focus on something else. They were thrilled to be reclothed. They were ecstatic when I pulled Murray onto my lap and Jordan onto the chair beside me. Jordan leaned against my shoulder, and Murray snuggled against my chest with a happy purr.

Then he bounced up and poked his cold puppy nose against mine as an intimate, reassuring gesture. The doctor glanced at us just in time to watch the show.

She swung her chair around and flipped the hair out of her eyes. "How precious!" she exclaimed, clasping her hands. "I wish I could have had boys. Boys just adore their moms! My girls are ten and twelve, and they have no good for their mom. But my husband *still* thinks his mom is the best woman in the world. I see it over and over—boys always love their moms best!"

New thought! My older brothers, Lloyd and Nathan, had trained me to believe that they thought all women and girls were stupid. (With the exception of a few names traced in the dust on the TMR mixer.) Their morose silence at the table and scornful remarks about any show of emotion, such as crying, had left no doubt in my mind. I had watched in amazement as they suddenly claimed girlfriends and enlisted my help to find the prettiest birthday gifts for them. They seemed to enjoy girlish things now!

I watched their sons, my nephews, to see if this female-disgust inflicted the next generation. They were sullenly silent at the table. They howled with disgust at the girls' foolish blunders in a ball game. *Just like their dad,* I told myself. But I was in for a surprise.

We gathered for a family reunion at my brother's place, and we arrived first. I was busy at the counter helping my sister-in-law with food preparation when her fifteen-year-old son came home from driver's ed. classes. I expected him to bolt for the stairs to change clothes so he could go outside with the men. Instead, his gaze swept the kitchen for his mother as he thumped his lunch box on the counter. "Hi, Mom," he called pleasantly. I nearly gasped. *He recognized his mother publicly!*

I want to be the kind of mother still loved by teenagers, I sighed to myself. I had been dreading the long years surrounded by stuck-up sons. Thus, I began to watch mothers with sons.

"Oh, I was so hard on my boys," my mother-in-law repeated frequently. "I didn't let them climb trees or wrestle or be reckless with machinery. And I raised them with an iron hand like I was raised."

My mind flew back to that distant day when my boyfriend, her son, said shyly, "I always thought my mother was the most wonderful woman in the world until I met you."

"But they loved you," I told my mother-in-law. "How did you do it?"

"Well, I certainly don't know. But I do know that I firmly believed that I should always respect their turn to talk. And I made sure they had a chance to say all they wanted to say (when it was something worthwhile)," she replied.

Lloyd and Nathan had told me something like that years before. "Marvin and Merlin say they really like their sister. She listens to everything they talk about and tries to understand even if she doesn't know anything about the subject." *Hm-m-m, those teenage boys liked their sister! And they weren't ashamed to say so!*

Evidently, what a woman *does* while listening is important too. My husband stops talking if I step outside to shake the tablecloth, even though I can still hear him. A middle-aged mother with a family of sons sent me a friendly letter with these lines included: "Amanda stopped by to visit me. She sewed, and I washed an accumulation of dishes. Some were from supper the night before. Amanda said she does not like to let dishes sit overnight. I don't either, but I think it is important to have time to listen to a boy tell his troubles—so the dishes wait." And it is obvious to others that she has a special place in the heart of her sons.

At a school picnic, I witnessed a mother make a dreadful mistake. Her son came to the group of women where she stood. He was eleven or twelve, overweight, awkward, and very uneasy. He was polite in asking for her attention, but he obviously did not want the others' attention. He backed away and beckoned for her, but she only turned halfway. Shyly, he whispered his request, and she turned with a giggle and blurted it to the surrounding group. The son's face was an agony of shame as he stood, betrayed by his mother. I would not blame him if he learned not to take his heart to her.

We joined Lloyd's family for supper one evening when we stopped by at a late hour. "Russ is about finished combining the soybean field," one nephew stated around a bite of chicken.

"Yeah, he said we're getting about thirty-five bushels to the acre," injected another brother.

"That's pretty good, isn't it?" their mother asked innocently.

"Naw!" growled the oldest. "Why, last year we got nearly fifty!"

"Yeah, and don't you remember the year before, it was sixty-five or seventy," added another.

My sister-in-law did not seem perturbed, but I blushed for her before I reconsidered. They were not being rude to her with their superior knowledge. Her unabashed ignorance gave them opportunity to excel and briefly claim the medal of manhood.

In comparison to the other training, this doesn't seem too hard. Make yourself available. (*Read: Stop working!*) Listen. Understand—if you can. Keep it confidential. Respect his reach for manhood. Admire! To him, you will be the best woman in the world for at least eighteen years. How rewarding!

Cutting Apron Strings

J ANN

Twenty-one years ago, I was pacing the floor with him at night. Tonight I slept fitfully. No, I was not pacing the floor with him, but my mind was.

"Mom," he whispered, "I'm leaving!"

I sat up in bed. It was 5:00 in the morning. I collected my wits and followed my son down the stairs.

Bryan was all smiles. He paused at the front door with his hand on the knob. In his hand was his wedding suit and new white shirt.

"Well, I suppose I will be on my way!" Bryan glowed with anticipation. His precious Emily was waiting 1500 miles away.

I put my hand on his shoulder. "Yes, it's time now. You must go!"

I waited in the doorway as he hung his suit in his car and walked around to the driver's door. "Thanks for being a good mom!" he called as he slid in behind the wheel.

I waved as he backed out, emotion stirring in my heart. *How did this happen so fast? To where did these twenty-one years fly?* I ran to the kitchen sink and waved from the window. Bryan blew the horn loud and long. I watched his car creep out the lane. The red glow of the taillights disappeared below the hill and he was gone... Gone! My tiny black-haired baby boy! A lone tear slid down my cheek. Then another...and another. I went back to the bedroom and fell on my knees. Then I cried! And cried! I didn't even know why! Shouldn't I be used to this by now? After all, this was our fifth wedding. I really did want this for our boys, didn't I? But, he was my baby boy!

I prayed. I prayed for his safety as he drove those hundreds of miles by himself. I prayed that the Lord would keep perfecting the work He had begun in Bryan's life. I prayed that God would keep him and his new bride from the deception and lure of the world. I prayed that God would guide them gently Home.

Yes, it was time to let go. Time to release my grip on my son and let him walk into the arms of his waiting bride. Time to cut the apron strings.

Then a beautiful thought struck me. Bryan was leaving home, but he was going to bring a lovely daughter to us! I had always wanted a girl!

There be three things which are too wonderful for me, yea, four which I know not: The way of an eagle in the air; the way of a serpent upon a rock; the way of a ship in the midst of the sea; and the way of a man with a maid (Prov. 30:18,19).

A Matter of
Perspective

It began innocently enough. The hefty telegraph box needed transported from the shop floor to the haymow directly above it. The only ladder to the haymow was a set of straight up and down hay-hole steps inside the barn. However, I'm getting ahead of myself.

First and foremost, I was (and still am!) an Only Sister. Besides the fact of being the only sister that each of my three brothers had, I was also younger. I felt life was unfair at times and prayed fervently for a little sister. Oh, to have someone to sleep with when a thunderstorm was raging outside during the night! Someone to stay in the house and play girl things with me while the boys ran outside! To work with me in the kitchen! To just be a GIRL with me!

With time also came enlightenment. The brother closest to me in age could be a far more realistic mighty preacher for my pretend-church services than a sister ever could be. He fervently preached even while I was out in the "nursery." Nevertheless, since I did not have that coveted sister to sit in the house with, I often sought out my brothers outdoors. One never knew what adventures awaited me there.

Brothers are great teachers! While playing ball, they insisted that I learn to pitch overhand. I actually pitied those girls at school who had to pitch underhand because God had not given them older brothers to teach them differently! As the years rolled on, my brothers also made sure I learned to use my side mirrors when backing a vehicle. They taught it effectively too! (To this day, I cannot identify with anyone who is scared to back up when all they need to do is watch their mirrors!) "Mirrors never lie," I can still hear them say.

Was life boring? How could it be? Not with brothers who would sneak me out of the house on a winter evening to haul me down the snow-covered road on their handcrafted toboggan, pulled by the garden tractor. Not when they would coax me up the narrow steps to their tree stand. Not when I was included in the party of rearranging their bedroom furniture, which usually called for propping the mattress against the wall to use as a sliding board while someone lay underneath the precarious arrangement waiting to get smashed! Not with brothers who would dump the empty muck bucket upside down on top of me and sit on it, waiting to see how long it would take me to get frantic. Not when they would build lovely hay tunnels in the haymow and make a surprise hole or a dead end in the pitch-blackness. Not when they would hide our stuffed bears, calves, and a raccoon all through the house and then draw up hunting seasons on the dry-erase board. They willingly equipped me with a handful of rubber bands, too, and what fun we had hunting and learning to abide by the rules!

Oh, my, no! How could I have been lacking for more entertainment? The conclusion of the issue was just a matter of perspective. At one point, my brothers were taken up with creating telegraph sets, learning codes, and operating them. Eventually, like most rages do, the buzzes stopped, and the equipment lay dusty and forgotten. The boys built a rather large and *heavy* box, and this was where all the obsolete telegraph paraphernalia was stored. But after it sat too long in their woodshop without any reason, they were ready to usher it to the upstairs of the barn.

As boys are, they schemed the best route to move the object efficiently to the floor above. As Only Sisters are, I was there witnessing the process. It was decided that the moving would work best using the haymow doors outside instead of inside the barn. They uncovered and rigged up some sort of pulley line (Or was it a block and tackle? You'd surely have to ask them!) and secured The Box to it. In order to get it fastened well, the box was turned on its side. The bottom of the box was now a side, and the opening was a side. The boys were all ready to crank it up the end of the barn when on a sudden boyish whim… "Don't you want to hop in and take a ride?"

I hopped in. The box wasn't more than a 2'x2'. There I sat, or rather, there I lay on my back with my feet in an Indian squat. My head stuck just far enough out of the lid to observe the beautiful Saturday afternoon around me. The boys p-u-u-u-l-led me slowly up all nine feet of the side of the barn, and what a lovely ride I had! I sure hoped Thelma was watching from her front porch. Our aging neighbor lady sat on her front porch watching us endlessly, day in and day out, and it was time to reward all her hours of watching. I made it safe and sound. I never panicked; I trusted my big brothers well. Why didn't Mom act enthused about it with me afterwards??

I had a new perspective of life… The world really did look different from my boxy viewpoint of lying flat on my back. Don't you see by now? If you need a new perspective of life, FIND SOME BROTHERS!

A SISTER'S VIEW OF BOYS AND NOISE

LORAINE J BATES

Within our walls, you'll rarely find
The one without the other;
For where there's noise, there's bound to be
An extra happy brother.
It seems they have a secret plan
To keep my ears a-ringing;
They love that look of dazed distress
When they are loudly singing.
They scream to hear how well they can
(Perhaps it's getting louder);
They chase each other through the house—
I'm sure they're getting wilder.
And when we're calmly eating lunch,
There's belching, and there's burping;
And if it happens to be soup,
There's such a lot of slurping.
They can't converse among themselves
In lower tones of talking;
They're stomping down the stairs so much
And hardly ever walking.
And when at last they leave the house,
They bang the door to top it;
I think if doors and walls could wish,
They'd wish those boys would stop it.
I only know that when they're gone,
I feel myself relaxing
And thanking God for boys and noise,
Although they're rather taxing!

Should Sis Groan or Grin?

D ROSE W

Cookie-gobblers, riddle-plotters, Daddy-lovers, mischief-makers, storytellers, totally lovable…well, mostly. Who would this describe? My brothers, of course! Being a teenager, second oldest in my family, and a sister to six wonderful brothers, you would think I would never be shocked at the noise level, manners, or outlandish ideas. Sometimes I am. Yet I like to try to laugh in those moments instead of giving the whole nine yards of a growly, unmerciful scolding. Really, boys should never be expected to act like girls!

This afternoon many unusual noises floated downstairs as four of the boys raided a shared closet that they had not looked into for awhile. What fun to rediscover their treasures! I was pleasantly surprised when they hauled two handfuls of garbage downstairs. *It is finally garbage in their eyes, too!* I thought. I decided to dwell on the things they brought down instead of all the treasures still in hiding. Funny how half the things they brought down didn't have a name. It was parts of things from who-knows-where. Oh, the adventuresome life that accompanies a house of boys! I have often wondered if other boy families face the same ridiculous (or not) problems that our family faces.

I really appreciate the rule my parents enforced a few years ago: if you burp with your mouth open, you are the dishwasher for the next meal. This rule works! If Matthew accuses Jordan of burping, and Jordan is positive that his mouth *was* closed, Dad or Mom is sure to remind them that it never hurt a man to wash the dishes. And should it make a difference whether they burped or not? They were told to wash the dishes. Talking back also results in doing the dishes or clearing the table around here. It works nicely! If they complain, they will be reminded that they need more practice to do it cheerfully, and are blessed with another turn!

Ever have the sloppy bathroom issues? Even when you think they are *surely* old enough to leave the bathroom as clean as they found it, they will still be the culprits! One rule seems to work quite well: If Mom sees any spots beside or on the toilet, she will keep an eye on it, checking the bathroom after a boy leaves. If it happens again, that boy will be the cleaning lady for the bathroom on Saturday. Occasionally, someone is in a big hurry again, but after the cleaning job, it seems the lesson sticks…until next time!

I suppose no household ever heard such thumping, bumping, and splashing as we hear when Lucas and Jordan are bathing! One Saturday night it was especially bad, and Mom questioned the boys when they came down as to the noises that were heard during their extra-long bath. Both boys eagerly began chattering.

"We were doing cannon balls!"

"You should have seen Lucas doing that belly flop!"

"That time when we both…"

It did not take Mom long to figure it out. I could tell she didn't know if she should laugh or cry. "Boys," she began disbelievingly, "you were diving into the tub?"

"Off the edge of the tub."

"Once we got *really* good at it, we could jump off the toilet!"

"You should have heard it!"

My sister and I could hardly contain ourselves as we scampered to the sewing room to hide our giggles. Mom ordered the boys upstairs to wipe up the bathroom. (How did she guess there was anything to clean up?!)

Awhile later, another disconcerting problem arose. I discovered it when I was hurriedly brushing my teeth one Saturday night. The shower curtain on the bathtub was wide open. Since that happens to be one of my pet peeves, I quickly stepped over to close it. I was mortified! It appeared as if someone had forgotten to pull the plug, and the water was three-quarters of the way up the sides of the tub! (It will never fail to shock me how DIRTY a boy's bathwater can become!) I knew without a doubt who had been using the bathtub last. Those boys! And *those boys* in particular! I grimaced, pulled up my sleeve, and tried to thank God for healthy brothers as I plunged my hand in and pulled the plug. A minute later as I headed down the hall to bed, three-year-old Kendall called for me.

"What is that noise?" he asked as he popped up from under the covers. The brother beside him appeared to be drifting off to dreamland.

"That's just the bathwater going down the drain," I answered as I shuddered again. "Someone forgot to pull the plug." I rested my gaze on Lucas while speaking loudly enough for him to hear.

"No," Lucas contradicted quickly, suddenly not asleep after all. "It was Jordan's turn to pull the plug. I remember him pulling it, so the plug must have dropped down again like it sometimes does."

I was appalled, and my imagination went to work. *So if the bathtub was fuller than this and two boys were sitting in it, the water was up to—where?* Needless to say, a reminder was in order.

I never figured out how the boys could possibly get such grimy ears. Mom likes to ensure that all their ears are clean on Sundays, especially doing an inspection after summertime baths. If they're not, oops! Look out! Mom plus washcloth attacks the boys, and that equals quite a hollering! No doubt about it, their ears are sparkling next Saturday night.

Two summers ago an unusual mystery occurred. We discovered that Matthew, known to be a little reckless, was having a terrible time with his shirt buttons. After keeping a lookout for it, Mom discovered that every one of his everyday shirts had a missing button. Always the same one!

Mom always has trousers to patch and mend. She didn't need a great pile of shirts with wandering buttons. Suddenly more boys began having button trouble. It was never more than one, and it was always in the same spot. We had had enough.

"Boys," Mom announced at the supper table, "we have a new rule." (The boys gave each other that now-what's-coming look.) "Every time I catch a shirt with a missing button, that boy will be sewing a new button on. What *is* happening to your buttons?" Our gaze followed hers to rest on an uneasy Matthew.

"I think I know," he began with a voice that said he *did* know. "After we're done with our chores, we climb up on the doghouse and jump onto the big pipes going from the grain bin up to the upstairs barn. And Mom, we can't help it. When we pull ourselves up onto the roof of the doghouse, there is a little ledge. But Mom, I *can't* help it! My button pops off right there!" he finished convincingly.

So the mystery was solved. But the rule remained. Of course, the boys thought it was only a girl's job, and definitely not a boy's thing. They became extra cautious about going over that ledge on their stomachs, but even so, the time came when Matthew lost a button. My sister and I were triumphant.

Matthew is one who does not spend unnecessary time caring about his looks. He seems to get a thrill out of being just a little different. He gets much joy at seeing his sisters irked at his quirks.

Thus when Mom told him to fetch a button from the button box, he picked the first one he saw and was back in a jiffy. My sister gasped. I groaned. "You can't use *that* one!" we cried.

Unfortunately, that made up his mind. "Why would you care if I have one white button with a blue rose in the middle?" he asked with a shining sparkle in his eye. "Mom said that the person who sews the button on may choose it!"

Suddenly he was very inspired to sew on his button. We girls were floored. We regretted having that button in the button box. Even though it had never been his favorite shirt before, he seemed to get a satisfaction out of making it his favorite one now!

To groan or to grin, to scowl and make it worse or to laugh and make a joke along with memories…that's what a sister has to decide. A lifestyle where the gas pedal, horsepower, and muscle far exceeds the importance of your diet, the condition of the brakes, and how many days you have worn that pair of socks… It's all right here!

"Lord, help me to be the sister they need, because one day these boys will be boys no longer. Thank you for all six of them. I love each of them dearly, although I sometimes fail miserably in showing it! And once again, I'll ask earnestly and humbly for every inch of patience you have to spare…."

boys' noise and joys
MARLENE BEILER

I am a mother of four boys;
"Lord, grant me patience with their noise."

Their tractors roar; their racecars zoom;
Their guns compel a noisy BOOM!
Boys make such sounds we girls abhor;
How much should Mama just ignore?

"Let's play ball!" here comes the shout;
Bats and balls are strewn about.
Sliding is a favorite thing,
Heedless of the dirt it brings.

A wad of socks inspires a kick;
My broom becomes a hockey stick;
A spoon is taken for a bat;
A mixing bowl creates a hat.

Shirts to sew and pants to lengthen;
Clothes to mend piled as a mountain.
Missing buttons, knees are worn;
Here's a sock, its heel is torn.

Yes, I'm a mother of four boys;
"Lord, help me treasure boyhood joys!"

A Sister to All Those Brothers

THE SISTER

An excited smile played around the corners of ten-year-old Kayla's mouth as she yanked another towel out of the basket and deftly folded it. Her thoughts tumbled over each other. *This is so exciting! It is two hours now since we came home from school and discovered Dad and Mom have gone to the hospital. Surely the phone will ring any moment. Oh, how I hope it's a girl!* Then her face grew troubled as she remembered the argument with her next older brother, Benjie, back when Dad had told them that God would be giving them another sibling.

"I sure hope it's a boy!" Benjie had declared with a sidelong glance at Kayla. "We already have two girls in the family, which is bordering on too many!"

Instantly Kayla had shot back, "It better be a girl! You boys have already doubled us girls in number!"

Oh, surely, surely, it will be a girl! We have the two older boys, Brendon and Benjie, then us two girls, then the twins, Justin and Joshua. A girl would be just right to keep the pattern going. And those sweet pink clothes! Kayla remembered the day last week when they had washed up the baby clothes. She and Kara had been delighted to finger the little pieces they had worn. The little blue sleeper had not looked as cute as the pink ones. *But,* Kayla sighed as she folded the last towel, *Benjie usually wins the argument, so he's sure to win this one too!* Scooping up the first stack of towels, Kayla headed towards the bathroom.

"Ring, Ring!" Hastily Kayla plunked the towels on the kitchen table and darted for the office.

"Hello?" Kayla held her breath.

"Hello!" It was Mom's voice, and immediately Kayla's heart sped up. "Praise God our baby is here!" Mom announced.

Kayla couldn't get the next words out fast enough. "Is it a boy or a girl?" she asked.

Then Mom dropped the bomb. "It's a boy!" Instantly Kayla's heart plummeted to her toes. Her shoulders slumped as all dreams of pink clothes evaporated. "We named him Clinton Eric, and he weighs 7 lbs. and 10 oz." Mom could not hide the excitement in her voice. "He is twenty inches long, and we think he looks like Brendon!"

Mom's mood was catching, and Kayla felt her spirits rising. After all, any baby was exciting if she could help care for it! After chatting some more, Mom concluded with, "Now don't forget to tell the others the news! Goodbye."

"Of course! I'll go tell them right away! Bye!" and Kayla raced out the door. Bounding up to the milking parlor door, she yelled, "Mom called!" She grinned as she watched Benjie and the maid, Doris, snap to attention.

Once the news was spilled, Benjie looked at Kayla with that triumphant gleam in his eye. "Clinton Eric Erb. So it *is* a boy!"

After shooting Benjie a dark look, Kayla sped to the feed room to tell Brendon. En route, she fumed, *Just because Benjie was right, doesn't mean that he has to rub it in!*

The next day when Kayla cuddled little Clinton for the first time, all disappointed thoughts were far away. *He looks so perfect and so sweet, it doesn't matter that he's not a girl!* She planted a kiss on the tiny head.

Brothers and Their Offerings

A week passed as everyone from fourteen-year-old Brendon to the three-year-old twins enjoyed the new blue bundle. "Kayla and Kara, please go and do your chores now," Mom instructed one evening.

Reluctantly Kayla stowed Clinton away in his swing and ambled toward the door, Kara close behind. Halfway across the yard, Kayla suddenly stopped in her tracks. "Oh! I forgot about the snakeskin!"

She recalled the horrible discovery of the evening before. They had been in the barn loft filling their wagon with hay for the sheep when they had noticed a snakeskin dangling from a stack of bales directly above them! It appeared as if the snake had slithered between the top and bottom bale, shedding its skin as it went. Imagine that snakeskin dropping down on them when they bent over to pick up hay! Both girls shivered as they stood in the yard, discussing what to do.

Then Kara spied Brendon, who had just stepped outside the feed room door. "Let's ask Brendon to take it down for us!"

"Wel-l-l," Kayla stalled, "but what if he chases us with it?"

"We'll just warn him not to chase us with it, or we will go and tell Dad. Then he'll be in trouble!" Kara planned.

"All right, we'll try it," Kayla agreed.

"Hey, Brendon!" the girls chorused.

Crossing the yard, they laid out their request and the consequences of any misconduct. "Oh, girls will be girls!" Brendon rolled his eyes in disgust. "Scared of such an innocent thing as a harmless snakeskin!"

Turning with the air of having to do his sisters a great duty, he headed for the barn. "Let's go and give the sheep their water now," Kayla suggested. "That way we are out of sight, and he'll be less likely to tease us."

Five minutes later the girls exited the barn. Glancing around, Kayla was relieved to see no Brendon. Approaching their hay wagon, Kara suddenly wailed, "Look what he did!"

There, tied to the wagon handle, was the snakeskin! "I just knew he'd do something!" Kayla sputtered in disgust. "Now how will we get our hay? I'm not touching that horrid old snakeskin!"

She looked around in desperation, but no Brendon was seen. *He's probably hiding in the feed room watching us and thinking he is real smart!* Suddenly she spied the twins in the sandbox. Hatching a plan, she called, "Justin and Joshua, come here, please."

Upon their arrival, Kayla mustered up her most beguiling voice. "Look, boys, see this snakeskin? If you take it off the handle, I'll give you each a candy from my collection."

"Oh, good!" the twins squealed with delight. Eagerly they reached for the snakeskin and soon had it removed.

After the chores were finished, the girls poured out their tale of woe to Mom. When they were through, Mom thought a moment. "I know Brendon shouldn't have done that, but do you realize that if you wouldn't make such a ruckus when he does things like that, he wouldn't get so much joy out of it?"

The girls rolled that thought around. It was hard to believe. Then Kayla spoke up, saying, "I'm glad though that at least the three youngest boys aren't old enough to tease us yet!"

The September sun shone down on the huddle of girls in the schoolyard. As Kayla unwrapped her cookie, she entered into the discussion of the Sunday afternoon activities each had been involved in the day before. "Brendon, Benjie, Kara, and I went down to the stream in the pasture and built another dam. We think this is our best one yet! Brendon put a pipe in it, so it won't overflow and get washed away. We want to go down next Sunday afternoon and see if it is still holding up."

Anne turned to Kayla and said, "I think you have it so nice to have older brothers to think up all that fun stuff to do."

"I think so too," piped up Anne's younger sister Gina. "We are the only ones in Room 2 that don't have older brothers."

"Yes, they are nice to have as long as they don't tease too much," Kayla agreed. There was some general agreement from the other girls who had big brothers. Then before Anne could ask any questions about the teasing and Kayla would have to own up to her reactions, Kayla quickly proposed, "Since we're done eating, let's get playing!"

Anne and Kayla shrieked with delight as they flew down the hill. Hopping off the sled, Anne said, "Let's go again! We don't have such big hills at our place."

"Sure," Kayla agreed. "I'm so glad you could come here after school tonight!"

The girls trudged slowly up the hill, talking all the way. Suddenly, Kayla heard Benjie's voice right behind them. "Look what I found in the barn tonight! A dead cat!"

Turning around, the girls came face to face with Benjie, who was holding the dead feline by the tail. "Ya want to come closer?" and he swung the cat toward Kayla.

Kayla let out a scream and jumped behind Anne, the only protection she could find on the wide-open hillside. Surely, he would not swing the dead cat at Anne!

"What a nice friend you are, Kayla, using your friend for a fort!" Benjie scoffed. Satisfied with the amount of screams he had gotten, Benjie headed back to the barn with his dead weapon hanging by his side.

"That's just what I mean, Anne, when I tell you big brothers aren't always nice!" Kayla exclaimed with a shaky sigh as the girls resumed their climb.

Brothers and Their Clutter

The years kept rolling by one by one. One Saturday morning fourteen-year-old Kayla headed toward the three youngest boys' bedroom with dust cloth in hand. Stopping just inside the door, Kayla surveyed the wreckage and felt impatience rising within her. *How am I ever supposed to dust when every surface is laden with rocks, feathers, snail shells, empty shotgun shells, candy wrappers...and of course, I wouldn't dare pitch the stuff!*

Later, passing through the kitchen, Kayla unloaded her thoughts to Mom. "I still wish sometimes that Clinton would have been a girl. Then there would be one less boy to help collect junk!"

"Oh?" Mom raised her eyebrows. "Think about this: Little girls like to collect treasures, too. If Clinton had been a girl, then there would be junk in *your* room."

"Oh," was all Kayla could manage as the thought sunk in. Maybe Mom had a point.

One evening the next week found Kayla sewing on her new dress.

Grabbing some pieces of the dress, she headed across the room to the ironing board. Suddenly, searing pain flashed through her big toe, and she gave a dance on one foot while she clutched the other one. She didn't even have to look down to see what the offending object was. The tattletale clink, clunk associated with experience told her that it was one of those miniature pieces of equipment.

"Mom!" she burst out. "Do the little boys have to always set up their farm around the ironing board? I've stubbed my toe on their toys for the twenty-third time!"

"At least it's not the twenty-fourth time," drawled Benjie from behind the farm paper.

Kayla didn't dare glance in the direction of the sofa. She knew she would see an amused grin, and that combined with her smarting toe would be too much.

"Please, not such a big outburst, Kayla," Mom chided. Then turning to the little boys she admonished, "Boys, I told you last week that if you set up your farm by the ironing board, we will be more likely to step on your toys and break them. Please put your farm over there," Mom said as she pointed across the room.

Still rubbing her toe, Kayla fumed, *Big brothers like to tease, and little brothers make so much clutter! I don't know which is worse!*

Kayla scurried into the kitchen to help Mom finish preparing the food. "I have the last-minute cleaning looked after, and Kara is setting up the tables and chairs on the patio, so what shall I do here?" she asked.

"Why don't you slice the tomatoes," Mom directed.

All the youth were invited over to the Erbs for supper. "Oh, here come the first ones!" Kayla announced as she shifted into a higher gear.

Mom welcomed the first youth at the door as Kayla grabbed the platter of cheese and hurried out to the patio with it. Passing through the dining room, Kayla caught her breath. There on one of the wooden chairs was a big jumble of toy equipment that she had instructed the little boys to take to their room when she was cleaning up. Typical of little boys, they had forgotten. Quickly depositing the cheese on the patio table, she silently slipped back into the dining room. *Good, looks like all the youth have their backs turned!* Stealthily, Kayla picked up the offending, loaded chair and noiselessly set it around the corner in the parlor. *I hope the youth never saw that! What would they think of our housekeeping?*

Cottage meeting was over at Shady Oak the next Tuesday evening. The youth were making their way across the parking lot to their cars when Anne and Gina paused and turned to Kayla. "We thought we should tell you how many laughs we've had about your clever chair move on Friday evening!"

Kayla's jaw dropped. So they *had* seen! Immediately Anne spoke up again, saying, "But don't be embarrassed. We have little brothers too, and the scene was so real of a little boy's forgetfulness and a big sister's remedy!"

Kayla joined their laughter. The joke really was on her. Everyone had enjoyed a good evening, and what did a chair piled with toys matter? There were little boys at this house!

Brothers and Their Merit

Kayla's brow knit in frustration. "I thought this arbor made from tree branches looked like such an easy project, but these old nails just bend and go in crooked no matter how hard I try," she muttered.

"Here, use screws instead of nails," the twins offered helpfully from nearby where they were working on their own project.

Kayla eyed the drill warily. "Screw heads always strip out for me; that's why I thought nails would be easier."

"We'll run the drill for you," the twins offered generously. "You just hold the pieces together and tell us where to drill."

Tired of her project going awry, Kayla gladly let them run the drill. To her amazement, the screws went in with little problem. *Working with tools must be inborn in boys,* Kayla thought. *Why, at seven years old, they can run a drill better than I can at fourteen!*

"Thanks, boys," Kayla said when they had the last piece screwed in place. "I guess the project will have to sit until I have time to go to the woods for more branches to cut. I need to go do chores now."

As busy day followed busy day, the project lay untouched in the back of the shop.

Kayla glanced around at each member of the Erb family. The whole family awake at 2:00 AM? With everyone gathered around the big van and trailer, Brendon's leaving was reality. He was leaving for Honduras for two years. Two whole years? Only four brothers around here for two years? Suddenly four brothers didn't seem like enough!

Now Brendon and his fellow travelers were saying "Good-bye" and jumping into the van to begin their long journey. As Kayla watched the taillights disappear, she realized more than ever how much her family meant to her. Even. Each. Brother.

"Looks like we certainly aren't the first ones here," Kayla commented as they neared Brother Ed's driveway. "People are already wielding wheelbarrows and chain saws."

"I can hardly find a place to park," Benjie stated. "I guess here on this strip of grass will be okay."

Just then, Kayla saw Anne pulling in. She waited until Anne was parked beside them before jumping out. "Hi!" Kayla greeted Anne as she emerged from her car.

"Hi, yourself!" Anne returned. "You're so fortunate to have a brother to drive you to these youth activities. You don't have to worry about where to park. I was glad you two pulled in ahead of me so I could follow your example. But you have a truck and I have a car. This spring ground is rather soft. What if I get stuck when I leave?"

"Oh, don't worry," Kayla assured. "If you get stuck, we'll help you out. I do agree, though, that it is nice to have a brother to come with. I think about how lonely you have it. But," Kayla laughed, "five years ago I would have thought *you* had it better with no big brothers!" Then she sobered, "But now I realize what good friends we can be, even if they still tease sometimes. Maybe we *are* growing up!"

"Soon Gina will be old enough to come too, and then I'll have some company. But now we'd better act grown up and get to work!" Anne said as she grabbed her shovel out of her car trunk.

"Yes," Kayla agreed, "or Benjie will walk by and tell me that I'm doing what girls do best: Talking!"

July 5, the day of Dad Erb's surgery, had come. The family praised the Lord that the surgery had gone well. As was expected, a week of recovery in the hospital was needed. Meanwhile, the Erb children pulled together at home to keep things going.

As Kayla lugged her bucket of cucumbers to the house, she glanced toward the barn. Noticing the chores seemed close to being finished, she quickened her pace to see if Kara needed any help finishing breakfast preparation. Brendon was home from Honduras, so Kayla had been relieved of all barn duties to keep things going in the house and garden. What a blessing it was to have five healthy brothers to keep the farm operating while Dad recovered!

Brothers and Their Influence

The years rolled on, and the day came when Kayla took her Sweetheart's hand in marriage. Of course, she moved away from all those brothers. Winston and Kayla really enjoyed it when there was opportunity for some of the boys to spend a day or two with them.

One by one, God blessed their home with children. How those little faces shone to see one of their beloved uncles walk through the door! Even though Kayla was busy with her own family, she was glad her brothers kept her informed about their lives.

"I thought I'd call and tell you where I'm planning to go this winter," Benjie told Kayla on the phone one day.

"Where is that?" Kayla wondered. She thought of the times he had helped in Honduras or in the southern states with disaster relief crews.

"To China, to smuggle Bibles," informed Benjie.

"I'm glad for you. That sounds like a worthwhile way to spend your winter," said Karla.

Karla sank into a chair beside Brendon's wife Lucy at the family gathering. "So it's only two more days until you leave for Honduras? It's hard to believe."

"Yes," replied Lucy, shifting baby Leon to her shoulder. "There is a lot to do before then. But it will be so nice to spend a couple months with the natives and renew friendships while we help with the work there."

The room was dark and all eyes were fastened on the pictures projected on the wall. Benjie, Justin, and Joshua had returned from helping with cleanup after a tornado in Texas. Dad and Mom had invited the family home to see the slides.

"Here is Mr. Cook's place. We worked here quite a bit," Joshua explained. "This stuff over here is debris from what was their house," he pointed out with his laser light.

As the Erb family took in one picture after the next, stories spilled forth from the boys. "This is Mrs. Hanson's place. While we were working there, she told us her experience when the tornado hit. She said, 'I was in the dining room watching the storm when suddenly the roof above me was gone. So I ran into my bedroom, and just like that, the bedroom roof left too! So I threw up my hands and said, "Lord, where do you want me now?"' She was very glad to let us have cottage meetings in her garage, and she would ask us lots of questions," Joshua related.

"A storm like that tends to make people recognize God's power and their own frailty. Therefore, they are more open to the truth. It's another way for God's Word to reach outlying areas," Dad commented.

Brothers and Their Sisters

Grandpa, Grandma, the four uncles, and one aunt still living at home were gathered at Winston and Kayla's for Heidi's sixth birthday party. "My, how sticky you are!" Kayla exclaimed to Wanda, who was just past a year old. "Was your roasted marshmallow good? Now we better take you to find some soap and water!" So saying, Kayla scooped Wanda up and headed for the house.

On her way back across the yard several minutes later, she suddenly stopped in her tracks and stared! There in the yard stood the tree branch arbor that she had dreamed about years ago. "How did this come about?" she finally managed to ask when the laughter had died down.

"Oh, we were cleaning out the shop this spring," the "little" boys admitted, "when we uncovered your forgotten, half-finished dreams lying in the back of the shop. We decided to surprise you and finish it for your birthday!"

"Thank you very much! That will look perfect at the end of our sidewalk!" Kayla declared. Her heart was touched that her brothers cared enough about their sister's clutter that instead of just throwing it out, they finished her dreams and surprised her!

Eagerly Kayla ripped open the envelope that had just arrived in the mail. A picture fell out, and she recognized Joshua's smiling face. Clustered around him, the small chocolate-colored faces contrasted sharply with his white one.

So these are the little African faces that Joshua sees five days a week in his classroom. "Children, come look at this! We got a picture of Uncle Joshua in faraway Africa. See his students?" Three little white faces gazed eagerly down at the little brown faces staring back from the picture.

After a thorough discussion about the picture, Kayla gave it an honored place on the refrigerator. As she returned to her work, her mind was busy. *All those brothers filling all those places of service. It seems like so short a time ago that they were "those brothers" all around me, teasing me and making clutter. And all that time they were little men, being raised for God's service. The cluttered dresser tops, snakeskin scenarios, and stubbed toes were more than worth it. If God had not given me five brothers, He would have five less workers in His kingdom. But they sure didn't grow to be useful because they had the most patient, loving sister there ever was.* Kayla's face turned a darker shade of pink. *Nevertheless, I do have a second chance to be patient and loving,* she mused as she glanced into the next room. Four-year-old Troy had his farm set up, complete with the little toy equipment that was perfect for stubbing your toes on. Her face grew grave. *However, there is a lot more at stake this time around, because I am the mom and not just the sister!*

The Meaning

of Big Sister

D ROSE W

I'm richly blessed by God—richly and wonderfully blessed to be called "Big Sis" by six healthy brothers! Therefore…

…I always have more than enough offers to run the "gas pedal" on my new sewing machine, and I would only need to comment on oiling it, and—presto! I would again have more hands offered than I need.

…Now that our gator is doctored up again, I have many offers to take out the garbage. I'm even asked, "Are you *sure* there's no garbage?" (Often more than once a week!)

…I get to witness and share my brothers' joy after a creative invention is completed. Whether it be a tandem bike, a bike on skis, or something else, it's always fun when they beg me to test-drive their inventions.

…I have the exciting job of cleaning boys' bedrooms and discovering *many* foreign objects that I might never have learned to recognize if I would not have so many brothers.

…I'm privileged to be able to double and triple recipes and still have the joy of seeing the food disappear like a marble rolling under the fridge. (It comes in very handy when I make a flop!)

...I am blessed with the challenge of trying to keep the pants labeled with the correct number of marks as they are passed down the row of boys.

...I have the satisfaction of seeing a wash line of freshly washed pants flapping in the sun. (Every size, it seems!) It's doubly rewarding if I know how they looked before washing.

...I get to hear interesting snippets of talk like this: "It smells like girl, doesn't it?" "Sure enough!" Then an exaggerated, "Peeeewheeee!" *Funny how I smell a whiff of my perfume on them now and then.*

...I have learned that brothers seldom forget wild reactions by me—they bring those incidents up at the most inappropriate times! (A good way to keep me humble!) My ten-year-old brother burst into the barn while I was doing chores tonight and asked excitedly, "Guess who's here?" Before I could guess, I had a drowned mouse dangling in front of my face. *And I'm not supposed to react?*

...I hear comments from others like, "How do you keep all the names straight?" or "I can never remember which is which!" I tell you, they are all vastly different!

...Last night wasn't the first time I heard Mom say, "Don't do such weird things with your eyes. Someday they might stick and stay that way. Can you imagine?"

...What is more satisfying than seeing my brothers dressed up in suits, ready for church on a Sunday morning, with hair neatly combed and faces shining? (Top shirt button closed and shirttail tucked in after a reminder.) Why, they look like good and proper gentlemen!

"Lord, thank you for blessing me with this influential role in life! Help me be the influence I should be to help these young gentlemen!"

My Brothers, My Friends

KRISTA J BATES

Brothers. That word brings many thoughts to mind. How familiar, so common, yet very precious. As the only girl with seven brothers, I had many chances to learn patience but few times to be bored. There were days I badly wished for more girl members in the family, but mostly I enjoyed my lot in life as the only sister. I could neither feel proud nor take offense when my brothers would tell me, "You are the best and worst sister we ever had." Like normal siblings we had our good times as well as our fights, but my brothers were my friends. As I grew older, I realized what a blessing and privilege it is to be in the middle of a family of boys.

When neighbors, customers, or people in town would ask about my family and learn I was the only sister of seven brothers, I usually got a lot of response: "You must have it pretty rough!" "Are they mean to you?" "Do they treat you good?" "Do you keep them all straight?" I was quick to assure them that they were good brothers.

When I was eight years old, I had appendicitis and spent five days in the hospital. I remember the strange feeling of lying in my hospital bed, and all my brothers coming into the room to see me. To them it was very different to see their usual lively sister looking so unwell. They told me they think the reason I got appendicitis was because I ate my hair and fingernails. I did not appreciate their reasoning.

One thing my brothers got a lot of practice with was washing dishes. Their ways of relating to this less-than-desirable job was as varied as their personalities. One brother would wash them at high speed. In a few minutes, the dishes were all in the drainer, and the boy was out the door. When we checked the dishes later, they were, surprisingly, usually clean. Another brother would take his good long time at it. Why not have some fun while you were at it? There would be experiments with soapsuds, bowls, and kettle lids. We always felt sorry for him when he was still trying to finish the dishes an hour later. Sadly, even with all the time, he still missed some dirt. I was always glad for their efforts. At least I had a break from the job!

Many memories were made with my brothers in the pea patch. We had many interesting conversations, and some of the boys could run their mouths much faster than their hands. Some of them thought sitting on their bucket to pick peas would make it a more comfortable job, but unfortunately, it also lessened the speed of the picker. One brother announced to us one year that he was picking peas the Biblical way: he was letting some behind for someone else.

My three older brothers and I, born within almost four years, did many things together. I trailed after my brothers, wanting to be involved with whatever they were doing. As we became teenagers and made the decisions to become Christians, we grew even closer. We shared a lot together with our parents as we faced life's struggles, decisions, and joys.

As my brothers got older, I looked forward to the possibility of sisters. I wanted my brothers to get married, but one part of me held back, wanting life to stay the same. I was thrilled when my oldest brother told me of the girl in whom he was interested. I thought the world of her and couldn't wait until she was my sister-in-law, but the morning of their wedding, I felt a mixture of feelings. As my big brother got ready to go out the door, he grinned at me. I was happy for him and yet sad to think of it never being the same again.

I admired the girl of Brother #2's choice as well. It was an answer to my prayers when she accepted him. I was happy for them when they joined hearts and hands, but another brother had left home. Again, I had to adjust to the change it made in our family life.

It was especially hard when my brother just older than me was interested in one of my very close friends. You would have thought I would have been thrilled, but I was not. My brother was taking my best friend, and my best friend was taking my brother. There was no changing their minds, so I had to change mine. They treated me nicely, and I was considered a friend to both of them. I had to learn to accept when envelopes came in the mail for him, not me. I also had to be careful not to share information that I knew they would want to tell each other.

My three older brothers all dated long-distance. Many times I rode with them when they drove the hundreds of miles to see their girlfriends. Sometimes they let me drive their cars, which I always thought was special. I was glad they trusted me, though they usually kept a good eye on me. I enjoyed conversing with them about their girlfriends and many other things. If I happened to talk to their girl-friend at a singing or some other service, they would always want to know what she said. I would try to repeat our conversations, and they would ask, "Was that all?" or "Did you talk about me?" On some trips, my brothers would not be in talking moods. Maybe they were preparing for a date or remembering one! I felt very privileged to ride with each one of them the last trip before their wedding. It was one last time to talk to them before they were a married man. Since they are married, I can still talk to them, but I also now enjoy the input of their wives. They have added a lot of spice to our family, and I feel a close friendship with each one.

A few months after my next older brother started courting, a young man talked to my father about his interest in me. My older brothers were informed, and they were not silent on the issue. They wanted to make sure he was the right kind of boy for their only sister. I waited prayerfully and hopefully, and when the letter arrived, I was so thankful to have my parents' and brothers' support to respond favorably. Through our courtship journey, we had much input from both my older and younger brothers. We enjoyed that for the most part. I was thankful to have their care and interest in our lives then, on our wedding day, and even now as a married couple. I was always assured they want what is best for me and us. I'm grateful they have accepted my husband into the family, and I enjoy watching him and my brothers interact.

Before my older brothers were married, I thought I would never be close to my younger brothers. It must have taken my three big brothers to get married to change that, because I now feel a close connection with my younger brothers. I had only a short four months between the time my next older brother got married and my wedding day. I wasn't really looking forward to being the oldest at home. Now I wish I had made better use of that time still at home with my younger brothers. We did have a lot of good times and talks, which I treasure. Since I'm married, I don't have as many chances to just sit down and talk with my younger brothers, but I love the times I can. I'm glad they want to talk to me, because I am very much interested in their lives and want to be an encouragement to them. I desire that they grow up to be strong men of God.

Recipes

Yummy Granola Bars
D ROSE W

My brothers always enjoy these bars. They're great for snacks, lunches, canoeing, hiking, or anytime!

Melt:
 ¼ cup butter
 ¼ cup oil   12 cups small marshmallows
Mix and add:
 ½ cup honey   ¼ cup peanut butter
In a large bowl, mix:
 4½ cups Rice Crispies   1 cup sunflower seeds
 1 cup graham cracker crumbs   1 cup coconut
 4 cups oatmeal   1 cup chocolate chips
Pour melted mixture on top and toss together. Press into 2 - 9"x13" pans. Cool and cut.

Muddy Buddies

M EBERSOLE

Sometimes it's dirty boys; this time it's a sweet treat!

9 cups Rice Chex, Corn Chex, or Chocolate Chex cereal (or combination)
1 cup semisweet chocolate chips
½ cup peanut butter
¼ cup butter or margarine
1 tsp. vanilla
1½ cups powdered sugar

Measure cereal into a large bowl; set aside. In a 1 qt. microwavable bowl, microwave chocolate chips, peanut butter, and butter, uncovered, on high for 1 minute; stir. Microwave about 30 seconds longer or until mixture can be stirred smooth. Stir in vanilla. Pour mixture over cereal, stirring until evenly coated. Pour into a 2-gallon resealable plastic bag. Add powdered sugar. Seal bag; shake until well coated. Spread on waxed paper to cool. Store in airtight container in refrigerator (if there is any left to store!). It's supposed to serve 18.

Brownie Cupcakes

M EBERSOLE

Easy enough for boys to make!

1 box Fudge Brownie Mix
1 package Reese's Peanut Butter Cups

Mix Brownie Mix according to package instructions. Pour into muffin pans lined with paper. Insert one Reese's Cup into center of each cupcake, pressing down until brownie batter comes to top of candy. Bake at 350° for 20-25 minutes.

Chocolate Syrup

MARTHA BEILER

This is easy to make and nice to have on hand to mix with milk for thirsty boys' stomachs!

¾ cup cocoa

3 cups sugar

3 cups hot water

2 tsp. vanilla

Mix dry ingredients. Add enough water to make a paste. Add rest of water. Boil 3 minutes and add vanilla. Cool. Keep refrigerated.

Buckeyes

NAOMI CROSS

Our youngest is the only one at home anymore, and his favorite kitchen creation is Buckeyes. They're always a treat for us! He often makes them when all the children and grandchildren come home. He melts the chocolate in a small two-cup crock-pot. When we hear the "tap-tap-tap" coming from the kitchen, we know we will soon be enjoying his Buckeyes!

1 cup graham cracker crumbs

½ cup powdered sugar

½ stick melted margarine

1¼ cups crunchy peanut butter

1½ cups Rice Crispie cereal

Mix well and form into small balls. Refrigerate for 1 hour. Dip balls into melted chocolate. Enjoy with the whole family!

Yogurt Parfaits

MARTHA BEILER

Great after-school snack!

yogurt

granola

fruit

maple syrup

I use small glass dishes and pour granola in first, then yogurt. Top it with fruit of your choice and drizzle maple syrup over it. Children are capable of creating their own, but my boys love when I make them, for they love being served by Mom!

Easy Fruit Slush
MARTHA BEILER
A refreshing after-school snack on a warm day!

1 jar canned peaches
1 jar canned pears
1 can crushed pineapple
½ pint frozen strawberries
1 tsp. stevia powder

Pour everything into blender and blend until smooth. Or for a chunky slush just mash with potato masher. This is delicious partly frozen or just chilled.

Good and Simple Bread
FONDA HEGE

One of our sons likes to work in the kitchen, making things and tasting them when they're done. Here are two bread recipes that he likes to make. They can be mixed in a mixer and are simple enough for a 10- or 11-year-old to make. Usually he relies on Mother to shape the loaves, but he likes to do everything else.

3 cups hot water
⅓ cup brown sugar
2 Tbsp. yeast
⅓ cup white sugar

Put in mixer, mix a bit, then let set 3 minutes. Add:

½ cup flour
1 Tbsp. salt

Mix and let set 3 minutes. Change to dough hook. Add:

¾ cup oil
8 cups flour

Add flour 1 cup at a time and knead 3 minutes at the end. Let rise 30 minutes. Knead and let rise another 30 minutes. Shape into loaves. Let rise. Bake at 350° for 30 minutes.

Wolf Bread

FONDA HEGE

This recipe comes from my friend, Sarah Wolf, and thus gets its name. It is whole wheat and so very soft!

½ cup molasses or honey   2 cups hot water
2½ Tbsp. yeast
Put in mixer bowl, mix, and let rise 10 minutes. Add:
2 tsp. salt   2 eggs
3 cups whole wheat flour (Prairie Gold is my favorite)
Mix 4 minutes. Add:
½ cup oil
Mix 4 minutes.
Change to dough hook and add around 4 more cups of whole wheat flour. Knead 10 minutes and let rise. Shape into loaves and let rise ½ hour. Bake at 350° for 20-25 minutes.

Children's Bag Bread

M EBERSOLE

A fun kitchen project that is surprisingly mess-free with results that are quite tasty!

Place in one-gallon Ziploc bag:
1 Tbsp. yeast   1 cup whole wheat flour
1 tsp. salt
Close bag tightly and shake until well blended. Open and add:
1 cup warm water   2 Tbsp. honey
2 Tbsp. oil
Close bag and squeeze until blended. Add:
1 cup white flour   ½ cup whole wheat flour
Close bag and squeeze again until combined well. Knead the dough, while still in bag, for 10 minutes. Let rise in bag, then take out and shape into a loaf. Place into a greased loaf pan. Prick and let rise again. Bake at 350° for 30 minutes.

Our Favorite Pizza
M EBERSOLE
This pizza is quick and easy. My seven-year-old can mix up the crust while I prepare the toppings.

Dissolve:
  1 Tbsp. yeast in 1 cup warm water
Add:
  1 tsp. sugar   1 tsp. salt
  2 Tbsp. oil
Stir in:
  2½ cups flour
Mix well. Cover and let rise at least 5 minutes. Grease pan. Flour fingers and spread crust in 16" pizza pan. (A half recipe fits in a 9" x 13" pan.) Add toppings. Bake at 425° for 18-20 minutes.

Chili
MARLENE BEILER
My go-to meal! Quick, nourishing, and easy cleanup!

1 lb. hamburger   2 cups corn (fresh or frozen)
½ cup brown sugar   1 pint salsa
1 Tbsp. chili powder   1 tsp. salt
  1 can (16 oz.) chili beans (pinto beans in chili sauce)
In large skillet brown hamburger. Add remaining ingredients; simmer until corn is cooked. Add water if needed.
Serving suggestions:
Serve over baked potatoes and top with cheese sauce and sour cream.
Top with cheddar cheese and sour cream and enjoy with tortilla chips.
Serve with breadsticks for a simple meal.
Serve on a bed of lettuce.

Beef & Rice Casserole

M EBERSOLE

This is my favorite quick dish, and my boys like it, which makes it all the handier!

1 pint canned ground beef (sometimes I use sausage)

1 cup dry rice

1 tsp. salt (use less if using sausage)

1 pint tomato juice

1 pint hot water

Mix in casserole dish. Bake covered at 350° for 1 hour. Stir in 1 cup cheese before serving.

For a one-dish meal, add canned beans before baking.

Variation: Replace ground meat with chicken and tomato juice with milk.

Popsicles

FONDA HEGE

A boy-pleasing snack!

1 small box Jell-O (3 oz.)

1 package Kool-Aid

1 cup sugar

Dissolve in 2 cups boiling water.* Add:

2 cups cold water.

Pour into popsicle molds and freeze.

*I like to use 1 qt. of grape juice concentrate in place of the water for "healthy" popsicles. In fact, I usually steam and can some white grapes so that I can make other colors of popsicles instead of all purple ones.

> Mother: "Is your tummy hungry?"
>
> Two-year-old son: "No. My mouth is hungry."

Some boys enjoy cooking and baking. During the job, they can taste it; afterwards they can eat it! Preschool boys enjoy the challenge of making granola. You can draw pictures to illustrate the ingredients for your sons. Following is the recipe I use.

Granola
MRS SHARLA BORNTRAGER

18 cups quick oatmeal

2 pkg. graham crackers, crumbled

3 cups coconut

2 cups brown sugar

Mom adds:

2 sticks butter, melted	1 Tbsp. vanilla
½ cup oil	1 tsp. soda
1½ tsp. salt	1½ tsp. cinnamon

Mix and pour over granola. Bake at 350° for 1 hour, stirring every 15 minutes.

Then boys add 1 or 2 cups chocolate chips or raisins.

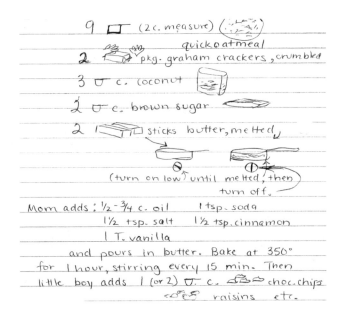

9 ☐ (2 c. measure) quick oatmeal

2 pkg. graham crackers, crumbled

3 ☐ c. coconut

2 ☐ c. brown sugar

2 ☐ sticks butter, melted

(turn on low until melted, then turn off.

Mom adds: ½ - ¾ c. oil   1 tsp. soda
1½ tsp. salt   1½ tsp. cinnamon
1 T. vanilla
and pours in butter. Bake at 350°
for 1 hour, stirring every 15 min. Then
little boy adds 1 (or 2) ☐ c. choc. chips
raisins   etc.

Kool-Aid Play Dough
FONDA HEGE

A nice soft play dough that our children have a lot of fun with.

2 cups flour   ½ cup salt

¼ cup cream of tartar   1 or 2 packages Kool-Aid

Mix in saucepan, then add:

2 cups water   2 Tbsp. oil

Stir over medium-high heat until mixture forms a ball. Remove from pan and knead one minute on a lightly floured surface.

We have a notebook that is turned into a boys' cookbook. The recipes are hand-written with interesting illustrations for decorations. All recipes have easy-to-follow directions. Here are some of their favorites.

Strawberry Milkshake
D ROSE W

Riddle: What does every boy like on a warm, sunny afternoon?
Answer: A shade tree and a cup of cold milkshake!

1. Fill your blender ¾ full of chopped strawberries—straight from the freezer.
2. Sprinkle 1 teaspoonful (a spoon that you use at the table to eat) of sugar on top.
3. Pour milk into the blender until it almost covers the strawberries.
4. Turn your blender on high speed until it looks smooth.
5. Take off the lid, scrap into cups, and ENJOY!

Peanut Butter Squares

D ROSE W

½ cup butter

2 cups graham cracker crumbs

1 cup Rice Crispies

1½ cups peanut butter

3½ cups icing sugar

1 cup chocolate chips

1. Put everything into a mixing bowl except chocolate chips. Mix until it does not stick to your fingers.

2. Press it into a 9" x 13" pan.

3. Melt the chocolate chips in the microwave and pour it over the top. Put it into the fridge for 1 hour.

4. Cut into squares and enjoy! Beware: You might not be able to stop!

Garlic Bread

D ROSE W

Garlic bread is something that is fun and easy to make—and the best part is that it's so-o-o good!

1. Spread a little bit of butter in the bottom of a cake pan.

2. Spread butter on 6 slices of bread with a knife—just like you would at the table. Lay the slices butter-side up in the pan. Then comes the fun part—snoop into Mom's spice cupboard and sprinkle your favorite seasonings on the bread.

3. Go to the oven and press "Broil" and then "Start." Put the pan into the oven and peek in every minute or so. Take it out once the butter is melted, and the bread slices are a little brown. Garlic bread is really good by itself or with soups or any other first course. Yum!

Fiber Balls

MARTHA BEILER

Great for lunches or an easy snack for hungry boys!

1 cup oatmeal

2 cups Rice Crispies

¾ cup honey

1 cup peanut butter

1 cup mini chocolate chips

¼ cup flaxseed meal (optional)

¼ tsp. salt

Mix honey and peanut butter; stir in remaining ingredients. Shape into balls with a cookie scoop. Freeze or refrigerate.

Specializing IN BOYS

FONDA HEGE

Grandma Mable was a cheerful person. You couldn't visit her without catching some of her cheerfulness yourself. Not that she didn't have reason to complain. She was a widow over one hundred years old. She was the only one left in her family since her siblings had passed on one by one. Sometimes she wondered if God had forgotten her. She longed to go to heaven. Nevertheless, she still had a radiant smile, a cheerful personality, and a determined spirit.

We visited her occasionally and, of course, took our little family of boys along. Almost every time, her face would crinkle into a grin when she would ask about our family and realize it was all boys. She would say, "I always said that we specialized in boys." She would explain how she had three boys and only one girl. The three boys married and her first four grandchildren were boys. Of her seventeen grandchildren, twelve of them were boys. Guess what else! Her first great-grandchild was a boy!

By the happiness that spilled from her voice, you would have thought that was the best thing that could have happened. What God handed to her, she accepted as good and counted it a pleasure. She specialized in boys and raised men of God.

Moms to the Rescue
Helpful Tips from Veteran Moms

Boys at Play

Outside

My favorite energy burner/mood enhancer is timing my boys while they are running laps around the house, the barn, or up the field lane, just so we can function peacefully again. Make it a challenge: "See my timer? How long will it take you to run around the barn ten times? Ready? Set? Go!"   MABEL REIFF

Did you know that when bicycles are turned upside down to rest on the seat and handlebars you can really spin the pedals fast? In addition, if you hold plastic cups or something else against the spinning tire, it makes terrific noises! Just don't do as one son who put his forehead lightly against the spinning bike tire until his forehead got warm. He regretted it when a seriously long burn welt appeared, and for weeks afterwards everyone asked what happened to him!   B Z

Do you have paper plates in the cupboard? Give your son one and tell him to wedge it between the seat and the rear bike wheel. When they ride, it sounds like a motor. Warning: You might be buying many paper plates!   MRS KUHNS

Our boys cut plastic rectangles from plastic jars or jugs in the recycling bin. They duct tape these to the spokes of the rear bike wheel for a "pleasing" motor sound.   MRS ALLAN MARTIN

Inside

A favorite pastime our boys haven't outgrown yet is making equipment and other things with Legos and K'nex. We found that to be a super investment. It encourages creativity and the sky is the limit. B Z

A tip I have often read is… "Get rid of toys with small pieces." However, even though we have to be vigilant of small pieces with a crawling baby, I think it is worth the many little pieces that seem to fly in all directions. We have an unused bunk, so I took the mattress out and let Matthias dump his K'nex, a fortunate Goodwill find, in that contained space.   S A R A   B O W M A N

Legos are worth their money. Our boys spend hours with them and they don't break. Dumping them on a large tray or cookie sheet makes for simpler cleanup. Do supervise toddlers—they might find a small round one that fits right in the nose!   M R S   K U H N S

Matthias draws a lot; we have some step-by-step drawing books he uses. (*Draw Write Now* has multiple volumes.) I keep crayons, colored pencils, and markers on hand. My husband brings large sheets of cardboard, brown paper, and scrap paper home from the cabinet shop, so we have an ample paper supply. When I send mail to someone, I often enclose Matthias' pictures. He uses clear tape and paper to make things—a boat, a fan…the imagination is limitless. We use a large sheet of cardboard to draw a road map. Matthias helps draw fields, barns, a river, and stores. Sometimes I outline him on cardboard or paper, and using a picture for a guide, let him draw and label the inside of the human body. He can cut it out and use sticky tack to attach it to his bedroom door.   S A R A   B O W M A N

Boys and boxes are a good match! Take the boxes apart—the boys can help—lay them flat on the floor and draw roads and a house for each boy. Add a few stores and anything else you or your boys can dream up. They can use their little cars and trucks to drive on it.

When they're done playing, it can be folded up and put away. If it gets too trashy looking, throw it away and make a new one.
MARY STOLTZFUS

Save boxes, large and small, to make things. A dollhouse for little sis can be made from a diaper box with pudding box furniture. Velveeta boxes turn into a pickup and van. Small check-size boxes make boats, with a drinking straw and paper for a sail or craft sticks and paper clips for oars and oarlocks. Draw a lion head, cut it out, and glue it to the front of a Velveeta or tissue box. Glue on short pieces of yarn for the mane. Twine with knots tied in the ends makes legs, feet, and a tail. Matthias has a lion catchall for colored pencils. An empty paper towel tube cut apart at the seams and then cut in half makes a snake that will wrap around your arm. All of these can be painted (Shhh! Don't tell Matthias!), covered with construction paper, or decorated liberally with markers. We have a Goodwill book, *Cardboard Carpentry*, which provided ideas, but when he got started, his creativity blossomed! SARA BOWMAN

I have found that my son likes to make cards for all his little friends. I got a farm stamp set and stickers, and he can spend quite awhile making cards. MARTHA SCHMUCKER

Paper grocery bags can be used to make an Indian vest. Or fold down the top and staple it shut; lay the bag on its side and cut an arched hole in the one end. Then decorate the outside with fiberfill snow, add leaves inside for bedding, and you have a den for teddy bear to hibernate. SARA BOWMAN

Let them use your table boards for sliding boards off the sofa.
FONDA HEGE

Our children followed their parents' footsteps in loving books. When they were small, reading books to them helped fill in that time between when Daddy-might-soon-be-home and when Daddy-actually-does-come-home. To a book-loving parent, a child's time with a good book is time well spent.   B Z

Give them washable markers and let them make fields or pens on a Formica-topped counter or table. They can use little tractors in the fields and put animals in their pens. Wash it off when they're finished.   FONDA HEGE

Let them string Fruit Loops or Cheerios on a double thread and a large blunt needle. They can eat their snack when they are finished. (Don't use yarn; they will not enjoy eating fuzzies with their cereal!) FONDA HEGE

Give your children washable markers and let them write on the front of your refrigerator. I've written a list of jobs for my son on the refrigerator. When he completed the jobs, he had the fun of erasing it. An old window blind that has a broken spring is also a nifty thing to roll out and let your children draw on with markers. Just roll it up for easy storage.   M EBERSOLE

Pour Rice Crispies on a large tray or cookie sheet. Let your sons use their small cars, trucks, and diggers in it like a mini indoor sandbox. MRS KUHNS

Pour rice into a plastic tote that fits under your bed. The boys can use it for an indoor sandbox. When you're tired of walking on rice, put the lid on the tote and slide it under the bed for another rainy day. M EBERSOLE

Over winter, the boys stretched the volleyball net at ground level in the basement and played tennis. It sounded terribly thumpy sometimes, and we cringed to think what might be getting damaged. However, energy was being released and made healthy bodies for the boys and healthy relationships for us all.   B Z

Boys' Occupations

Any project you give your boys, no matter their size, will take a little money and parental supervision. Not that you need to be at their elbow every minute. That defeats the purpose of keeping them occupied. They will have questions and need a bit of guidance here and there. Time spent with them in this way is not wasted time.
> F O N D A   H E G E

Give boys the opportunity to learn and experiment at their parents' expense. (You'll need to purchase things like tools and fasteners, etc.) This does not mean that they need to ruin expensive tools or deface buildings or other property just because they are boys!
> A N O N Y M O U S

When our boys were quite young, they raised bunnies. The rabbits became pets and were very tame. Especially Cocoa. He was a chocolate-colored one who was content to ride around on the boys' shoulders. Quite often the boys would bring him into the house to play. Cocoa would jump up on the boys begging to be chased. How he loved that! Of course, the boys loved it too! N A O M I   C R O S S

Rabbits, lambs, chicks, or any small animal can provide your boy with responsibility. It's amazing how a sleepy boy can wake up in the middle of the night to bottle-feed an orphan lamb.
> F O N D A   H E G E

Building a tree house utilizes many hours. A N O N Y M O U S

For many years, we raised Lady Finger popcorn, which kept our boys busy in the fall and winter as they helped husk, clean, and shell the popcorn. In the summer, we raised produce. We didn't make much money on the produce, but we did learn to work together.
> N A O M I   C R O S S

Let boys plant something of their own in the garden. The possibilities are endless—popcorn (try Power Puff Popcorn from E & R Seeds), pumpkins, Indian corn, watermelons, red beets... Let them take care of the watering and weeding, but be interested in their project and praise their progress. Our boys loved to have their own things when they were young, and now they often run the tiller for me. Plant a love of gardening in them when they are young!
FONDA HEGE

Something profitable for our boys was the job of stripping the scraps of wire the electricians left behind from our house addition. They spent many hours stripping, and even the two-year-old said, "Coppa (copper) is like pennies."   B Z

Make sure they have a place of their own that can be as cluttered as they want: an old shed, shop corner, or even an old truck body moved in for that purpose. Give them plenty of sticks of wood, drill and screws, hammer and nails, a small scroll saw and thin sheets of wood to cut shapes, and leftover paint to decorate the finished results. Buy how-to-build books to inspire them.   ANONYMOUS

Our boys enjoyed working in the shop with woodworking tools. (Caution: One son came in with a bloody finger and said his big brother told him to put his finger against the wood planer to feel it tickle. Well, it tickled too hard and took a chunk of finger!) B Z

Get a wood burner and wood. Our boys started out on scrap wood for practice. It should have a smooth surface and a close grain or it will be frustrating to them. When they get good at it, get them plaques to make mottoes.   FONDA HEGE

Let boys collect junk appliances to dismantle or fix. Just remember, no microwaves! Microwaves can carry current even after they are unplugged. Be sure they understand the dangers of electrocution.

Always tinker unplugged! Maybe Dad could remove the cord before they get the appliance. A N O N Y M O U S

My brothers spent lots of time with old lawn mower engines and finally succeeded in building their own go-cart.
A N O N Y M O U S

There is no shame in learning to do housework so well that boys can keep house by themselves before they are married.
A N O N Y M O U S

Cleaning

In the winter, I often list jobs as I think of them and hand each boy a paper after school or copy the jobs on one big list for them to take their pick. But the fun jobs wait for last. I learned housecleaning chores need to be done before they run outside to work or play. Our boys are pros at "forgetting" to come back inside.
M A B E L   R E I F F

Let boys play as they work. Pretend they are skid loaders as they pick up toys, or tractors as they tow trash bags to the burn barrel or haul slop out to the field. Dirty dishes can be cars going through the car wash. Give them a spray bottle of water and a rag! Squirting water is a lot of fun, and they hardly even realize they just washed your floors for you!   M A R I L Y N   W E A V E R

When it's time to pick up toys, I often tell them to each pick up twenty or thirty toys. When they're drying dishes, I tell them if they get finished with what's on the drainer in five or ten minutes, they don't need to do the rest. This way it doesn't look so overwhelming, and it motivates them. A N O T H E R   M O T H E R

For the boys in the house, I found charts worked best. The same person didn't always do the same job without me having to remember whose turn it was. I also found charts worked well for paying children to brush teeth or make beds. But they lost money when I had to turn dirty socks right side out or pick up their shoes, jackets, or clothing. Over the years we also had many charts to overcome bad habits; with each mark, extra jobs were given. Often when a child saw they were getting marks that the other siblings were not, it helped them overcome more quickly.   A MOTHER OF SONS

If there was a lot of housework to do, I tried to divide the work as evenly as possible. For example, everyone took thirty pieces of clothing off the wash line, washed twenty dishes, cleaned five windows, or picked up and put away fifty things.

A MOTHER OF SONS

I got each of my boys his own cleaning bucket. (Wal-Mart had all kinds of plastic buckets during Easter season, and they even had pictures on them!) I put one job on an index card with instructions of how to do the job and what kind of cleaner and rag to use. On cleaning day, I hand out the job cards. The boys can wear their tool belts and stick the cards in the pockets. Of course, they love little rewards too!   MRS KUHNS

If you would ask my boys what's the worst thing about housework, they would quickly say, "The weekly cleanings!" I find it works best to make a list of chores and let them take turns picking out their jobs and initialing them. Keep the jobs down to what they can do in an hour or so and then give them an outside job. Another thing that has worked well also is putting all the jobs on slips of paper in a container. They get to pick out a slip of paper as they do them. Make sure to put in extras, like "give everyone a piece of candy," "sing a song," "run around the house," or "play with the dog for two minutes."

THANKFUL FOR MY BOY BLESSINGS

A boy's way of cleaning a room likely isn't the same as a girl's would be, but I try to tell myself that if they do the best they can, it's okay. I'm thankful my husband lets our boys help me in the house. He even helps too, which is a good example for our sons. I have various ways to solicit the boys' help with cleaning. One way is to tell each one to pick up twenty pieces in each room. Sometimes I sweep everything on a pile (or piles!), and they put the things away while I clear off furniture or sweep another room. Another method they enjoy, but don't do often, is to take turns being the foreman or boss of a room. For example, the boss of the kitchen gets the others to help him get the kitchen in order. After the kitchen is tidied, another boy is boss for the next room they clean. It is interesting to watch. It brings out each boy's personality a bit. Some sit on a chair to boss, while one will boss and still pitch in and help!   S U S A N   S H E T L E R

Turn your little boys loose with a window spray bottle and window rags. It makes them feel grown up, and your windows will look a little better though maybe not perfect. A simple Windex recipe I've used over the years is 1 pint alcohol, ½ cup ammonia, and 1 gallon of water. If you want it to look store-bought, add a few drops of blue food coloring.   F O N D A   H E G E

One thing I find of great value and worth every cent is disposable disinfectant wipes. (I buy the store brand.) With these, the boys can clean the bathrooms at a young age. No soap gets squirted who-knows-where! No water spills either! The wipes also come in very handy for those bathroom accidents for which boys are so popular for causing!
T H A N K F U L   F O R   M Y   B O Y   B L E S S I N G S

Sewing

My boys all know how to sew. They can sew on missing buttons and even mend pants. I have had boys sew up their own shirts and make

their own pajamas. Right now my six-year-old is sewing a comfort top complete with a sash. A couple of his older brothers have done the same sewing project and are the pleased owners of a comfort. Sometimes it is a big bean bag chair, stuffed with peanuts or grocery bags, that is being sewn, or maybe a hassock made with layers of foam. One time there was a pair of hunting pants that took on a unique look. The lad had taken a pair of brown pants and camouflaged them by sewing brown and green flippy-floppy strips of material all over the fronts.
        EVELYN FISHER

Do they like to sew? Our one son has cut out and sewn up his own (and his daddy's) pajamas. Who sees if they are not perfect? They are so much more fun to wear if the boy made them himself! Pillowcases are another easy thing to sew, especially if you get cute material with monkeys or tools on them.   FONDA HEGE

Baking

We rarely eat cookies at our house. Cakes and bars are so much faster. Even a five-year-old can mix up a cake mix with a bit of supervision, and you can add some diversion. Melt chocolate and peanut butter and layer it on the cake or use the Jell-O recipe on the bag and pour it over the cake. Refrigerate. Our bent and dent store has quite a variation of flavors that we enjoy. And no matter what you add to the cake, it tastes so much better to the five-year-old who made it!
        NORMA STEINER

Do you need crushed Oreos or crackers for a recipe? Put it in a double plastic bag and tell your sons to bring their toy hammers. You'll have the finest crumbs!   MRS KUHNS

My boys enjoy making granola. They pretend they are dumping coconut snow on oatmeal mountains.
        MRS ALLAN MARTIN

As our boys got older, we learned how to make noodles. In the winter, that was an after-school job to fill extra time. Boys can think of anything to keep a job behind the crank from being boring!

B Z

I have a container of paper slips for table-setting for the preschoolers. It inspires a boy to enjoy setting the table. Save the paper slips and reuse daily. Here is an example of what the slips look like:

(8 plates)   (8 spoons)   (1 ketchup bottle)

MRS ALLAN MARTIN

Boys Away from Home

We find a simple packed lunch to be handy on evenings that we go away for nursing home singings or such like. It's standard that we have sausage burger sandwiches. It's quick to pat the meat onto cookie trays and grill it under the stove broiler while you pack other lunch items.   N O R M A S T E I N E R

For going on trips, I find it helpful to pack my boys' clothes by the day. For example, I make a pile of all the clothes Boy #1 will need for Saturday, a pile of all the clothes he'll need for Sunday (including his Bible and shoes), a pile of all the clothes he'll need for Monday, and so forth. I do the same for each boy, then I put each set of clothes into a plastic grocery bag, and using a marker, I mark whose clothes are in the bag and for what day he is to wear them. I usually have a bag marked "Extra" for each boy for just-in-case, because you never know with boys! It prevents the soup in the suitcase that can occur when boys start digging around to find their clothes. And no one can complain that "Brother took my socks!" When they use the clothes out of the bag, their dirty clothes are then to be put into the bag.

M E B E R S O L E

Boys' Clothes

How did I know whose clothing was whose when I had almost every size in boys' clothing? It is rather hard to keep track when clothing gets passed on to the next younger child each year. For coats and hood sweaters, I found it was easy to fasten a snap onto the tag on the inside of a coat, and then make fabric name tags for each child with the other part of the snap. As the child outgrew the jacket, the name tag could be snapped off and fastened to the next coat. For boots, we initialed with paint markers. If they got passed on the next year, it was worn off enough to write over top. For laundry, I marked all the clothing by the sizes with permanent marker and added an "X" if it was everyday. Even that can be confusing if you have boys that are ages eight, nine, eleven, and thirteen, and the shirts are marked 8-10, 10-12, 12-14 or if your boys are bigger or smaller than their age. When folding wash, I used different baskets for each child, and at times found it necessary to put a sticker on the basket on which to write the size clothing that child was wearing.

A MOTHER OF SONS

Mark your boys' clothes with tally marks. Just add a tally mark when you pass it down to the next boy. One mark for boy number one, two marks for boy number two, four marks with a diagonal slash for boy number five, and so on. NORMA STEINER

My mother thought I was spending too many precious minutes ironing shirts. She suggested I just throw the shirts into the dryer for a few minutes immediately after washing and then promptly hang them up. Now I rarely iron the little boys' shirts, especially during suit coat season. Of course, it helps to not bunch Sunday shirts in the bottom of hampers! I sigh and keep on trying.

NORMA STEINER

My sister-in-law shared her laundry detergent recipe with me, and it serves us very well. It is simple to make, and it cleans better than cheap Wal-Mart brands. During some busy summer months, I was using bought soap until I noticed how dirty and stained the barn shirts were getting. It's probably not better quality than Tide, but I don't like Tide prices. The following ingredients are all together in the soap aisle at Wal-Mart.

1 bar Fels-Naptha soap	1½ cups Washing Soda
3 quarts water	2 quarts hot water
1½ cups Borax	11 cups water

In a big kettle, melt bar of soap and 3 quarts water. (Shredding the bar of soap makes for easier melting.) Remove from heat and add Borax and Washing Soda. Mix well. Mixture will thicken. Add 2 quarts hot water. Stir. Add 11 cups water. Mix. Stir occasionally. Ready to use in 24 hours. (I don't always wait.) Use ½ to ¾ cup per load. (I use a generous amount per load and freely use fabric softener for scent.

NORMA STEINER

Our five boys are extremely fussy with how their socks fit. We struggled with our oldest son with this issue for quite a few years. He was even late for school a few times because his socks just did not feel right to him. The day I started buying better socks was a good thing indeed! I have learned it pays to buy good brand-name socks that fit snugly on their feet. It has created so much less stress for all of us! Department stores usually carry good ones. Our boys like the PUMA brand, and they seem to last pretty well.

MARTHA BEILER

Handy Hints

Keeping super glue on hand is a necessity at our house. It will glue together the nasty cut that would otherwise send us to the ER. Drip in only a little so that the glue doesn't hold the skin apart. Squeeze the cut together. Cocoa butter may be applied to help those ugly scars to vanish even after it's healed.　　NORMA STEINER

Do I get tired of my son's stuff? YES! However, I remind myself that he has spent many hours creatively; and once his creations are no longer played with or are torn up, he can usually be persuaded to throw them away. "You have to throw the old things away so you have room for new things" is a sentence I repeat when we are cleaning his bedroom.   SARA BOWMAN

Save yourself some precious minutes! Baby Gold peaches are good with the peelings on. We actually like the texture. Even potatoes don't always need to be peeled.   NORMA STEINER

As the school year ends, I compile a list of things that can always be done at a glance. When boys need extra chores, a punishment, or just something to keep them busy, I have a job ready for them.

Here is what my list might look like:

Scrub the patio and sidewalks
Wash basement floor
Check lawn for any trash
Sweep the lean-to
Sweep down cobwebs in basement
Weed strawberries (or pick)
Clean chicken coop
Bake (That's a favorite, BUT they need to completely clean up the mess!)

Sometimes the chore can be repeated each day. Some weeks the patios and basements sparkle every day! They soon learn that if the job isn't done correctly, they will need to do it over. If they are not playing nicely, they can expect another chore to be coming their way.
A MOTHER OF TEN

Build Your Own Articulating Tractor!

D ROSE W

This is a pattern invented by my dad to make wooden tractors. It is very basic, and the only limit is your imagination. Schools have used this pattern for boy projects. My brothers enjoy it as well, but not every boy is a carpenter.

Materials

Wood - 2" x 6½" pine (or 2" x 8" spruce) 8' long
Small piece of ¾" x 4½" pine (or 1" x 4") 5" long
Round dowel - ⅝" x 2'
3" door hinge
4 pc. of washers approx. ¹¹⁄₁₆" hole in the center
Hook or eye screw for hitch
Screws - 17 - 2½" and 6 - 1"
Paint (opt.)

Tools

Pencil
Speed square
Jigsaw (or equivalent)
Sander (small bench-top belt sander works good)
4¾" hole saw
Expansion bit (or 2¼" bit)
³⁄₁₆, ⅝, and ¹¹⁄₁₆ drill bit
Screwdriver (or impact bit) to fit screws
Straightedge or level
Drill press and/or drill
Woodburner (opt.)

To Start

Trace two tractor patterns - Cut out with jigsaw and screw together using 6 long screws.

Trace one roof - Cut out and sand.

Cut 4 wheels - 4¾" diameter.

Cut 4 more wheels approximately ¾ the way through wood, then use expansion bit set at 2¼" and drill approximately ⅜ the way through each of the 4 remaining wheels. Use 4¾" hole saw to complete cutting out the wheels. (These will be the outside wheels.)

Screw 2 wheels together to make 4 sets. Use ³⁄₁₆" bit to pre-drill 2 screws from the inside of wheel into the outside wheel.

Sand wheels.

(A drill press will work best for the next 2 steps.)

Drill ⅝" hole through center of wheels for dowel.

Drill ¹¹⁄₁₆" hole through tractor frame for axles.

Sand or cut a notch into back of tractor frame ¼"-⅜" for tractor hitch. (So hitch does not stick out past the back tractor wheels.)

Some sanding can be done on tractor frame. Top of hood in front of cab can be sanded narrow. Corner posts of tractor can be sanded.

Cut tractor frame in half behind tractor cab (along dotted line). Use a square to mark.

Both frame pieces will need to be sanded or notched on the sides along this last cut to allow the tractor to turn. Sand or notch close to the middle, taking a bit more out of the front frame than the back.

Take frame pieces apart and lay 1 front piece and 1 back piece on the workbench. Put a straightedge along the bottom side of tractor frame pieces with the middle side of frames facing up. Lay the open hinge between front and back frame with hinge flush at the bottom by straightedge. Trace hinge size on front and back frame pieces. Sand a notch as deep as the hinge is thick—approx. ³⁄₁₆" out of the front and back frame pieces.

Put the opposite 2 frame pieces on workbench along the straightedge and fasten hinge with 6- 1" screws.

Fasten frame pieces back together in the same screw holes.

Install roof piece using 3 screws.

Cut 2 dowels (length will depend on the thickness of wood used) for axles.

Put washer between tractor frame and wheel - 4 pieces.

Optional additives: fenders; exhaust; front side weights; mirrors; dowel caps to keep wheels on axles; paint any color; woodburn additional details.

To build this tractor you can use the pattern on the following pages.

Articulating Tractor
Wheel Pattern

Back and Front Wheel

Articulating Tractor

Roof Pattern

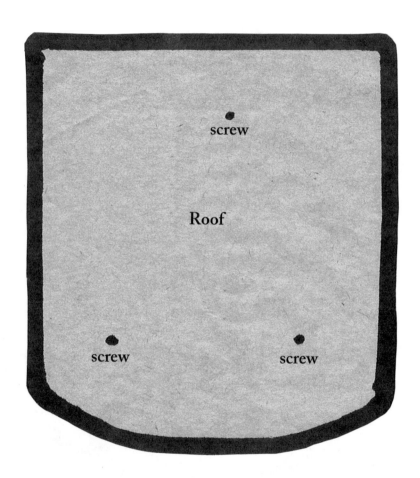

screw

Roof

screw   screw

You may cut along this line

Articulating Tractor

Body Pattern Front

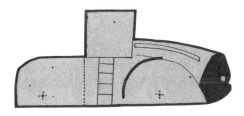

"A"

Tape "B" here

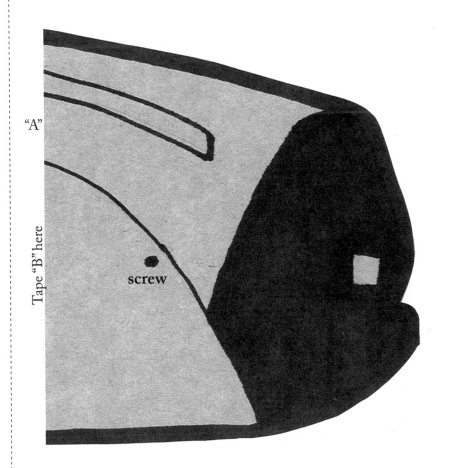

screw

Articulating Tractor

Body Pattern Middle 1

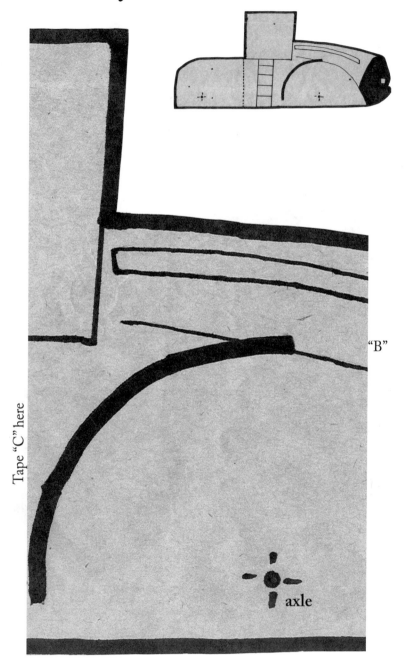

"B"

Tape "C" here

axle

Articulating Tractor
Body Pattern Middle 2

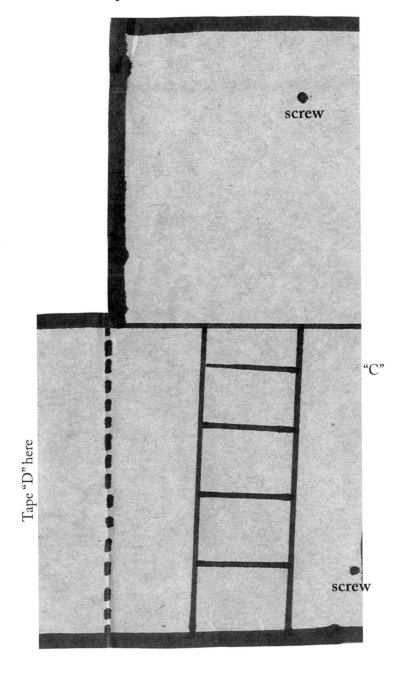

Articulating Tractor
Body Pattern Back

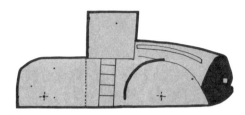

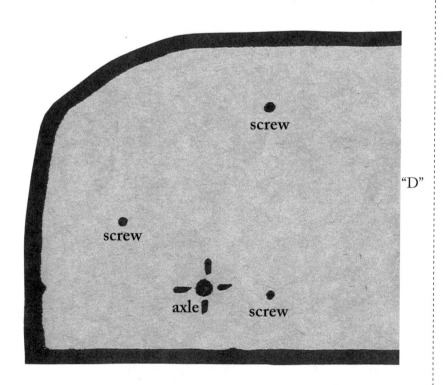

"D"